THE GREAT UPHEAVAL

THE GREAT UPHEAVAL

• • • •

Higher Education's Past, Present, and Uncertain Future

Arthur Levine
and
Scott Van Pelt

JOHNS HOPKINS UNIVERSITY PRESS | Baltimore

Johns Hopkins University Press
2715 North Charles Street
Baltimore, Maryland 21218-4363
www.press.jhu.edu

Library of Congress Cataloging-in-Publication Data

Names: Levine, Arthur, author. | Van Pelt, Scott, 1988–author.
Title: The great upheaval : higher education's past, present, and uncertain future /
Arthur Levine and Scott Van Pelt.
Description: Baltimore, Maryland : Johns Hopkins University Press, 2021. | Includes
bibliographical references and index.
Identifiers: LCCN 2021003075 | ISBN 9781421442570 (hardcover) |
ISBN 9781421442587 (ebook)
Subjects: LCSH: Education, Higher—Aims and objectives—United States. |
Education, Higher—United States—History. | Educational change—United States.
Classification: LCC LB2322.2 .L49 2021 | DDC 378—dc23
LC record available at https://lccn.loc.gov/2021003075

A catalog record for this book is available from the British Library.

To our children and grandchildren.
The future belongs to them—
Ian, Isaac, Jamie, Linnea, Nate,
Rachel, and Torin.

CONTENTS

PREFACE

This is a book about the future of higher education in a time of profound, unrelenting, and accelerating change of a magnitude and scope unequaled since the Industrial Revolution. The United States is hurtling from a national, analog, industrial economy to a global, digital, knowledge economy.

We decided to write this book for four reasons. First, the transition makes higher education more essential than ever before. It is the engine that powers the global, digital, knowledge economy by producing knowledge, preserving knowledge, and disseminating knowledge. In contrast to industrial economies, which are rooted in natural resources and physical labor, knowledge economies are fueled by minds and information. They have an endless hunger for research and demand the most highly educated citizenry and labor force in human history.

Second, higher education will be transformed in the course of the transition just as it was during the Industrial Revolution. The reason is that today's colleges and universities, like all of the nation's social institutions, were built for the passing industrial era. In the emerging knowledge economy, they work less well than they once did; to some they appear to be broken. The incongruence between the industrial era model of higher education and the needs of the emerging knowledge economy will increase over time. Higher education will need to be refitted for the global, digital, knowledge economy. This can be accomplished either by renovating the existing institutions or by replacing them. It may entail institutional adaptation to changing conditions or the changes may be of such magnitude that they disrupt the existing institutions, rendering them obsolete and making room for new actors. Regardless of the method by which change occurs, higher education will be transformed in the years ahead.

The rapidity of this transformation was accelerated by COVID-19. The pandemic caused a number of anticipated changes to occur far more quickly than expected, including the closure of colleges and universities owing to declining enrollments and finances, the ballooning of online education, the expansion in the number and the enrollments of nontraditional higher education providers, and the demand for short-term, nondegree training and retraining programs to meet changing labor market realities.

Third, the term *transformation* is imprecise. It speaks to a broad range of possibilities regarding the potential depth, breadth, and scope of change that higher education will experience. There is widespread agreement on the forces that will drive the transformation: changing demographics, the rise of the knowledge economy, and the advance of digital technology and globalization. These are the known forces; COVID-19 demonstrates the power of the unknown.

However, there is fundamental disagreement, even among the experts, regarding the impact of these forces on higher education. At Harvard University, for example, president Lawrence Bacow says higher education will incrementally adapt to changing conditions as it has historically, maintaining its current mission and structure. In contrast, one of Harvard's most prominent business school professors, the late Clayton Christensen, argued that the changes will be of such magnitude that they will disrupt higher education as we know it, rendering the existing model obsolete and driving a majority of colleges and universities to bankruptcy.

Recent years have witnessed an outpouring of publications about the future of American higher education, which mirror this split and everything in-between. There have been calls for change, pleas for preservation, and visions of what lies ahead, ranging from the utopian to the apocalyptic. Taken as a whole, this writing is largely ahistorical, projecting the future on the basis of what is going on today and expected future trends rather than examining how we got here and the lessons the past teaches. It also tends to focus on higher education in isolation, ignoring the pressures and changes other knowledge industries experience. It is often rooted in one of the multiplicity of changes occurring in society, usually new technologies. Too often advocacy, what the author wants higher education to become, overshadows the analysis.

The point is this: understanding the future of higher education must not be a guessing game or a matter of personal opinion. The stakes are too high.

Fourth, we believe a dramatically different approach is required to understand the future of higher education or any other organization than is currently being employed. It requires us to look in three directions—backward, forward, and sideways. Over the past four decades, Levine's research and writing has used these three perspectives independently to understand the current condition and future prospects for higher education. This is the culmination of that work, harnessing the power of the three perspectives—looking backward, forward, and sideways—in tandem. Taken together, these three perspectives tell us what, how, when, and why higher education will change. It offers guidance on what institutions of higher education, policy makers, funders, and the public should do.

This is why we wrote this book. We want to be equally explicit about what we wrote—what this book is and what it is not.

This volume is a report on the findings of a research study. It is not a work of advocacy. It doesn't make a case for what we want or hope higher education will become in the years ahead. In fact, we undertook this study as agnostics. We didn't know what it would reveal, and we had no bias in terms of what we hoped it would reveal. Put simply, we had no skin in the game. Only after we completed the book did we write a final chapter at the suggestion of reviewers, reacting to the findings, which were not all to our liking and offering recommendations for institutions and policy.

This is a book not only about colleges and universities but also about the larger universe of postsecondary education, the full range of education opportunities available to students after twelfth grade and increasingly before. It discusses the proliferation of new and nontraditional providers, for-profit and non-profit; the content they offer; the delivery systems they use; the assessments they employ; the certifications they award; and the students they enroll.

Historically, the mission of higher education has been described as teaching, research, and service. This book focuses on only one of those activities, the teaching or education function and how it can be expected to change in the years ahead.

This book is about higher education in the United States, but in varying degree, the challenges facing it and the directions in which higher education will change are similar around the world. Levine has been awarded a Fulbright Fellowship to replicate this study in India in 2021–22.

This is a book we hope will be read by college and university administrators, faculty and trustees, higher education policy makers, graduate students in higher education, media, government, funders, and college students and their families. They need an accurate picture of what the future of higher education will be and the actions they need to take to shape it.

But this book is also intended for two other audiences. One is general readers. Sixty-one percent of Americans over the age of 25 have attended college, and 45 percent have earned an associate's or bachelor's degree. For this reason, we hope they might be interested in reading a book written in a journalistic fashion, without jargon, about how college as they know it is being transformed.

The other audience is people who work in nonprofits other than colleges and universities, organizations such as museums, libraries, zoos, and symphonies. The tripartite methodology—looking backward, forward and sideways—used in this volume can be applied to studying the future of any of those organizations. The forces projected forward in this volume are precisely the same challenges they face. The looking sideways profiles of three knowledge industries—movies, music, and newspapers—are just as relevant to other nonprofits as for higher education.

For all three audiences, this is a unique moment in history, a moment that must not be squandered. We should not and cannot wait for the future to happen to us. We have a chance now to shape the future that awaits our nation's colleges and universities as well as organizations facing the same challenges. Not since the Industrial Revolution has a generation been offered this opportunity.

ACKNOWLEDGMENTS

This book would not have been possible without the support of Vartan Gregorian and the Carnegie Corporation. Vartan was a friend and mentor, a giant who made the world a better place.

We can't thank Faith Hamlin, senior agent at Sanford J. Greenburger Associates, enough. Faith was there from the very beginning as a cheerleader, motivator, critic, counselor, agent, and first and always a dear friend.

Greg Britton, editorial director at Johns Hopkins University Press, was a creative thought partner for this volume, whose wisdom, warmth, and advice enabled us to turn our manuscript into a far better book.

This book would not have been possible without the assistance of many people. We are grateful to education historian James Fraser, professor at New York University and formerly senior vice president for Programs at the Woodrow Wilson Foundation, who convinced Arthur to write this book and discussed the findings with him for years throughout the research and writing.

We thank Noah Kippley-Ogman, now assistant director of Institutional Advancement in the Bard College Prison Initiative, whose work on this study while completing his doctorate at New York University was invaluable.

We are grateful to Professor Anna Neumann who leads the Teachers College Higher and Postsecondary Education Program for introducing the authors.

We thank Julie Wilson, executive director of the Institute for the Future of Learning, who served as the Sherpa or guide for the authors introducing us to a new world of nontraditional education providers.

We are especially thankful to Deborah Quazzo, managing partner of GSV Advisors, who was our teacher. She gave us her wisdom, time, contacts, counsel, vision, and opportunities to present our work and meet the leaders inventing higher education's future.

We are thankful to many, many people who discussed the ideas in this book with us, read many drafts of this book, and/ or provided opportunities for us to present the findings of this book with key audiences. They include David Asai, Norman Atkins, George Blumenthal, Lee Bolman, Frank Britt, Sean Buffington, Mary-Mack Callahan, Patrick Callan, Gerald Chan, Terah Crews, Carol D'Amico, Amber Garrison Duncan, Richard Ekman, Greta Essig, Jonathan Fanton, Carl Ferenbach, Abigail Frank, Chris Gabrieli, Sameer Gadkarree, Barbara Gellman-Danley, Lev Gonick, Fred Grauer, Matt Greenfield, Daniel Greenstein, Deborah Hirsch, Dennis Holtschneider, Jim Honan, Stephanie Hull, Alberto Ibargüen, Zoe Ingalls, Farnam Jahanian, John Katzman, Jan Krukowski, Vijay Kumar, Paul Le Blanc, Richard Levin, Ellis Levine, William Lilley, Carolyne Marrow, Ajita Menon, Jamie Merisotis, Michael Moe, Matthew Pittinsky, Scott Pulsifer, Deborah Quazzo, Shep Ranbom, Rafael Reif, Shai Reshef, Patrick Riccards, Beverly Sanford, Sanjay Sarma, Bror Saxberg, David Shane, Mark Strickland, Peter Taylor, Jay Urwitz, and Ralph Wolff.

Arthur Levine is particularly grateful to his wife, Linda Fentiman, an emeritus professor at Pace University Law School, who did all of the things she has done throughout their marriage—supporting, encouraging, tempering, being his best friend, colleague, partner, and counselor. Plus, she wrote a book at the same time a lot faster than we did.

Scott Van Pelt feels fortunate to have studied with some of the most creative minds in higher education; in particular, the faculty and staff of the Higher and Postsecondary Education Program at Teachers College, Columbia University, who challenged him to critically explore the past, present, and potential futures of higher learning. He is especially thankful to his partner, Erica, whose patience and support has been unyielding.

THE GREAT UPHEAVAL

. . . .

Where You Look Determines What You See

American higher Education is the envy of the world. It is absurd
to describe it as mired in the past or unwilling to change.
Change is inherent and constant in higher education
—new research, new faculty, new courses.
—Henry Rosovsky, 2019

History is littered with examples of industries that, at their peril,
failed to respond—or even to notice—changes in the world
around them, from railroads to steel manufacturing....
Institutions of higher education risk falling into the same
trap...increasingly characterized by obsolescence.
—US Department of Education, *A Test of Leadership: Charting
the Future of US Higher Education Spellings
Commission Report*, 2006

Fifteen years from now more than half of the universities
will be in bankruptcy, including the state schools.
—Clayton Christensen, 2013

It has become trendy to predict that higher education
is on the verge of collapse.
—*Inside Higher Education*, 2017

The United States is experiencing profound, unrelenting, and
accelerating demographic, economic, and technological change.
The nation's population is changing racially, aging, moving,

and coming from abroad. The country is undergoing a transformation from an industrial to a knowledge economy. New digital technologies have emerged with the power to recast our lives and the world around us.

Change of this magnitude and scope, which last occurred during the Industrial Revolution, is rare. One consequence is that our social institutions, which were created for the passing era, are compelled to change to meet the demands of the emerging order. This is a book about the future of one of those institutions: higher education. It asks in what ways, how, and when higher education can be expected to change in the years ahead.

An army of commentators have already opined on this subject—academics, journalists, researchers, investors, and entrepreneurs. Their conclusions fall into two major buckets. The first is the *adaptive bucket*, which predicts that the existing model of higher education will be fundamentally sustained. It is premised in the belief that higher education is continually reinventing itself, that perpetual change is built into its DNA. It holds that higher education will adapt to current societal changes as it adapted to changes of the past through a process of reform and renovation. It dismisses the value and need for disruptive change. This was Henry Rosovsky's point in the quote that opens this chapter as well as that of a host of publications, such as Steven Brint's 2019 article "Is This Higher Education's Golden Age? Pessimism Reigns, but America's Universities Have Never Been Stronger."

The second bucket can be labeled disruptive. It foresees a break with higher education's historic past and a fundamental remaking of the enterprise. The name most closely associated with this school of thought is Rosovsky's Harvard colleague, the late Clayton Christensen, also quoted at the beginning of this chapter, and his sentiment is shared in publications such as "College Disrupted: The Great Unbundling of Higher Education" by higher education entrepreneur and investor Ryan Craig (2015).

What we are left with are polar visions of the future of higher education, promulgated by renowned and well-respected experts and a cacophony of other voices spanning the poles.

The reality is that, depending on where you look, both conclusions are plausible. There is an optical illusion named Rubin's Vase created more than a century ago. It is a black-and-white drawing in which one can see either two faces or a vase but not both at the same time. If the black of the picture is perceived as background, then two faces appear, one on the right side of the drawing and the other on the left. If the white is seen as the background, a vase appears at the center of the drawing.

The world of higher education is similar. If one looks at the nation's colleges and universities as the foreground, one picture emerges, which argues for adaptation. If one views traditional higher education as the background and the larger postsecondary world beyond the mainstream campuses as foreground, another very different image appears, making the case for disruption. Let's consider each in turn.

Rubin's Vase

Looking at Traditional Higher Education

If you focus only on the nation's nearly four thousand non-profit colleges and universities, offering two-year, four-year, and more advanced degrees, higher education certainly does not appear to be an enterprise on the verge of collapse, even after the damage inflicted by the COVID-19 pandemic.

The roots of higher education in the United States are deep, with an uninterrupted and eminent history of nearly four hundred years, spanning colonial to modern times, including a transition from an agrarian to an industrial nation. It has been the first choice of students coming from abroad, enrolling 24 percent of foreign students globally (Study International, 2018). However, COVID-19 and Trump administration immigration policy have combined to affect enrollments, which declined by one-sixth during the 2020 fall term as the pandemic raged (Baer & Martel, 2020).

Nonetheless, higher education is a growth industry in a knowledge economy that demands a more educated and continually reeducated labor force. Between 1969 and 2019, college enrollments rose steadily, increasing more than two and a half fold with modest declines adjusting for demographic and economic changes (National Center for Education Statistics, 2019a). In that time, the number of associate degrees awarded increased by a factor of five, the number of baccalaureate degrees more than doubled, and master's and doctoral degrees tripled (National Center for Education Statistics, 2019b).

The failure rate of institutions had been low. Since 2002, the number of college closures for the most vulnerable institutions—small private colleges—has varied from one a year to a high of eleven in 2018, which is a closure rate of less than 1 percent per year (Seltzer, 2018). To put this into perspective, the five-year failure rate for small businesses is 50 percent

(Desjardins, 2017). However, the pandemic dramatically inflated those numbers in both sectors. University of Pennsylvania professor Robert Zemsky projects college closure rates of between 10 percent and 20 percent (Korn, Belkin, & Chung, 2020). If realized, that's a very large number, but it doesn't rise to the level of a collapse. Rather, it is the telescoping of losses that would have occurred over a far longer period. Endangered, financially troubled institutions, still hanging on, were pushed over the brink by COVID-19 revenue losses.

There is also evidence that higher education has been cautiously and disparately adapting to the new demographic, economic, and technological realities, though often reluctantly, largely by augmenting or supplementing their existing operations. Internet and mobile technologies have become campus staples. While one in three students had taken an online course before COVID-19, in a matter of days the number jumped to nearly 100 percent. Nonetheless, colleges and universities remain more analog than their students. To a far lesser extent, big data and artificial intelligence have appeared in initiatives, such as the Georgia State University's adaptive, or personalized, learning program. Virtual and augmented reality is visible at Georgetown University School of Medicine, where students use virtual reality to simulate the experiences of aging patients (O'Neil, 2019).

There are large- and small-scale experiments in areas ranging from outcome-based education and time variable instruction to alternative credentialing, and growing interdisciplinary fields such as learning and data sciences. Partnerships are being formed between higher education and nontraditional providers, such as StraighterLine in general education, Credly in microcredentials and badging, 2U in online programing, Trilogy in career skills, Civitas in data use for student success, and General Assembly in coding boot camps. On a grander scale, the proprietary chain Kaplan Higher Education with thirty thousand students merged with Purdue University to form Purdue Global, and the University of Arizona purchased the for-profit Ashford University, which enrolls about thirty-five thousand students. Arizona State University, Carnegie-Mellon, MIT, Olin College, Southern New Hampshire University, and Stanford University have become nationally recognized leaders, labs, showrooms, and incubators for imagining a new future for higher education. Innovations such as massive open online courses (MOOCs), courses with unlimited enrollments that have exceeded one hundred thousand, originated in higher education. These will be discussed in chapters fourteen and fifteen.

At the same time, it must be recognized that higher education is facing some very real challenges, beginning with COVID-19 recovery. Criticism of its performance and worth has increased. Its cost and student debt are urgent problems. Access and graduation rates are too low, particularly for the nation's fastest-growing populations. Digital technology adoption has been slow, though COVID-19 demonstrated it could be done much more quickly. Demands for greater accountability and competition from nontraditional providers are on the rise.

However, there is nothing in this situation that argues against an adaptive response to the changes and challenges facing higher education. Until the pandemic, the pace of that change had been slow, spotty, and restrained, but there was movement and COVID-19 accelerated it.

Looking Beyond Traditional Higher Education

If the world of higher education seems established, staid, complacent, and unhurried, the world of postsecondary education beyond traditional campuses appears disorderly, brash,

vibrant, and impatient. It is a grab bag of diverse and independent for-profit and nonprofit institutions, organizations, programs, and services that begin at the periphery of mainstream
colleges and universities and extend far beyond. There are new
and nontraditional institutions that have abandoned key elements of mainstream higher education—emphasizing digital
technologies, rejecting time- and place-based education, creating low-cost degrees, adopting competency- or outcome-based
education, focusing on the growing populations underrepresented in traditional higher education, offering pioneering
subject matters and certifications, and more. There are mom-
and-pop proprietary schools as well as chains of for-profit colleges. There are knowledge organizations, ranging from libraries and museums to media companies and software makers,
that have entered the postsecondary marketplace, offering content, instruction, and certification. There are entrepreneurial
firms attempting to poach higher education's most profitable
programs in areas such as general education, business, and
education and seeking to offer cheaper, faster, better, and more
convenient versions. In his book *A New U: Faster + Cheaper
Alternatives to College*, Ryan Craig (2018) listed more than two
hundred postsecondary alternatives to college.

Historically, the postsecondary sector, which has mushroomed in recent years, has filled the gaps in collegiate education. It has in practice served as an opportunistic competitor to
traditional institutions seeking to capitalize on their perceived
shortcomings in areas such as pricing, calendar, location, services, programming, and access. In this manner, it has also
served as a lab for innovation, pioneering new approaches to
teaching, learning, and certification.

•   •

The relationship between the two sectors has always been frac-
tious, not surprising when one is built on the deficiencies of the

other. Mutual criticism tends to revolve around the practices each employs or fails to employ.

The authors are products of mainstream higher education. It's where we went to school and where we've worked. About twenty years ago, Arthur Levine began hearing the names of a growing number of education organizations and people he didn't recognize. It was initially like learning about a shadow world that surrounded traditional higher education. He found the equivalent of a Sherpa to introduce him to its leaders and its initiatives, which began a fascination with the multibillion-dollar world of postsecondary education. Over the years, for both authors, it has turned into reading an avalanche of reports and studies; visiting postsecondary institutions and enterprises in the United States and abroad; meeting with and interviewing postsecondary CEOs, entrepreneurs, funders, and policy makers; attending postsecondary conferences and meetings; and even sitting on a few boards and advisory committees.

Perhaps the single most instructive introduction to this world is the annual Arizona State University+Global Silicon Valley (ASU+GSV) Summit, which brings together more than five thousand education entrepreneurs and leaders, foundation and venture fund executives, industry CEOs, top government officials, researchers, and media representatives. It is the education equivalent of Davos. The three-day gathering is intended to be a "catalyst for elevating dialogue and driving action around raising learning and career outcomes through scaled innovation." A mouthful. In the course of the event, participants attend talks, panels, and performances by the likes of Barack Obama, George Bush, Colin Powell, Condoleezza Rice, Malcolm Gladwell, John Legend, Bill Gates, Laurene Powell Jobs, Common, Tony Blair, and Priscilla Chan. There are presentations and discussions of cutting-edge innovations in education both in operation and on the drawing board. But the big draw is the hallway and out-of-session conversations. It's a deal maker's heaven.

Here's what we learned. The postsecondary leaders we read, interviewed, and listened to consistently criticized higher education for being overpriced, low in productivity, slow to change, dated in content, and poor in leadership. They echoed the sentiments of two former governors, James Hunt of North Carolina and Thomas Kean of New Jersey, subsequently a university president, who have said the financial model of higher education is fundamentally broken.

• •

They viewed today's colleges and universities as anachronistic and heading toward the "obsolescence" the Spellings Commission warned of, built for the industrial era rather than the emerging knowledge economy. A fundamental difference between the two eras is that industrial societies are rooted in common processes and knowledge economies are focused on common outcomes.

In reality, today's colleges employ designs and values that reflect their industrial era roots. They are modeled on one of the most successful technologies of industrial America, the assembly line. In the main, students attend two- or four-year programs, generally consisting of two fifteen-week semesters annually. During each semester, most full-time students enroll in four or five courses, which generally meet three times a week for fifty minutes per session. When students complete a requisite number of courses, they are awarded a degree.

It is a higher education system tied to the clock. Students progress on the basis of seat time, the amount of time spent in class with a professor. The unit of currency for measuring seat time and academic progress is the Carnegie unit, or credit hour, created by the Carnegie Foundation in 1906 as a means of standardizing high school and college courses of study. The result is a unitary model of higher education in which both the time and process of education are fixed and the outcomes are variable.

In contrast, many postsecondary educators seek to create a dramatically different model of higher education, which they believe the global, knowledge economy demands. This model emphasizes outcomes over process. Outcomes would be fixed, and the process and time to achieve them would be variable. The focus of college would shift from how long students are taught to what they learned from teaching to learning and from the professor to the student.

Because students learn different subjects at different rates and in different ways, a one-size-fits-all approach to education won't work. Rather, education would need to be individualized, which digital technology makes increasingly possible. It also extends the capacity to conduct anytime, anyplace education and to extend higher education's demographic reach.

Because time would become a variable, the Carnegie unit would no longer be relevant in measuring student progress. Instead, an education accounting system grounded in learning outcomes, rather than the clock, would be necessary to replace it. Degrees, which are time-based would also need to become outcome-based, which would permit the development of new forms of certification such as badges and microcredentials that might signify the mastery of clusters of related outcomes in areas such as coding and foreign language rather than a full degree.

In many respects, the postsecondary sector is a rehearsal, setting the stage for that world. If one sorts through its mélange of institutions, organizations, programs, and services, there are a multitude of pioneering initiatives seeking to create the knowledge-era university. There are pilots, experiments, and start-ups in outcome-based, time-independent, individualized, low-cost, twenty-four seven, anyplace, microcredentialed, technology-driven education. When we asked postsecondary entrepreneurs why they were doing these things, they gave us four answers.

First, they believed the changes required in higher education could not be addressed by adaptation or tinkering with the existing higher education model. They thought higher education needed to be reinvented or at least supplemented with postsecondary products and services, such as tutoring, online course management, and specialty instruction such as coding.

Second, they believed higher education had neither the capacity nor the will to make the required changes.

Third, they saw the changes as inevitable and almost universally believed they knew what the knowledge-era university should look like and had the expertise to create it.

Fourth, for-profit entrepreneurs thought they could make money in higher education, believing higher education was ripe for a private-sector takeover much as health care had been in the past. They pointed to some very appealing qualities of the industry as well as its challenges, as noted earlier. It's a growth industry. It's publicly subsidized. It's paid for prior to consuming the product, meaning tuition is paid before taking courses. It's countercyclical in revenues; enrollments rise when the economy declines. It's a long-term, high-price purchase in contrast to items such as milk and soap. And it's now a slow-moving, expensive industry in a time of rapid change.

Bottom line, disruption is both needed and inevitable.

Looking Elsewhere

We have two dramatically different visions of the future of higher education. One is retrospective and the other prospective. The knee-jerk response from the higher education community is that, based on the past and expectations regarding the future, the current model of higher education will prevail, and any changes will occur through reform and adaptation to the new realities confronting it. In contrast, the go-to response from the postsecondary sector based on its current activities and a starkly different view of the future is that higher education will be transformed. The existing model will be replaced through a process of disruptive change.

Perhaps the difference is generational. The leaders of the higher education community are older than the postsecondary sector. The age disparity means higher education leaders grew up in a time when America's colleges and universities were thriving, and based on this they assume with any needed tweaks and repairs they will continue to thrive. The younger postsecondary sector population never knew such a time. To their minds, higher education has always been broken and in need of replacement.

We decided to write this book because there is no evidence to suggest that either of the two schools of thought is correct. Accepting either comes down to a leap of faith.

We employ a different methodology to look at the future than others have used. We believe that to understand the future of higher education or any other organization, it is essential to look in three directions—backward, forward, and sideways.

"Looking Backward" is a historical perspective, allowing us to study the past and to learn how higher education responded to similar societal conditions. In this case, it is a time of profound social change like the present, specifically the Industrial Revolution when the last transformation of higher education occurred. This perspective is most useful in gaining insight into *how* change is likely to occur rather than *what* changes can be expected in the years ahead. The substantive changes are period or time specific.

"Looking Forward" is concerned with trends. It examines the major forces that are changing American society—demographics, the knowledge economy, digital technology, and globalization—and projects their impact on higher education into the future. This perspective is concerned with *the what* of higher education change, the substance of the changes that are likely to be necessary in the future.

"Looking Sideways" is a comparative perspective. It is the study of organizations facing pressures similar to higher education that were compelled to change more rapidly. In this case, it is three knowledge organizations—newspapers, music, and motion pictures—facing the same demographic, economic, technological, and globalization forces as higher education. This perspective is concerned with *what* the organizations did, *when* they did it, and *why* they did it to better understand the pressures that higher education may experience.

Seeing the same object from three very different perspectives offers the potential for both a panoramic and nuanced view. It offers the possibility to compare and contrast, to assess both consistencies and inconsistencies. It is an antidote to the tunnel vision of seeing the future of higher education from only the perspective of higher education or postsecondary education. It is as close as we can come to seeing faces and vases simultaneously.

This volume is divided into four sections—one for each of the three perspective and a final section integrating their findings—discussing what, when, and how higher education can be expected to change with recommendations for higher education and policy makers.

Let's start by looking backward.

Part 1
LOOKING BACKWARD

Looking backward is all about context, the study of historical precedents that shed light on the present. Part one focuses on the Industrial Revolution, the only other time in American history in which the nation experienced change of the scope, duration, and depth it is undergoing today. America and its colleges were transformed during that era as the nation shifted from a local, agrarian society to a national, industrial economy. Then as now, America's colleges were products of the passing era. As the society around them changed, colleges were perceived as dated and out of touch with the times. Over the course of a century and a half, higher education was remade to meet the new realities through a messy and disorderly process that included resistance to change, prolonged and heated debate, wide-ranging experimentation, emergence of model institutions, diffusion of their best practices to mainstream higher education, standardization of practice and policy, and scaling and integration to create the modern industrial system of higher education.

By studying these changes, we are being offered a window to view their context, their nature, their proponents and opponents, and the process by which they occurred. We are being presented with an opportunity both to better understand the present and to glimpse the future that may lay ahead for the nation's colleges and universities.

Chapter one is an account of the Industrial Revolution, how it changed America and triggered a revolution in higher education. The second chapter focuses on the early stages of higher education's transformation: criticism, denial, and experimentation. Chapter three discusses the flowering of transformation—the establishment of new models of higher education and their diffusion to mainstream higher education. The fourth chapter studies the final stages of the transformation—standardization, integration, and scaling to create the Industrial Age system of higher education. Chapter five discusses what looking backward tells us about the future of higher education today and the coming transformation.

Let's begin our look backward with an examination of the Industrial Revolution to set the stage for the changes that followed in higher education.

1

· · · · · · ·

The Industrial Revolution and the Transformation of America

Washington Irving's 1819 tale "Rip Van Winkle" is an allegory for the Industrial Revolution. It's the story of a man who wakes up after sleeping for twenty years, believing he has slept a single night. Having fallen asleep before and awakened after the Revolutionary War, he finds an unrecognizable, incomprehensible, and overwhelming world. So stark is the change that Rip Van Winkle, nearly mad, screams, "Everything's changed and I'm changed and I can't tell what's my name, or who I am" (Irving, 2011). The scale of change during the Industrial Revolution was so swift, deep, unrelenting, and all-encompassing that the image of a person sleeping a night and feeling as if twenty years had passed captures the times.

In 1800, the United States was an agrarian nation of east coast villages with widely scattered homes populated by farmers, artisans, and laborers. A century later, America had become a nation stretching from the Atlantic to the Pacific, built of steel, powered by petroleum and electricity, illuminated by gas and electric light, and crisscrossed by railroad, telegraph, and telephone lines. More than two out of every five Americans lived in cities, and a minority worked on farms.

The Industrial Revolution remade the nation, its economy, communications, transportation, demographics, social institutions, and daily life. This revolution happened in two stages—the first occurred in the seven decades before the Civil War and the second in the half-century that followed. Both were characterized by an outpouring of often competing inventions, practical applications and continuing improvements in those inventions, and rapid expansion of successful applications. An example would be the invention of the steam engine, which gave birth to the steamboat and locomotive, which in turn produced transoceanic steamship lines and a transcontinental railroad system.

The Second Industrial Revolution built on the first, simultaneously eclipsing, disrupting, and accelerating the earlier changes. If the First Industrial Revolution were described as a whirlwind of change, the second would have to be characterized as a tornado.

The First Industrial Revolution

America's First Industrial Revolution, powered by water and steam, was imported from Britain or more accurately stolen from Britain, following in the time-honored tradition of developing countries appropriating the inventions of their pre-eminent peers. In this case, Britain's textile technologies were pilfered, brought to the United States, and turned into mills in New England. To add insult to injury, America improved on the original designs and produced a cornucopia of uniquely domestic innovations that moved the US far beyond Britain in industrial productivity, even before the Civil War.

The Connecticut River Valley, where the earliest factories

were built, became the Silicon Valley of its day. Concentrations of industrial inventors congregated there, giving birth to an age of innovation, which flowered between 1800 and 1860. Patents ballooned, increasing more than a hundredfold from 41 to 4,588 annually in six decades (Hindle & Lubar, 1986, 79).

The First Industrial Revolution produced what today would be called disruptive innovations in four distinct but interrelated areas—manufacturing, agriculture, transportation, and communications.

In manufacturing, the principal innovation was the factory. The first factory in America, a water-powered textile mill, was established in 1790. By the start of the Civil War, there were 131,000 factories in the US (National Park Service, 2015).

The factory system moved America from a handicraft economy of artisans, craft workers, and cottage industries to mass production manufacturing. Indeed, in the thirty-year period between 1825 and 1855, household textile production dropped from 16.5 million yards annually to 0.9 million yards (Taylor, 2015).

The factory increased worker productivity fortyfold and geometrically expanded the number of units produced while dramatically lowering costs and prices (Ayers, 1989). And as more and more of the manufacturing process was mechanized and interchangeable parts made replacement of worn equipment fast and cheap, productivity continued to soar.

Beyond making cheap consumer goods available to a hungry domestic and international market, the factory fundamentally changed workers' lives, the kind of work they did, the way in which work was organized, and where workers lived. Factories tied work to the clock, which made a clock as much a staple in American life as the sun had been on the farm. The railroad, with its need for timetables, reinforced and even standardized the move, requiring the creation of time zones.

Factories, demanding a division of labor, also changed the nature of work. Laborers shifted from being generalists, each performing all of the tasks involved in production, to specialists, assigned a limited number of largely repetitive tasks in the making of a product. Unlike the subsistence farms from which many factory workers came, not only were they specialized but so were the factories where they worked—clock making in Waltham, Massachusetts; cloth making in Lowell, Massachusetts; and gun making near New Haven, Connecticut.

Rather than the relatively flat preindustrial distribution of wealth, wealth became increasingly concentrated, flowing to owners and away from workers. The gap continued to grow throughout the nineteenth century.

The manufacturing boom was supported by dramatic changes in agriculture. The agrarian South resisted industrialization, instead exploiting the labor of four million slaves. However, even before abolition, mechanization came to the fields. First, there were the cotton gin, reaper, and steel plow. By 1857, *Scientific American* enumerated the minimum machinery necessary for a hundred-acre farm as a reaper and mower, a horse rake, a seed planter and mower, a thresher and grain cleaner, a gristmill, a corn sheller, three harrows, a roller, and two cultivators (Morris, 2012, 49).

As with factories, agricultural productivity skyrocketed. The cotton gin, which separated seeds from cotton, alone increased worker productivity by a factor of fifty and cotton production more than twentyfold. In 1801, the United States produced 100,000 bales of cotton. By 1850, that number had risen to more than 2.1 million bales (Ayers, 1989, 16–17; Olson, 2015). As a consequence, farms required fewer workers but more capital for equipment. Opportunities for work in factories and cities rose as the need for farm labor decreased, encouraging the urban migration of the First Industrial Revolution.

Americans followed the jobs. They moved from farms to employment-rich urban areas. In 1800, three-quarters of employed Americans worked in agriculture. By 1860, that number had declined to slightly more than half. It was only a third in the Northeast, the home of US manufacturing (Margo, 1992, 213).

The population also moved west. In 1830, 43 percent of Americans lived in the Northeast and 13 percent resided in the Midwest. Three decades later, the proportions were 34 percent and 29 percent, respectively (Morris, 2012; Haines, 2000, 189). The ten largest cities in the country were located in the East in 1800. By 1860, four were located in the Midwest and South. Indeed, the states and territories, comprising the United States in 1800, stretched only as far west as the Mississippi River. By the start of the Civil War, they spanned the entire continent from ocean to ocean and from Florida to Washington.

At the same time, immigration boomed. From the 1840s through the first decades of the twentieth century, a period when the nation's population tripled, immigrants, willing to work long hours at low pay, consistently composed between a quarter and a third of the nation's population growth (Morris, 2012). The new arrivals garnered the opprobrium of many for keeping wages low and taking jobs away from native-born whites. After the war, the previously enslaved people freed by the Thirteenth Amendment also began migrating north for better economic opportunities and were often met with comparable hostility and racism.

A revolution in transportation speeded the mass migration. Roads multiplied during the First Industrial Revolution, but the game changer was the rise of canals, steamboats, and railroads, which exploded in scale and consequence and allowed for moving goods quickly and cheaply to market.

Canal networks nearly tripled in size between 1830 and 1840, from 1,277 miles to 3,326 miles of canals (Taylor, 2015,

59). Steamships on the western waterways alone increased more than fortyfold between 1817 and 1855, from 17 to 727 ships (Taylor, 2015, 64).

The railroads, however, expanded most rapidly, were the most financially successful, and gained ascendancy among the new modes of transportation. Railroads were introduced in the 1820s, gained momentum in the 1840s, and boomed in the 1850s (Taylor, 2015). The number of miles of track rose by a factor of more than four hundred, from 76 miles of track in 1830 to 30,636 miles in 1860 (Taylor, 2015, 79).

Together canals, steamboats, and trains changed America from a nation of subsistence farmers and local trading to a fledgling national economy. The Erie Canal, which opened in 1825, is a vivid illustration of their impact. Joining Lake Erie with the Hudson River and thereby the port of New York, the Erie Canal knit together New York, New England, and the Great Lakes states. In so doing, it slashed the time necessary to bring goods to market. In 1817, it took more than fifty days to ship merchandise from Cincinnati to New York. The Erie Canal reduced that to eighteen days, and railroads, which would replace most of the canals, cut it to six to eight days (Taylor, 2015, 79).

The Erie Canal also dramatically reduced the cost of shipping from an average of over $100 per ton to $4 and enabled producers to reach the largest consumer markets in history (Mooney, 2011). In this way, the Erie Canal created a national and, by virtue of the port of New York, an international market for goods produced from the Midwest to New England. The railroads completed the job, spanning the continent in 1869 from the Atlantic to the Pacific and from Mexico to Canada.

In the same fashion, the telegraph remade communications in America. Developed early in the nineteenth century, its first long-distance use in 1844 connected Washington, DC, and Baltimore; two years later it joined Washington and New York and soon after linked New York and Boston. By 1850, telegraph lines connected population centers across the East and Midwest, and in 1861, there was a transatlantic cable allowing international communication with Europe.

Like the transportation innovations, the telegraph reduced the cost and time for communication. But it did something far more profound. Until its advent, communication was hand to hand. It was synonymous with transportation; communication was only as quick as a message could be physically delivered from one person to the next. The telegraph made communication nearly instantaneous. The effect was to make news immediate, to make politics national, to promote democracy and to build a common American culture, to speed commercial activity, and to connect the US to the world.

The First Industrial Revolution challenged America's social institutions and the ways in which Americans had historically lived their lives. It raised fundamental questions about the nation's values and expectations for the future. It planted the seeds for the even more dramatic changes to come in the Second Industrial Revolution. It gave birth to a new and emerging world order and caused an old and familiar world to recede. By the time of the Civil War, the United States had emerged as a transcontinental nation, but a nation in transition from a known agrarian society to a still inchoate and as yet unimaginable industrial economy. It was a nation deeply divided, not only over issues such as slavery and states' rights but split too by those determined to reclaim the agrarian past and those committed to building an industrial future. It was a fight for the soul of America and a time of instability and gridlock in Washington, rooted in feelings of profound loss and extraordinary promise.

The Second Industrial Revolution

During the Second Industrial Revolution, change was faster, deeper, and more extensive. This was a revolution powered by petroleum and electricity rather than by water and steam. It was a revolution built of steel rather than wood. The process of change was similar—invention, application, and scaling continued, but standardization and consolidation at a level never before realized were new.

The Second Industrial Revolution rested on four inventions, three occurred in the decade before the Civil War and the fourth a decade after. In 1856, the Bessemer process for converting iron to steel was created. Three years later, the first oil well and the internal combustion engine were developed. The invention of the electric dynamo, or generator, followed in 1876. The result was the steel, oil, the petroleum engine, and electricity that gave birth to a revolution. Between 1875 and 1920, steel production rose over 150-fold from 380,000 tons to 60 million tons (Kennedy, 1987, 200). Similarly, petroleum production experienced a thirty-five-fold increase between 1850 and 1900, rising from 216,000 tons to 7.6 million tons (US Department of Commerce, 1975, 588). Coal dominated the late nineteenth century but was joined by oil and other petroleum products in the twentieth century. Electrical power moved more slowly. It wasn't until 1895 that the very first large-scale generating station began operation. Located in Niagara Falls, it had the capacity to power the city of Buffalo twenty miles away.

A cornucopia of inventions followed in their wake. In communications, there were the telephone and radio. It took twenty-five years for the telephone to reach a 10 percent adoption rate, but it would transform communications, creating a direct, immediate, personal, verbal, extended, interactive medium that would change business, family, civic, and consumer life.

The radio, a product of the late nineteenth century but not a consumer reality until the twentieth century, was a means of communication that went far beyond newspapers, with the capacity to reach all Americans, even those who were illiterate. It changed seemingly everything it touched from advertising, music, and news coverage to politics, entertainment, and sports. It would remake America's social, public, and commercial life and form the backbone of a common American culture.

·   ·

There were inventions in entertainment—the phonograph and motion pictures were created. The former, along with the radio, would bring entertainment into the home and the latter would take people from their homes to be entertained in numbers larger than live theaters or concert halls could accommodate. Beginning with nickelodeons, Hollywood and movie stars would emerge.

There was the electric light, which would fundamentally alter domestic, work, and personal life, affecting everything from birth rates, being described as America's most effective form of birth control to work hours, making it possible for business to operate twenty-four seven. The interior wiring required in homes and offices to make electric lights possible also created the capacity to easily add other appliances.

In transportation, although railroads continued their rapid expansion to 193,346 miles of track crisscrossing the country in 1900 (Gordon, 1997), new means of transportation were created—the automobile, subway, electric streetcar, and airplane. They would further shrink the continent; cement America as a nation; promote cities; spawn suburbs; change where and how people lived; transform commerce, work, leisure, and family life; and provide a degree of freedom to the populace never before possible.

It was a society that demanded a progressively more educated citizenry and workforce. Old jobs changed: the farm and factory evolved with advances in technology and science. New jobs emerged: office and white-collar jobs exploded for managers, clerks, secretaries, and bookkeepers. The professions ballooned. The numbers entering the historic professions such as law and medicine multiplied. Vocations previously learned through apprenticeship training became professions, requiring formal education in universities in fields such as engineering, business, nursing, dentistry, and teaching.

America became a truly urban nation. By 1900, 40 percent of the US population lived in cities, two-thirds in the Northeast. Twenty years later, a majority of Americans were urbanites (US Census Bureau, 2012). Between 1800 and 1900, the percentage of non-farmworkers in the country increased from 26 percent to 60 percent of the labor force (Lebergott, 1966).

Cities, constructed of steel, illuminated by gas and later electric lights and populated increasingly by elevated buildings that reached to the skies, materialized, and boomed. In 1850, ten American cities had populations larger than fifty thousand, none exceeded a half-million. By 1900, there were seventy-eight cities with more than fifty thousand residents and three—New York, Chicago, and Philadelphia—had populations of more than a million (US Department of Commerce, 1975, 11). The migration west and from abroad grew commensurately as well.

The consolidation of these inventions was led by the first generation of industrial natives, men born after the advent of canals, steamboats, factories, railroads, and farm technologies. Among the best known were Andrew Carnegie in steel, John D. Rockefeller in oil, Jay Gould in railroads, and J. P. Morgan in banking, all men born between 1835 and 1839. They integrated their industries vertically by buying their competitors and horizontally by purchasing the related businesses they depended on—from the mining of raw materials to the distribution of finished products and the rail systems required for both. Called robber barons and titans, they created business monopolies.

Morgan was the merger and acquisition financier, who dominated industrial consolidation and is credited by many for creating modern industrial era banking. Among the 42 major consolidations he engineered or financed in the late nineteenth and early 20th centuries were US Steel, AT&T, General Electric, American Harvester, and 24 railroads.

The railroads are exemplary of the scaling up, standardization, and consolidation that occurred. When Abraham Lincoln died, it required 10 different railroad lines to take his body from Washington, DC, to Springfield, Illinois, where he was buried. In 1865, the nation's railroads consisted of more than 300 independent lines (Taylor, 2015, 86), developed largely by local entrepreneurs and municipalities. Tracks were of different widths and sizes prohibiting passage of trains from one line to the next. Rails were made of iron, which wore out quickly, and for a paucity of bridges, trains often needed to be ferried across bodies of water (Morris, 2012, 6–7).

By 1900, this mélange was consolidated into a half-dozen loosely connected systems with six times as many miles of track as in 1860 (Morris, 2012, 235). Those tracks were made of much more durable steel and their gauge was becoming standardized.

The scale and power of the consolidated enterprises and the power of the industrialists who led them was new to the country, having extraordinary and largely unfettered reign over the nation's economy, politics, and social conditions—fixing prices, establishing low wages, and creating deplorable working conditions. America was a nation with a legal and regulatory system created to govern an agrarian society, incapable and owing to the political power of the industrialists who were largely unwilling to change, which prompted Mark Twain to say the United States had "the best government money can buy."

• •

While the Washington gridlock over the agrarian-industrial future of the nation continued with battles over tariffs, immigration, and hard money, labor, populist, and progressive movements were born to combat the abuses of the monopolies and the resulting concentration of wealth. The last great battle over the agrarian versus industrial future of the country was the presidential election of 1896 in which industry vanquished agriculture with the victory of William McKinley over William Jennings Bryan. Government—legislative and judicial—moved in successive actions to adopt with agonizing slowness and powerful opposition the laws, regulations, and regulatory apparatus necessary to govern an industrial society and confront the new reality of monopoly and other abuses of the commonweal in the emergent economy. The old rules no longer fit. New rules affirmed the permanence of industrial America.

It would be impossible for this explosive growth not to change America's colleges.

2

. . . .

Criticism, Denial, and Innovation

Following in the wake of the national changes, the transformation of higher education took place over the course of more than a century in a herky-jerky fashion, with more the appearance of a three-ring circus than the orderly progression of a play. One of the few constants was a never-ending debate, often heated and invariably self-righteous, about the purposes and future of higher education, much like that going on in the country over industrialization.

Criticism of higher education mounted during the antebellum era. Colleges were increasingly thought to be anachronistic and out of step with the times. They responded both by defending their existing practices and by accepting the new realities and experimenting with a panoply of largely piecemeal or ameliorative reforms, ranging from who they enrolled and how they taught to what programs they offered and which degrees they awarded.

A wave of far more substantial innovations followed after the Civil War, most notably the founding of new and dramatically different types of higher education institutions. The lion's share of the experiments and innovative institutions failed, but those that succeeded were improved upon by successive iterations with varying rates of adoption within higher education.

The result was a crazy quilt of institutional types, practices, and policies, which brought about efforts to standardize or establish common policies and practices across higher education and then to scale and integrate the various resulting bits and pieces into a whole. It was a process not dissimilar from that occurring in industrial America and gave birth to the modern industrial era higher education system. That's how the story ended. Let's go back to the beginning.

The American college of 1800 had changed relatively little since the founding of Harvard in 1636. It remained an institution designed to meet the higher learning needs of a sectarian, agricultural society. The college curriculum consisted of Greek, Hebrew, Aramaic, rhetoric, grammar, arithmetic, geometry, astronomy, history, and the nature of plants. There were no courses. Students studied one subject a day from 8 a.m. to 5 p.m., Monday through Friday and a half-day Saturday (Friday was not a party night; actually, neither was Saturday). The methods of instruction were lectures, recitation-repetition of assignments orally and verbatim, and disputation—formulaic debate using Aristotelian syllogisms on themes such as "we sin while we sleep."

There were twenty-five degree-granting colleges in 1800 that together enrolled fewer than one thousand students, who varied in age from tweens to twentysomethings. In the main, they were much younger than their contemporary peers, typically matriculating in their mid-teens, some even earlier. High schools had not yet come into being, so colleges occupied the position of secondary schools, and students enrolled after completing what would now be considered a middle school education.

The first decades of the nineteenth century were hard on higher education. The number of institutions, following the westward migration of the country, doubled between 1800 and 1820 and multiplied another fivefold by the start of the Civil War. The growth of potential college students didn't keep pace with the expansion, causing enrollments to drop at a number of institutions, particularly in New England.

Financial pressures mounted, exacerbated by the widespread belief that college was too expensive and the classical curriculum was of doubtful value. Competing noncollegiate vocational programs and apprenticeships in industry and the professions thrived.

Colleges responded in two ways. Some experimented with more modern, vocational, and abbreviated alternatives to the classical curriculum; others rejected the criticism and denied the need for change.

The Dawn of Innovation

The antebellum efforts to create an alternative to the classical curriculum were largely unsuccessful. They failed for lack of funding, internal institutional opposition, bad timing, and unpopularity with students and their families.

Harvard was an early reformer and the driver was Professor George Ticknor, a graduate of Dartmouth and, in 1815, one of the very first Americans to attend the research universities of Germany. Hired as professor of French and Spanish at Harvard, he was appalled by what he encountered in Cambridge—from an antiquated library and intellectually unchallenging program to an idle faculty and poor teaching. Ticknor wanted to remake Harvard in the image of the great German universities, embracing academic freedom and scholarship.

In 1825, he proposed a menu of reforms for Harvard, which had until then responded to the criticisms and pressures on higher education by adding a few professorships like his and supplementing its classical curriculum with a sprinkling of new elective subjects and courses such as modern language, which he taught. Ticknor called for elective classes to supplement Harvard's prescribed curriculum, tutorials and lectures, pedagogies and assessments demanding deeper questioning of students, the creation of academic departments, student uniforms, grouping students by ability, advanced graduate studies, and the admission of nondegree students to shorter programs that would come to be called partial courses.

Faced with the Great Student Rebellion of 1823, in which nearly half the senior class was expelled for rioting just before graduation, and mounting discontent with the situation in the Massachusetts legislature, the Harvard Corporation, a board of trustees, approved the Ticknor plan for the college. But, for the most part, the reforms bombed. Actually, they were never really adopted.

Harvard president John Thornton Kirkland was not a supporter, and the faculty opposed the changes. In fact, they sabotaged them. For instance, as required by the Harvard Corporation, the faculty divided students by ability, but they gave them all the very same assignments. In the end, only one department carried out the Ticknor reforms, the department he chaired. Kirkland's successor was not nearly as supportive of the Ticknor reforms as he had been, championing an unadulterated classical curriculum and rejecting the need for change. A frustrated Ticknor resigned in 1835.

At Amherst College, it was the faculty and board that called for change. In 1826, the faculty reported to the trustees on "the inadequacy of the prevailing systems of classical education in this country" (Amherst Faculty, 1827, 1). They argued, "One fact ... is becoming more and more obvious every day. The American public is not satisfied with the present course of education in our higher seminaries. The great objection is that it is not sufficiently modern and comprehensive to meet the exigencies of the age and country in which we live" (5). "While everything is on the advance our colleges are stationary or if not quite stationary, that they are being left far behind by the rapid march of improvement" (5–6).

The faculty proposed that the college adopt a parallel course of study, an alternative track to the baccalaureate. In addition to its classical curriculum, the college would offer a "theoretical and practical mechanics" program. It wouldn't really be an alternative though because the admissions requirements for both would be the same, including Latin and Greek. The new program would offer instruction in modern languages: French and Spanish, perhaps Italian and German; English literature; mechanical philosophy; chemistry and physical sciences; architecture and engineering; natural history; modern history; and political and civil law. But the students who chose this new route would still be required to take a great deal of the classical curriculum: ancient history; geography; grammar; rhetoric; math; natural, moral, and intellectual philosophy; political economy; and theology.

The faculty also proposed that Amherst place a major emphasis on the science of education, create a professorship, and establish a department in the area. While parallel courses of study were often part of the reform agenda during the antebellum period, education science was a uniquely Amherst idea.

The board was excited by the faculty report and had extracts published in the hope that the report would be read by other colleges, government, and the public. They asked the faculty to turn it into an actionable plan.

That's pretty much as far as reform went at Amherst. The college didn't have the money to implement what would become a hotly argued critique of the nation's colleges and an explicit

road map for change, which may seem modest by today's standards but was considered radical at the time.

The big success story of the antebellum years, at least during
that period, was Union College in Schenectady, New York, at
least for several decades. Striving to be "the university of its
times," Union was an innovator from its founding in 1795. It
was a proponent of democratic rather than elite access to college; a critic of the dead languages, requiring French instead;
an advocate of public schooling for all children, a relatively
new idea at the time; and the home of America's first collegiate
fraternities.

In 1815, Union adopted a pioneering parallel course of
study, blending modern language, science, and technology that
awarded the same degree as its classical curriculum. The accent
at Union was on the applied sciences. In the years that followed,
Union would offer America's first engineering course, beat out
Yale to hire a professor of chemistry, and fail in an attempt
to establish an Institute for Science that would be home to
a faculty engaged in teaching, research, and development in
the "application of science to the useful arts."

However, Union proceeded cautiously. It dropped the option of allowing students to substitute French for Greek out of
concern that parents wanted a classical curriculum for their
sons. Although Union required students to read modern think-
ers such as Locke and Newton, it did so in defense of religion
rather than as a challenge to it, as proof of God's orderly universe and man's role in perfecting it. The college seal demonstrated the same careful balancing act in linking the classical
with the modern. While picturing the Greek goddess of wis-
dom, Minerva, Union combined it with a motto in French,
"Under the laws of Minerva, we all become brothers."

Union thrived. The parallel course proved very popular;
enrollment boomed, increasing from 160 students in 1815 to

255 six years later (Hislop, 1971, 166–183). By 1830, Union graduated more students (96) than any other college in America, more than Yale (71), Harvard (48), and Princeton (20). It remained among the top three through the start of the Civil War and its graduates became leaders in higher education; of those graduating between 1804 and 1866, 86 became college presidents (Hislop, 1971, 224–233; Fox, 1945,16).

Why Union thrived is a story of location, leadership, money, and a unique program. With the advent of the Erie Canal, the city of Schenectady prospered, becoming a center of trade, water-powered manufacturing, and transportation. Union was very nicely located.

As for leadership, for sixty-two years Union was headed by Eliphalet Nott, the longest-serving college president in US history, which seems like the stuff Dante might have written about. Nott, a minister, inventor, and entrepreneur, was unique as an educator. He captured the spirit of his times and served as a bridge between America's Christian and rapidly advancing civic cultures. Rather than seeking to impose a borrowed European cast on the college as Ticknor attempted at Harvard, Nott advocated a uniquely American vision of higher education, blending the nation's sectarian and secular roots.

Nott was also a rainmaker extraordinaire who made Union the wealthiest college in the country. At a time when legislatures weren't all that friendly to higher education and Union was in deep financial trouble with partially constructed buildings, he convinced New York's legislature to support the college and ultimately to turn over the management of the state lottery to Nott and two Union trustees. Union made $512,687 and Nott received $451,045 from the lottery, which in current dollars would be about thirty times larger (Hislop, 1971, 300–346).

In response to student complaints of poorly heated dormitories, Nott invented stoves. Thirty patents later, Nott had created the anthracite steam boiler that powered much of the steamboat traffic on the nation's canals and waterways.

Nott, who also married well to a wealthy widow, had a propensity to commingle the college's finances and his own. Early in his presidency, this worked to the advantage of Union. He and trustees also aggressively invested the college's money in real estate and that, too, initially boosted Union's fortunes.

It all fell apart after the Civil War. Enrollments plummeted after the war, dropping from 437 in 1860 to 89 in 1879. Union's peerage with Harvard and Yale ended (Hislop, 1971, 556–567).

Nott died in 1866, nearly blind, having spent too many years in office. By the end of his term, Union lagged behind the times rather than setting the standard. Yale and Harvard created scientific schools before Union announced its intent to establish the ill-fated Institute of Science. Not only was the college late, but competition to offer the scientific programs that in earlier years distinguished Union had increased substantially. With the growth of the railroads, the prosperity engendered by the Erie Canal waned, reducing Union's geographic advantage. Finally, the aggressive real estate investments ultimately ate up the college's operating funds and the commingling of Nott's and the college's money worked against Union and became a source of continuing litigation.

The scientific schools at Harvard and Yale represented a different approach to reform. Rather than creating a parallel track like Amherst and Union, these colleges established what amounted to parallel colleges, separate units—the Lawrence Scientific School at Harvard and the Sheffield Scientific School at Yale.

The stories of the two are similar. Both began with a science-math professorship, of the sort Ticknor held in modern language, supplementary and outside the classical core. Harvard hired its first science and math faculty member in 1728. But science education truly started nearly a century later with an 1814 bequest by the scientist and inventor Benjamin Thompson, Count Rumford to establish a professorship in the Application of Science to the Useful Arts. Harvard appointed the botanist Joseph Bigelow, who not only wanted the practical arts to be added to the Harvard curriculum but also built a sizable collection of industrial machines at the college, including a full-size cotton loom.

Yale, which was the epicenter of the old order, hired Congregational minister Jeremiah Day as professor of mathematics and natural philosophy. Day was the author of the nation's first algebra textbook and would become president of the college and one of the nation's most ardent defenders of the classical curriculum.

In the years that followed, both institutions added more science faculty, eminent scientists who would constitute a critical mass for the useful arts. In 1827, Bigelow left Harvard College to join its medical school faculty, a more congenial place for his work and the endowed Rumford Chair remained vacant for seven years, which is a pretty good indication of the importance of the useful arts in Cambridge.

Finally, embarrassed at the hiatus, Harvard hired Daniel Treadwell, the president of the Boston Mechanics Institute to fill the professorship. Though Treadwell called for more practical education in Cambridge, he was not viewed as a threat to Harvard's classical curriculum. It was his colleague, Benjamin Pierce, America's most renowned mathematician and a consummate Harvard insider, which gave him the capacity to pursue more radical change. Pierce led the effort to establish an alternative to the college's classical curriculum; he persuaded the institution to adopt elective courses in math and recommended that Harvard create an engineering school.

At Yale, a father and, later, son team, supported by a growing coterie of distinguished colleagues, drove science education for much of the nineteenth century. In succession, a chemist and a geologist, Benjamin Silliman Sr. and Jr. determined the Yale science curriculum as well as shaped the sciences in America. They wrote voluminously; gave thousands of public speeches; created journals and professional societies; served as consultants to America's entrepreneurs, playing a major role in the development of the petroleum industry; prepared the next generations of scientists; and recruited outstanding faculty to Yale.

The Industrial Revolution and its demand for applied scientists—engineers, chemists, and geologists—spurred the rise of the sciences at America's colleges. In 1828, there were approximately sixty science faculty nationally. By 1850, there were more than three hundred (Geiger, 2015, 262).

But what got Harvard and Yale to establish scientific schools were mega-gifts from industrial entrepreneurs. In Harvard's case, it was Abbott Lawrence, an importer, exporter, and textile magnate who championed railroads. In 1847, he gave Harvard the unprecedented sum of $50,000 to establish a school to prepare engineers, chemists, or men of science who would apply their skills to practical purposes. He gave the gift believing the nation's future depended on highly skilled technical and scientific talent, while knowing he was unable to find skilled mechanics and technical workers for his own factories. The result was the Lawrence Scientific School.

Yale's Sheffield Scientific School was funded a year later with a $130,000 gift from Joseph Sheffield, a railroad entrepreneur who had earlier in life worked on the Erie Canal.

The schools differed. Though both offered three-year programs, they awarded different degrees—a bachelor of science and a bachelor of philosophy. Lawrence was more theoretical and Sheffield more practical, which was reflected in their curriculums and methods of instruction. Lawrence was a confederation of disparate, semiautonomous academic programs with widely varying standards, while Sheffield operated as a single unit with common academic requirements for its students. Lawrence received support from Harvard, and Sheffield was proprietary, funded on the basis of student tuition and external support, though both were chronically underfunded and required support from their hosts.

Both schools suffered from common problems. Each was looked down on by its parent college owing to the quality of its faculty, students, and programs. Both had low admission standards and high attrition. There was competition for students between the colleges and their scientific school. Both scientific schools became enclaves for innovation at their institutions— awarding new degrees, including the first PhD in America at Sheffield; offering programs of unconventional lengths and content, including a one-year bachelor of science degree in civil engineering at Lawrence; and employing faculty with differing backgrounds, interests, and values. This served only to highlight the divergence between the units rather than being perceived by the parent as a lab for experimentation. At bottom, there was a fundamental clash of cultures between the colleges and their subunits, between practical and classical education.

In the end, their paths were different, but the results were the same. Harvard tried several times to merge Lawrence with the Massachusetts Institute of Technology. Sheffield sought to make itself more like Yale, adding more liberal arts to its curriculum. The courses of study were lengthened at Lawrence. There were continuing reorganizations at both universities, a euphemism for making the scientific schools like the universities, transferring their programs to the university, or limiting scientific school operations. Over the years, the desirable Lawrence and Sheffield programs were absorbed by their parent institutions, and the scientific schools faded away. A shorn version of Lawrence morphed into the Harvard School of Engineering and the remaining shadow of Sheffield was officially closed in 1956. The lesson here is that an innovation needs to be compatible with the values of the university that hosts it.

One of the grandest and saddest failures of antebellum reform occurred at Brown. In education reform, timing matters a lot. That was the problem at Brown. It anticipated the reforms that would sweep higher education in the aftermath of the Civil War, but it did so beginning in 1842, a quarter century before Americans wanted them.

Francis Wayland, the fourth president of Brown, was a Baptist minister who attended Union College, served as professor of moral philosophy and professor of mathematics and natural philosophy at Union, and was recommended for the Brown presidency by Eliphalet Nott.

A popular choice for the job, Wayland arrived on campus in 1827 to lead an institution with falling enrollment, declining admission standards, poor student discipline, an angry faculty, and a diminishing reputation. He made immediate changes, beginning with student discipline. Wayland imposed much stricter rules of conduct, required regular room checks after curfew, and demanded all faculty members live in campus housing and participate in student discipline, a rule that effectively closed the medical school by driving the nonresident faculty out.

Academically, what Wayland did sounds modest by today's standards, but in his time, it was radical, going right to the heart of how students were taught. He challenged the established practices of recitation, formal lectures, textbooks, and memorization by banning textbooks in recitations with the goal of forcing students to comprehend and explicate rather than memorize and regurgitate.

In 1842, his fifteenth year on the job, Wayland wrote a very well-received book entitled *Thoughts on the Present Collegiate System in the United States*. It called for deep and far-reaching reform of the American college, pointing to its declining enrollments. The number of colleges and the population of the country were increasing, but student attendance wasn't keeping pace. Wayland concluded the public didn't want what colleges offered. He argued the price of college was already low, but even so, colleges were having difficulty giving away the education they offered. The problem was that collegiate programs were out of date, created for "a society very different than our own" (Wayland, 1842, 12). Wayland criticized the uniformity of the nation's colleges, with few exceptions, consisting "of a four-year course, terminating in graduation, all the students pursuing the same studies, the same labor being required from all, and the same time being allotted to each" (9–10). He charged that established colleges refused to deviate from this approach and newer institutions judged their success imperfectly, replicating it. Wayland dismissed recent reform efforts as inconsequential and said the public wanted improvement.

President Wayland went beyond simply including a set of recommendations in his book; he asked the Brown board and faculty to adopt his proposals the year before his book was published. Little came of it, and in 1849, with continuing enrollment declines, he offered his resignation, shocking the college community and the board. To get Wayland to stay, a study commission was formed, his proposals were adopted, and a campaign was launched to raise $125,000 to support them. The New System, as the program was called, was a work in progress—a combination of actual program changes and aspirational goals to guide future changes.

The New System established three distinct degrees. Two were new—a bachelor of philosophy degree was created for students who wanted a shorter, more specialized partial course and a three-year master of arts degree was instituted, which was essentially the old classical baccalaureate program. The third degree retained the name bachelor of arts but was reduced from four to three years and included fewer liberal arts requirements, affording students the opportunity to choose their own courses and study the practical arts. Each degree was awarded based on examinations rather than on actual time spent in the classroom. The duration of each program was to be based on the subject studied and the pace at which students completed it.

Student choice was paramount, though parental wishes superseded choice. Students were not obliged to complete a degree. They could select the courses they wished to study, and a certificate of proficiency would be awarded for each course completed.

More practical studies were added to Brown's program, such as science and engineering, thus encouraging concentrated partial courses. Wayland envisioned that a mechanic might come to Brown and study only physics to the good of the mechanic and the country. Partial courses were seen not only as a lifesaver for Brown, boosting enrollments and generating cash, but as a vehicle for democratizing collegiate education, opening the doors of higher education to middle- and working-class families. Toward this end, Brown would adopt new courses to meet community needs, sort of an early version of extension education. For example, in 1852, Brown offered lectures on calico printing and in 1853 on the chemistry of precious metals. Both lecture series were aimed at tradesmen of Providence, Rhode Island, and were well attended. The chemistry lectures drew more than three hundred people.

The college also democratized its admissions requirements as supporters explained it or lowered admission standards as critics charged merely to increase enrollment in the partial course. Latin and Greek proficiency, for instance, were elim-inated as admissions requirements, and in some programs, a primary school education was sufficient to matriculate.

The New System also sought to transform faculty compen-sation, first by increasing salaries and then by tying salaries to enrollments. This was a nonstarter with faculty, though there was a good deal of enthusiasm for the raises.

The New System was a bold program that anticipated by de-cades the development of the elective system at Harvard, the creation of land-grant colleges straddling the classical curric-ulum and the useful arts, the advent of the community college with its local service mission and commitment to expanded access, and the rise of the university, promising any person, any study.

But the New System ultimately failed. It didn't produce the enrollment increases Brown needed and it diminished the col-lege's reputation. Less lucrative, shorter duration partial course enrollments flourished while the number of traditional bacca-laureate students increased initially and then dropped. Democ-ratizing access to college reduced Brown's standing, driving away its traditional clientele—parents and children who did not want to rub shoulders with the working class. They applied instead to schools with higher and more traditional standards.

Some parts of the New System just didn't work. For instance, earning degrees by demonstrating what students knew on ex-ams rather than the fixed amounts of time they spent in classes was a revolutionary idea that placed a premium on student learning, promised to individualize each student's program, and broke the formulaic collegiate approach Wayland criti-cized. But the tests were "superficial," undemanding, and had very low passing scores; proficiency was set at a score of 25 per-cent (Bronson, 1914, 291). A faculty committee reported that four and a half days of devoted study would be sufficient to pass the master of arts exam (Bronson, 1914, 291). This both defeated the educational rationale for the change and further weakened Brown's academic standing.

The elective curriculum never really materialized. Only two to four of the nine requisite courses for the bachelor's degrees were chosen by students and just three of twelve for the master's (Bronson, 1914, 290–291). The problem was economic. The student body and faculty were too small to support the number of courses an elective system actually required. Plus, there was the matter of faculty who wanted students to take their courses and so required them.

There were also unexpected consequences. Student discipline suffered under the New System. The lack of curricular rigor, the reduced length of the bachelor of arts degree, and the absence of pressure to complete a degree gave students more time for hijinks. Newly hired faculty, recruited for their scholarship, didn't maintain discipline as firmly as Wayland wanted and soon left the college.

Wayland, at the height of his career and fame, resigned in 1855 for health reasons. His successor quietly declared the New System a failure and dismantled it.

Brown after Wayland came very much to resemble Brown before the New System. Entrance requirements and languages were restored quickly along with the older degree requirements. The master and baccalaureate of arts were merged and the baccalaureate was once again a four-year degree. By 1861, Brown was returned almost entirely to the collegiate norm, and the reversal of Wayland's reforms was cheered by undergraduates who in particular didn't like being grouped with their social inferiors who took only the partial course (Bronson, 1914, 325).

Defense of the Status Quo

All of these changes—at Harvard, Amherst, Union, and many other colleges that attempted similar reforms—were repudiated and denounced as injurious to collegiate education by the most prestigious college in America, Yale. In 1828, the college issued the best known and most influential of the defenses of the classical curriculum, the Yale Report of 1828.* At Yale, which then had the largest enrollments and the most geographically diverse student body, students studied Latin, Greek, and mathematics for the first three years with a dollop of science, astronomy, geography, history, rhetoric, and grammar stirred in. Senior year was devoted to metaphysics and ethics.

At the time of the report, Yale was 127 years old. However, its enrollments were in flux—down 20 percent one year then up 40 percent the next. College finances were tenuous. Increasing amounts of the endowment were being used to cover annual operating losses. An alumni solicitation effort produced disappointing results, and the Connecticut state legislature, which supported Yale, was unwilling to provide a supplemental appropriation.

The Yale board, president, and faculty were by all accounts quite satisfied with the academic program and college life, but not everyone was equally enamored. Yale students had staged a demonstration to protest both the quality of the college's teaching and the food it served, though not necessarily in that

*This account relies on several sources: the Yale Report of 1828, published in 1829 as "Original Papers in Relation to a Course of Liberal Education"; a case study of the Yale Report entitled "Locke College" which Arthur wrote with the assistance of Joseph Zolner; *The American College and University: A History* by Frederick Rudolph; and Melvin Urofsky's article on the history of the Yale Report, "Reforms and Response."

order. The faculty were criticized for adhering to a curriculum that stressed memorization over thinking and that emphasized dead languages over useful subjects.

During this same period, the Connecticut legislature carried out a review of the college, concluding that the quality of its program was declining and costs were too high, though Yale tuition was lower than many of its competitors. The curriculum was thought to be poorly matched with the business needs of the nation. The college was taken to task for staunchly adhering to an antiquated curriculum and giving too little attention to career preparation.

In light of Yale's precarious financial position and plans to lobby for additional state support, both President Jeremiah Day and the board viewed the student rebellion and critical legislative review as serious attacks on the institution. In response, Senator Noyes Darling, a Yale alumnus, college trustee, former judge, and state legislator, proposed the creation of a board committee to consider reform of the curriculum, specifically the expediency of dropping "the dead languages" from the course of studies. Darling was a proponent of Connecticut industrial development, who believed the state should turn away from outdated ideas that were embedded in the past. He worried that the old Yale curriculum was out of step with an age that took progress, symbolized by the Erie Canal, for granted.

In September, the Yale board approved Senator Darling's suggestion and created a blue-ribbon committee that included the governor of Connecticut to review the curriculum. In April, the committee asked President Day and the Yale faculty to address the question of curricular change.

The result was a report, not only on Yale and the value of dead languages, but an exegesis on collegiate education in America with a carefully reasoned defense of the classical curriculum and a dismissal of the reforms urged on higher education by its critics and even adopted by other institutions. It had the enthusiastic and apparently unanimous support of the faculty. Indeed, if there was any faculty dissent, it was well masked.

The Yale Report began with a recognition that collegiate education was imperfect and needed improvement but said it would be a mistake to believe colleges were unchangeable or had been standing still, a dismissal of the Amherst statement. The Yale Report argued that, in recent years, colleges had made important updates to their courses of study, expanded their methods of teaching, added new fields of inquiry, and toughened admissions standards. There was confidence that improvements would continue as rapidly as possible, without hazarding achievement already attained.

The document acknowledged in this era of profound change that it might be a good idea to pause and consider whether gradual change would be adequate or whether more sweeping institutional transformation was required of colleges. Indeed, critics had argued that colleges required dramatic redesign, needed to be new-modeled, and were incapable of adapting to the changes occurring around them. They would as a consequence lose students because they were unable to meet the needs of the work world. The report said that these ardent critics were posing the wrong question. Instead of asking, *What type of change is necessary?* (small or large, immediate or gradual), the question they should have been asking is, *What is the purpose of a college?*

Yale's response constituted the heart of the report. The fundamental purpose of collegiate education, the authors declared, is to develop "the discipline and furniture of the mind, expanding its powers, and storing it with knowledge." The work of the college is to lay a foundation for superior learning—"broad, and deep, and solid" through a prescribed course of instruction, which would develop in students' attention, memory, analysis, discrimination, judgment, balance, discipline, imagination, and character. This could only be achieved with a classical curriculum, more specifically the Yale curriculum; the report explained how each component of that curriculum—subjects and methods of instruction—contributed to these outcomes and declared that no other subjects or pedagogies should be included in the curriculum. While no specific institutions were named in the report, this was an implicit shot at colleges that were adding electives and modern languages to their programs.

• •

Nor, the authors warned, should the curriculum of the American college seek to ape the European universities. This was an attack at Harvard for importing elements of the German university.

The report also set its sights on colleges offering partial courses in science and engineering, saying it was not enough to develop only certain thinking skills or to study only a few subjects. Curricular balance and comprehensiveness were essential.

Vocationalism and professional education were dismissed as well. The report argued that the purpose of collegiate study was not to complete a student's education but to lay a foundation, to teach students how to think and what to think about throughout their lives. The authors accordingly excluded professional education from the curriculum. It was too narrow, failing to develop a person fully in thinking and knowledge. Since life entailed more than just earning a living, far more than a vocational education was needed to serve family, community, and nation. The report insisted that this broader conception of education would not grow up spontaneously amid the bustle of business. A classical curriculum should serve as a precursor to professional study.

The report asked, "What is a [person] fit for, when he takes his degree? Is he qualified for business?" The report says no if he stops there. His education is begun but not completed. The college should not be reproached for failing to accomplish that which it has never undertaken to perform. The analogy is made to complaining about a mason who has laid the foundation of a house, saying that he has done nothing of purpose because he has not finished the building and the product of his labor is not habitable.

The report also countered the anti-elitism that would sweep Andrew Jackson into the White House later in the year, stating that the kind of education Yale espoused was not for everyone. Some would lack time; while others would lack resources. For these individuals, a two-year program stressing a professional field or an area of specialization would be appropriate. While the report labeled such programs defective education, it also went on to say that "a defective education is better than none."

• •

Disdain was also expressed for smorgasbord programs that gave students a "smattering of almost everything." "A partial education is often expedient," noted the report, "a superficial one, never." This was an implicit attack on the new university Thomas Jefferson was building in Virginia.

The report advised that despite pressures to democratize, not to mention to increase enrollments, colleges must maintain competitive admission standards and bar vocational studies. The challenge facing colleges is not a competition for numbers but for excellence.

The report concluded with an inquiry into the condition of the Yale curriculum. It asked whether it was up to date, whether it had kept pace with advances in knowledge. The answer was absolutely.

Moreover, no question has engaged the attention of the faculty more constantly, than how the course of education in the college might be improved, and rendered more practically useful. The charge, therefore, that the college is stationary, that no efforts are made to accommodate it to wants of the age, that all exertions are for the purpose of perpetuating abuses, and that the college is much the same as it was at the time of its founding are wholly gratuitous. The changes in the country, during the last century, have not been greater than in the college. ("Original Papers in Relation to a Course of Liberal Education," 349–350)

Yale, the institution that produced the greatest number of college presidents in the country, had spoken. The board accepted the report. For the next half-century, the college continued to teach the trivium and quadrivium. When new subjects were added, it was not as electives but rather as add-ons to be taken in addition to the classical curriculum (Urofsky, 1965, 61).

The report had extraordinary impact on higher education, although Yale was not the first institution to make the case for the classical curriculum. Columbia did so eighteen years earlier but not as cogently or thoroughly or with the status of Yale.

Colleges across the country embraced the Yale Report, particularly the new institutions in the Midwest and South from Indiana, Ohio, and Wisconsin to Georgia, North Carolina, and Virginia. Presidents sought for their colleges the instant academic credibility that came with the Yale imprimatur. The first Beloit College catalog went so far as to say its program was "drawn up exactly on the Yale Plan" (Urofsky, 1965, 62). Historian Melvin Urofsky concluded the Yale Report made the case for the classical curriculum so forcefully that it wasn't until after the Civil War that the reform movement regained the initiative (63).

The antebellum years served as a rehearsal for the coming transformation. It made clear who wanted change and who didn't. In the main, the nation's colleges and the families that traditionally attended them resisted change. The supporters were government and employers.

Second, each failure at reform revealed more about the requirements for success. Money, leadership, support within the academic community, compatibility with institutional norms and values, and timing were essential as were garnering enrollments and the willingness of families to send their children. A good location was also an asset.

Once implemented, the changes needed to work, to accomplish what their authors said they would, and they needed to be profitable to the institution adopting them in terms of the college's revenues and reputation. The centripetal force of inertia that pulled colleges toward the tried and true was a continuing threat.

Third, despite opposition to change even at the most resistant schools, change still occurred. Over time, Yale, as its report noted, added faculty and coursework in the useful arts, such as science and modern languages, though these subjects were generally not required and were seldom offered as replacements for any portions of the classical core.

3

·······

New Models and Diffusion

The real transformation of American higher education occurred after the Civil War, during the Second Industrial Revolution. The depth, scope, rapidity, and character of the change mirrored but followed in the wake of the larger society's changes. A new generation of leaders emerged. They teamed with government and industry to turn the nation's colleges into universities. They built new institutions, varying models of what that university might be, rather than attempting to reform existing institutions as their predecessors had. Diffusion followed. At a quickening pace, mainstream higher education adopted the reforms. Standardization, scaling up, and integration followed.

A New Generation of Leaders

Three presidents are usually credited as the architects of the postwar transformation: Andrew Dickson White at Cornell, Daniel Coit Gilman at Johns Hopkins, and Charles Eliot at Harvard. Unlike their predecessors, they were not ministers, and they were not born in the eighteenth century. They were industrial natives, born in the 1830s, the same decade as Carnegie, Gould, Morgan, and Rockefeller. They were cosmopolitans, well acquainted with higher education in Europe; products of the antebellum reform efforts, who learned from the leading reformers and faced their opponents. They were academic entrepreneurs who worked well with their counterparts in business, prompting the economist Thorstein Veblen to christen them "captains of erudition" (1918, 59). They were simultaneously managers and visionaries who viewed higher education not as a religious calling but as a summons to build the future of education and the nation. Though differing in their views on what that the future should be, they shared a new and uniquely American vision of higher education for a new era.

Daniel Coit Gilman, born in 1831, grew up in a business family. His father was a well-to-do mill owner, and his grandparents on both sides were wealthy merchants. He attended Yale where the future "revolutionary" lived with James Kingsley, the Yale professor of Latin who had been a principal author of the Yale Report.

He was in the same class and close friends with Andrew Dickson White; together they traveled to Europe after graduation. Gilman wrote about the experience and published an article on "Scientific Schools in Europe" in the *American Journal of Education* in 1856, which ended up being used at Sheffield as a fundraising piece.

Gilman returned to Yale where he built his career, beginning as assistant librarian, then librarian, and finally professor of physical and political geography at Sheffield, where he sat on its board and argued its case in the state legislature, the press, and the homes of wealthy donors. Gilman, who played a key role in creating Sheffield's partial course, was a powerful proponent of the advantages of technical and scientific schools over the classical college.

In 1867, he was offered the presidency of the University of Wisconsin and three years later the presidency of the University of California. He turned down both because he wanted the Yale presidency and the chance to transform his alma mater into a real university.

That opportunity came in 1870. Gilman was one of two finalists for the job. The other was Reverend Noah Porter, an alumnus and professor of moral philosophy at the college, who was committed to maintaining the dictates of the Yale Report. Yale chose Porter. And Gilman accepted a renewed offer by the University of California, where he spent three frustrating years in battles with the legislature before being called to Baltimore by the board of Johns Hopkins.

Like his friend Gilman, Andrew Dickson White, born in 1832, also grew up in an affluent family. His father was a wealthy merchant and banker in Syracuse, New York. White spent one year as a student at Geneva College, which he found to be a waste of time and then enrolled at Yale, where he was influenced by Noah Porter, first his teacher and later friend. During the time abroad with Gilman, he studied at the Sorbonne and the University of Berlin, completing the tour by becoming attaché to the US minister to Russia.

On his return home, White enrolled once again at Yale for a master's in history. Based on advice from Francis Wayland that the best place for graduates was the West, he wrote to "influential friends" and secured a faculty position at the University of Michigan, then presided over by President Henry Tappan. Tappan had been educated at Union during the Nott years and was attempting to transform Michigan into a research university— replete with an elective curriculum, graduate school, research faculty, labs, and professional programs in fields such as engi-

neering and applied science. A proponent of the German research university over the British college with its classical curriculum, Tappan's vision inspired White, who thought of himself
as a revolutionary, though few others concurred; he dreamed
of creating a great university. Tappan, by the way, was fired in
1863 by a largely rural board that saw him as too aristocratic
and guilty of the sin of trying to Germanify their college.

The Midwest proved not to White's liking, so he returned to
Europe and then came home to Syracuse, where he ran for and
won a seat in the New York State Senate. There, the new chair
of the Senate Education Committee met fellow Senator Ezra
Cornell, a farmer who had made a fortune as a contractor and
developer of telegraph lines. Together they decided to create
that Great University.

Charles Eliot, the third member of the triumvirate, born in
1834, was scion of a prominent Boston family and had Harvard in his blood. He attended Harvard and taught at both the
college and the Lawrence Scientific School. His father, who had
been mayor of Boston, was the college's treasurer and institutional historian. His grandfather endowed a professorship
of Greek in 1814. Jared Sparks, Harvard president when Eliot
attended, was a close family friend. Two of his uncles, George
Ticknor and Andrews Norton, were Harvard professors. And
Eliot himself was elected an overseer, a second board charged
with review of the corporation's actions, in 1868.

After graduating from Harvard, he spent a year away volun-
teering as a teacher and rejoined the college as a mathematics
tutor in 1854. Eliot, who chafed at the limits of the recitation
system, preferring practical demonstrations and challenging
traditional oral examinations, focused his efforts at Harvard
on curriculum change and instructional improvement. Accordingly, as a tutor, he worked closely with his undergraduate chemistry teacher Josiah Cooke to expand the chemistry

program at the college. A natural at administration, President James Walker used him to perform a wide array of administrative tasks. In 1858, Eliot was promoted to assistant professor of math and chemistry.

But Eliot was a lightning rod whose officiousness, combined with his strongly held and bluntly expressed opinions, produced conflict throughout his tenure teaching at Harvard. In 1859, he had a falling out with Cooke and left the College for the Lawrence School.

At Lawrence, where he rose to acting dean during the war, Eliot threw himself into improving teaching and strengthening the school's administration. He made examinations more rigorous, expanded laboratory instruction, and even reduced pilferage of lab equipment. However, he clashed with Louis Agassiz, one of the world's foremost scientists and founding head of Lawrence, who created a school emphasizing theory over practice and formal lectures over experimentation. Abbott Lawrence's original gift had been intended to create the kind of practical scientific school Eliot yearned for, but the hiring of the reputed Swiss scientist, Agassiz, who really wanted to build a museum, changed the direction. Agassiz hired colleagues of comparable persuasion and interests.

So not surprisingly, Eliot was passed over for the Rumford Chair, which he desperately wanted and believed he earned, in favor of Wolcott Gibbs, a more prolific scholar and an Agassiz acolyte. Embarrassed at not having been selected and insulted by receiving as a consolation prize a poorly funded professorship and an administrative position as laboratory manager, Eliot left Harvard for a two-year study of science and technical education in Europe, where one of the things he witnessed was the powerful connection between science and business.

As a next step, he thought seriously of abandoning academe for a career in business. His family had been hit hard by the

Panic of 1857, and he had a job offer in hand, which paid much more than a professor's salary. Given his skill set, pedigree, and connections, Eliot would likely have been equally successful and become a lot wealthier in the private sector. But he couldn't bring himself to do it. So instead in 1865, he joined the chemistry faculty at MIT, an institution far better suited to his practical orientation than Harvard.

Four years later, Eliot published two articles in the *Atlantic Monthly*, a favorite magazine of the Boston intelligentsia, entitled "The New Education," which were widely read, highly praised, and embraced by the business community. The focus was on scientific schools, explaining their importance for the nation and the need for them to be separate freestanding institutions. He bashed Lawrence and exalted MIT. Eliot also offered a vision for the new American university. He wrote:

> [It] must grow from seed. It cannot be transplanted from England or Germany in full leaf and bearing. It cannot be run up, like a cotton mill, in six months to meet quick demand. Neither can it be created by energetic use of the inspired editorial, the advertising circular and the frequent telegram. Numbers do not constitute it and no money can make it before its time.... When the American university appears, it will not be a copy of foreign institutions, or a hot-bed plant, but the slow and natural outgrowth of American social and political habit.... The American college is without a parallel; the American university will be equally original. (Eliot, 1869a, 216)

Those articles became a bible for MIT, and got Eliot a new job a few months later. A troubled Harvard, suffering from a series of short-term presidencies, uncertain direction, declining fortunes, and an inability to find a new president, asked Eliot to accept the position. The new president focused first on the Lawrence Scientific School, seeking a merger with MIT. Revenge is best served cold.

Models of the New American University

The American university was built exactly as Eliot said it would be. It was a work in progress, a matter of successive iterations of competing visions. White, Gilman, and Eliot offered three distinct and different models, or prototypes, of what that university might look like.

The models were new institutions; replacements for the existing colleges rather than efforts to repair them. They provided clean slates. There was no need to uproot current practice or to win over established faculties or boards.

During the antebellum period, in addition to the expanding number of traditional colleges, there had been a steady stream of new, nontraditional postsecondary institutions—both collegiate and subcollegiate. Some targeted populations historically denied access to mainstream higher education—women, blacks, laborers, and farmers; others offered training for careers that colleges excluded, including the military, engineering, law, mechanical sciences, and teaching. The most ambitious was Thomas Jefferson's University of Virginia, established in 1825 as a nonsectarian college with a largely elective curriculum and wide-ranging programs, including traditional fields such as ancient language and moral philosophy, professions such as medicine and law, and new subjects such as modern languages and the sciences. Few of these new and innovative colleges succeeded for much the same reasons as the antebellum reforms in established colleges.

One of the postwar models resembled Jefferson's College, the land-grant college. In 1862, the federal Morrill Act gave states an opportunity to establish colleges designed to straddle the agrarian and industrial eras. Washington offered each state a grant of thirty thousand acres of land for each senator and representative it had in Congress. The land was to be used or sold to fund at least one college that combined the liberal and practical arts, offering instruction in agriculture and the mechanical arts "without excluding scientific and classical studies and including military tactics" (Morrill Act, 1862).

Sixty-five colleges in what would become fifty states, six territories, and the District of Columbia were established. Sixteen additional colleges were created in the aftermath of a second Morrill Act of 1890, which provided direct funding to the colleges but barred racial discrimination. Southern states established sixteen new "separate but equal" black colleges.

Some states used their land-grant appropriations to fund existing public and private liberal arts colleges or established agricultural schools. The former often created disconnected agricultural and technical units and the latter tended to merely expand what they were already doing. Other states bypassed existing colleges, founding new universities or A&Ms, agricultural and mechanics colleges. Some states established one land-grant college; others divided the money among several.

The results were disappointing. State politics were messy and often defeating. The quality of the institutions was mixed; many were weak academically. Too many were only add-ons. Admission standards were generally low. Funding was inadequate, particularly in states that divided their funds. Farmers showed little interest in attending the land-grant colleges, believing experience was a better teacher than formal education. Black students were barred from enrolling in land grants in the South. The purposes of the land-grant college were vague. In a study of the outcomes of the Act for the US Commissioner of

Education in 1872, Gilman was very critical, charging that the resulting colleges were subcollegiate, merely industrial schools that trained farmers and people who applied science to industry rather than studying science for science's sake and engaging in essential research, as Sheffield, which Connecticut had designated a land-grant college, did (Gilman, 1872, 427–443). There was confusion about whether the goal of the act was to promote research and prepare agricultural and technology scientists or to better educate farmers and mechanics. Most assumed the latter, and the 1887 Hatch Act was passed to ensure the former.

Cornell was the undisputed jewel among land-grant colleges, and it was the Land-Grant Act that brought Ezra Cornell and Andrew Dickson White together to found it. As New York State senators, White chairing the education committee and Cornell, a member of finance and construction, both wanted to use the land-grant appropriation to fund a single "truly great" institution, fighting the legislative pressure to divide it among several. They had differing views of what that institution should be. Cornell, a poor farm boy who made his money in new technology, was a pragmatist like Abbott Lawrence. He envisioned a university rooted in the useful arts and applied sciences, providing its students with the knowledge and expertise the new economy demanded. White dreamed of the research university that Tappan failed to realize. They joined their visions and $500,000 from Cornell to create a university, where "any person can find instruction in any study."

Cornell University was founded in 1865 and opened its doors in 1868 as the largest institution of higher education in the country with an enrollment of 412 students. It was a nonsectarian, coeducational institution, defying two of the norms of traditional higher education.

Classical and professional studies were given equal status,

another departure from tradition. The university was divided into two divisions—one for academic departments in science, literature, and the arts, housing both ancient and modern languages and another named "special science and arts," consisting of nine professional fields, including agriculture, architecture, engineering, industrial mechanics, and history and political science, intended to prepare students for careers in public service.

White dismissed the philosophy of "discipline and furniture of the mind" in favor of allowing students to direct their own learning, abandoning yet another established tenet. The curriculum was elective. There were five routes or courses of study students could choose. They took a classical course to earn a bachelor of arts degree. They could study science for a bachelor of science degree. A combined course, a mix of the classical and practical, including Latin, modern languages, math, and science, led to the bachelor of philosophy. There was a wholly elective bachelor's course and a nondegree option called specialized study, the Cornell version of a partial course.

A doctoral degree was offered from the very beginning, but the first was not awarded until 1872 when the first earned master's program was also established. A true graduate school was decades off. Indeed, the Cornell faculty went through endless debate and revisions regarding the degrees to be offered and the requirements to earn them.

•   •   •

Democratizing higher education was another goal of the university. Not only were women admitted but the common social class and race bars were broken. In the earliest years, students were young, local, rural, and often academically unprepared. New York State scholarships and a short-lived manual labor requirement made it possible for them to attend, though only about one in ten members of that first class earned degrees.

Over the years, both the academic credentials and socioeconomic status of students rose substantially.

White's hope had been to recruit a faculty of distinguished senior scholars, but that wasn't possible, so he hired promising young professors and sprinkled in a few eminent short-term visitors such as Louis Agassiz. The Cornell faculty, treated as academic professionals, was relieved of the student policing duties expected at most other colleges.

Ezra Cornell died in 1874, and White, whose tenure was repeatedly interrupted by bouts of government service, including a stint as ambassador to Germany, retired in 1885. In their partnership, Cornell's vision was realized to a greater extent than White's. The research mission White cherished didn't become a reality until after he departed.

Together White and Cornell founded a university that preserved what they believed worthy from the classical college and embedded it in a modern university, rooted in practical and advanced studies, student choice, expanded access to higher education, and a more professional faculty. This was the land-grant ideal. It was Wayland's Brown magnified, not Tappan's research university.

That university would await the 1876 founding of Johns Hopkins, a second model of what the American university might be—a graduate school and research center. In his will, Johns Hopkins (1795–1873), a Baltimore merchant, banker, philanthropist, and one of the wealthiest men in the nation, left a $7 million bequest (over $140 million today), largely in Baltimore and Ohio railroad stock, to establish an orphanage for children of color, a hospital, a nursing school, a medical school, and a university to oversee it all. Lacking guidance from Hopkins on what he wanted in a university, the university's twelve trustees, who were not knowledgeable about the subject themselves, were left to establish a university and hire a president to lead it.

• •

The trustees conferred with leading names in higher education—Eliot, White, Porter, and others—who disagreed about the potential mission and even the prospects for the new university but concurred that the person to hire was Daniel Coit Gilman.

Gilman, thrilled to be leaving California and eager for the opportunity to create a great university, one unlike any other in the nation, became president of the entire Hopkins legacy in 1875, after the obligatory university study trip to Germany.

At the center of the enterprise was Johns Hopkins University, the institution Gilman envisioned to train scholars, advance knowledge, and apply research to solving social problems, which connected the university to the other organizations in the Hopkins bequest. Gilman wanted the new university to be only a graduate school, awarding doctoral degrees to its graduates, but that raised a storm in the local community, which found no value in such a precious and esoteric institution for Baltimore. So Gilman, always the pragmatist, added a small undergraduate college to his plan, which would offer a three-year baccalaureate program.

He built the university scholar by scholar, professor by professor. People, not buildings or subject matters, would be the foundation of his new university. Indeed, one could easily have mistaken the university's lone, unprepossessing building for an old factory. Not only was this what Gilman wanted, but Hopkins's will forbade the use of endowment principal for construction; only the interest could be used for building.

Gilman created the nation's first faculty-centric university. The principal of *Lehrfreiheit*, literally teacher freedom but more familiar as academic freedom, was imported from Germany. The academic departments, organized around subject matters, or disciplines, had complete freedom to plan their own activities, which caused curricular disarray but spawned a community of scholars inside and outside the classroom.

Faculty were supported with purchases of needed lab equipment and by aggressively building a library to enable their work. But the largest expense was reserved for recruiting a student body that would stimulate them intellectually. This was no mean feat since in 1870 there were only two hundred graduate students in the United States. Those who could afford it studied at the far superior universities in Europe (Bishop, 1962). So Johns Hopkins bought the most distinguished students in the country with the lure of large graduate fellowships. The first class consisted of fifty-four students from across the nation, all of whom were required to have baccalaureates and, almost as an afterthought, thirty-five less academically distinguished local undergraduates. As the size of the university grew, the proportion of undergraduates declined and the number of graduate students increased.

The first Hopkins programs were in the arts and sciences; professional schools followed. *Lernfreiheit*, the freedom of students to choose their own studies, was extended to all students. The PhD required one major and two minor subjects, literacy in French and German and a thesis. Hopkins originated the terms major and minor in America, adopted from the German, *Hauptfach* and *Nebenfach*. While Cornell continued with pedagogies such as recitation, instruction at Hopkins was rooted in the lecture, laboratory, and seminar.

The medical school, the first in the nation to admit women and require a baccalaureate for admission, regarded as the premier institution of its type, also proved a leader in pedagogical innovation, employing clinical education ("bedside learning"), research projects, and lab training. The 1910 *Medical Education in the United States and Canada*, known as the Flexner Report, pointed to Johns Hopkins as one of North America's two model medical schools.

Gilman recognized that, if Hopkins was to change higher education, it needed to do more than educate new scholars and engage in its own research. The result was an effort to build a national scholarly network by establishing Johns Hopkins University Press, the oldest university press in the nation, and creating academic journals and scholarly professional societies.

For a small institution, Johns Hopkins played a powerful and oversized role in the transformation of American higher education. By the turn of the century, it produced more PhDs than Harvard and Yale combined. Its graduates were eagerly sought by the top universities for their faculties. Within twenty years of its founding, sixty American colleges had at least three staff with Hopkins degrees. The University of Wisconsin employed nineteen; Columbia had thirteen, and ten worked at Harvard. A 1926 study found that of the 1,000 leading academics, 243 were Hopkins graduates (Brubacher, 2017, 149).

At bottom, what Hopkins did was create a new profession, demanding a new set of research skills, the university professor, whose work was research, teaching, and service. Unlike Yale and Union, the principal destination of Hopkins graduates in academe was not presidencies. Hopkins produced graduates who built academic fields—John R. Commons (history), John Dewey (philosophy), Abraham Flexner (education), Walter Hines Page (journalism and publishing), Josiah Royce (philosophy), Florence Sabin (medicine), Frederick Jackson Turner (history), and Woodrow Wilson and Herbert Baxter Adams (political science).

• •

As Eliot admitted, Johns Hopkins pushed him and other university presidents to emulate it. They embraced the research and advanced studies it modeled and an emerging industrial society demanded.

Gilman retired in 1901, but in the decade before his departure, the primacy of Johns Hopkins as a graduate school had diminished as Baltimore and Ohio railway stock crashed and other institutions made sizable investments in research and graduate studies. Thereafter, Hopkins kept pace, but it no longer set the pace.

The third model is one Eliot spotlighted in his first *Atlantic Monthly* article, the Massachusetts Institute of Technology (MIT), where he had been one of the first faculty members, designed its chemistry program, and coauthored two textbooks for its chemistry lab. However, the founder of MIT was William Barton Rogers, who spent much of his career trying to create a model scientific school. Born in 1804 to a family of scientists, his father was a doctor trained at the University of Pennsylvania who failed at starting a medical library, medical practice, and apothecary before becoming a professor of chemistry at the College of William and Mary. Rogers and his two brothers were homeschooled, which prepared them for careers in science but also left them disappointed in their peers and the quality of college teaching.

Rogers began honing his idea for MIT at an early age. After graduating from William and Mary, he founded an academy with his brother and then gave public lectures at the Maryland Institute for the Promotion of the Mechanic Arts, where he created a collegiate program in the practical arts before succeeding his father as professor of natural philosophy and chemistry at his alma mater.

Seven years later, in 1835, Rogers was hired away by the state of Virginia to conduct the commonwealth's geological survey. Actually, Rogers lobbied hard to get the job. The survey

focused on three issues: (1) categorizing the state's rock forma-
tions, (2) identifying resources of farmers and industry to use,
and (3) developing theories of geological change. The survey
provided him with quite an education. He found there were
no people appropriately trained to work with him, so he was
forced to use the survey as a vehicle to train them; it became
a school of practice.

Rogers also learned that a geological survey was a high-
stakes enterprise that placed him in the teeth of a political buzz
saw as farmers, industry, politicians, and different regions of
the state pushed hard to get the results they wanted. In short,
applied scientific research had great value and a large non-
scientist consumer base.

He also learned about the politics of academe. (A Teachers
College trustee once explained the difference between the
business world from which he came and the university, saying
in business it was dog eat dog, but in academe it was just the
reverse.)

Rogers repeatedly butted heads with Harvard's Louis Agassiz, first over the proper way to categorize rocks and then over
whether the American Association for the Advancement of
Science should welcome applied scientists as members and
whether funding should be sought for pure or applied research.

After the survey, Rogers retreated to a professorship at the
University of Virginia, which he found modestly more appealing than William and Mary because it offered students limited
choice beyond the classical curriculum. As a professor and
later dean, he worked on a plan for the Franklin Institute in
Philadelphia to create an applied science education program
emphasizing laboratory work. It wasn't adopted.

A decade later, Rogers sent a comparable proposal to entrepreneur John A. Lowell Jr. in Boston. Nothing came of it, though
Lowell's good friend, Abbott Lawrence, provided funding to

create a similar school at Harvard. Rogers turned down an offer to join the faculty of the Lawrence school after he learned of the directions Agassiz, the founding head, planned to take it. Francis Wayland learned of Rogers's proposals and consulted him as he drafted his 1850 proposals for Brown. But no new scientific school materialized.

Rogers, who married a Boston Brahmin, left Virginia and moved to Boston in 1853, where he set about drafting yet a third plan and variations thereafter. By 1860, it had the catchy title of "Objectives and Plan for an Institute of Technology Including a Society of Arts, a Museum of the Arts and a School of Industrial Science, Proposed to be Established in Boston." During those years, Rogers ran a gauntlet of promising developments and bitter disappointments.

The Society of Arts, a scholarly association for those with interests in the applied sciences and technology, which entailed no real costs, was easily established in 1862. The museum to collect and display new technologies was never created. A poorly funded school of industrial arts was founded in 1861 as the Massachusetts Institute of Technology. Named one of three Massachusetts land-grant colleges, the other two being Lawrence, which fought for the entire grant, and the state agricultural college in Amherst, MIT was able to open its doors in 1865 with a student body of fifteen. The institutional motto, "mens et manus" (mind and hand) captured the essence of the new university and its model of educating applied scientists for the new economy.

It offered two programs, a day school with a degree for regular full-time students as well as a partial course for special students and a night school, providing a lecture series for working people with an interest in technology. Special students outnumbered regular students until 1880.

Admissions requirements were rigorous, though a departure

from the classical language requirements prevailing in higher education. Students needed to be at least 16 years of age and have passed entry exams in arithmetic, algebra, plane geometry, English, grammar, and geography.

MIT's curriculum was dramatically different as well. The four-year baccalaureate program consisted of a modern common core in science, math, modern language, history, and economics and an elective specialization in one of six areas: (1) building and architecture, (2) civil and topographical engineering, (3) geology and mining, (4) mechanical engineering, (5) practical chemistry, and (6) general science and literature. The core, concentrated in the first two years of study, extended throughout the entire program. In year one, students studied algebra, solid geometry, elementary mechanics, trigonometry, chemistry, English, German, and drawing. The next year, the curriculum covered calculus, spherical trigonometry, analytical geometry, astronomy, surveying, physics, qualitative chemical analysis, English, French, German, and drawing. There were fewer core requirements in the third and fourth years to accommodate the students' specialization. The third-year core consisted of physics, geology, history, the US Constitution, English, French or Spanish, and German. In the final year, students studied political economy, natural history, French or Italian, and German (Eliot, 1869a, 217–218).

The faculty and methods of teaching were geared to MIT's practical approach, employing professors who were engaged in research, wrote about it, and shared the beliefs and experiences of Rogers and Eliot. Instruction favored the laboratory over traditional recitation, lecture, and demonstration. The laboratory was the most difficult element of the program to get right, necessitating, for example, that the mechanical engineering lab be located at the mechanics shop of the Boston Navy Yard. This aspect of the program went through constant revision as faculty attempted to gear labs to the latest developments in fast-changing technologies, the conditions in which applied science was actually taking place, and how applied science research was conducted. They were inventing it as they taught on a shoestring budget.

MIT proved a success story. Enrollments passed two hundred in 1870, rose to three hundred fifty in 1873, and hit one thousand in 1894, at a time when Lawrence enrollments were declining. The university that emerged was not a trade school, as early critics charged, but instead the leading science and engineering university in the country. It transformed the standards and design of the nation's scientific schools. It raised the status of the applied sciences and created the curriculums and pedagogies other universities emulated. It set the bar for training and research in the applied sciences and engineering, and its faculty and graduates powered the Second Industrial Revolution.

Assessing the Institute's accomplishments in his 1894 annual report, President Francis Walker (Rogers had passed away on the podium during Walker's inauguration in 1882) wrote the MIT model of engineering had spread to universities in every state of the union, concluding "if indeed imitation is the sweetest form of flattery ... the surviving founders of the Massachusetts Institute of Technology ... have reason to rejoice, the battle of New Education is won" (MIT, 1894).

When asked where he would send his son to college, Thomas Edison replied without hesitation, the Massachusetts Institute of Technology (Edison, 1929).

Diffusing the Models: Transforming Mainstream Higher Education

Charles Eliot was the pivotal figure in the transformation of higher education. He was the banished prince who had become king, presiding over America's oldest and one of its wealthiest and most prestigious colleges, located in the cradle of the Industrial Revolution. In the course of his forty-year tenure, he was by turns a reformer, an arbiter and legitimizer of innovation, and a consolidator, a standardizer, and an integrator of change.

Eliot created a very different model of the American university than White, Gilman, and Rogers. Eliot's was not a distinctive prototype—not a land-grant university, not a graduate research university, not a scientific school. Over the course of his five decades in office, stretching from 1869 to 1909, Eliot amalgamated all three of those models.

• •

Instead, the model he created was a bridge. It was a bridge between the antebellum era and the present, demonstrating the earlier experiments had come of age. It was a bridge between the three new models and mainstream higher education, taking their visions of the university from the periphery of higher education to its very center. It was a bridge between one of the nation's most vaunted colleges and its traditional peers, modeling how a college could be transformed into a university.

Eliot became president of Harvard at a time when sixty-three thousand students, 1 percent of the college-aged population, were attending the nation's 563 colleges, where they almost universally studied a classical curriculum (National Center for Education Statistics, 1993, 64). He rocked Harvard and the world of higher education with his 105-minute inaugural address on October 9, 1869, calling for a set of reforms closely mirroring Cornell's minus nonsectarianism and coeducation. He focused on free electives, equal standing for classical and modern subjects, raising professional school quality, and excellent teaching. Eliot did not want to prune the Harvard curriculum; there was room and a need for all subjects in Cambridge. The problem, Eliot said, was "not what to teach but how to teach"

(Eliot, 1869c, 31). Believing the best pedagogy is that which best fits the subject being taught, he called for reducing the use of recitation and other forms of rote learning in favor of broader, deeper, and more intellectually enlivening instruction. Toward this end, students needed to be treated like grown-ups with fewer rules, higher standards, and increased autonomy. Raising faculty quality was a priority. Professors had to be paid higher salaries. Class sizes and workloads needed to be cut, beginning with eliminating faculty responsibility for petty student discipline. And the pressure to carry out original research had to be resisted.

Eliot's address embraced White's and Cornell's vision of a university that straddled the classical and the modern but rooted it in the realities of Cambridge. While he tipped his hat to the importance of democratizing collegiate education, he talked only of Harvard's practice of enrolling poor and wealthy students. Though he stressed the importance of the sciences and the need to raise professional school standards, he did not speak of agricultural education, the mechanic arts, or even Lawrence and the scientific schools.

Eliot's presidency and the roles he played in higher education's transformation can be very roughly divided into three overlapping phases. During the first, which extended to the mid-1880s, he was the reformer who turned Harvard College into a university and demonstrated for traditional institutions how transformation could be accomplished. Because it was Harvard that adopted these reforms, Eliot made a statement nearly as powerful as Yale's about the need for and propriety of change.

Eliot did what he proposed in his inaugural address. The adoption of the free elective system, which continued throughout his presidency, required far more than permitting students to choose their own studies; it demanded a fundamental curricular redesign of the college. Harvard's program, like those of most traditional colleges, was integrated, organized around the subjects and books students studied during their first, second, third, and fourth years at the college. Electives necessitated breaking up the unified, yearlong curriculums into courses to make student choice possible (Geiger, 2015, 319).

A year after Eliot's inauguration, the Harvard catalog began to list its courses by subject rather than by student class. Within six years, the college's few remaining requirements were relegated to the freshman year.

These requirements were also on the chopping block but were far more sensitive matters, since they necessitated eliminating the cornerstones of the classical curriculum—Latin and Greek. That set off a firestorm at the Corporation, which threatened Eliot's tenure but when approved left him in a far more powerful position. By the early 1890s, all of the requirements were gone, and students only needed to pass eighteen courses to graduate, marking an end to the fixed four-year baccalaureate program. Depending on how many courses students took each term, they could graduate in three years, a practice Eliot endorsed, believing they would continue on to professional studies after graduation, and the fourth year was becoming increasingly a time of sloth for students who had already passed the requisite number of courses (Geiger, 2015). In 1902, Eliot persuaded the faculty to abandon the four-year requirement for the baccalaureate, and by 1906, 41 percent of students were graduating in three or three and a half years.

The elective system also made it possible to recruit a stronger faculty and improve teaching. Class sizes dropped as common requirements ended. Faculty introduced advanced studies into their courses and were no longer responsible for overseeing petty discipline. Student rules of conduct were modernized and simplified. Eliot also raised salaries.

Eliot's other immediate target for change was the then autonomous professional schools. When he took office, there were four: medicine, divinity, law, and a new dentistry school. President Eliot would add a school of business and a graduate school of arts and sciences.

Eliot brought the professional schools into the university, appointing deans, supportive of his plans, to head each. They raised entrance standards to require a baccalaureate or suitable alternative for admission. They increased the length of professional school programs from three terms at the law school and two terms at the medical school—to three years. They mandated rigorous graduation exams. Until then, law and divinity had no exit exam and the medical school required only the passage of five of its nine ten-minute exams. The professional schools sequenced their courses, and they replaced their faculties of practitioners with academics. The Harvard professional schools came to be leaders in their fields with the law school pioneering the case method of teaching and the medical school embracing lab and clinical education (Geiger, 2015, 320).

Eliot also made changes that were not announced in his inaugural. He established a sister institution for women, Radcliffe, in 1879. Eliot secularized the university to the extent of making chapel voluntary in 1886. Harvard became more hospitable to black, Catholic, and Jewish students than other major universities, with the accent being on *more*, not hospitable as Eliot favored quotas. He tried to build a model scientific school by repeatedly attempting, almost successfully, to have MIT merge with Lawrence. When that failed, Eliot downsized Lawrence, shipped its best programs to the university, and turned what was left into the Harvard engineering department.

As a reformer Eliot drew inspiration from the Cornell and MIT models, adapting elements of each to the realities of Cambridge. In the next phase of his presidency, he would add the

Johns Hopkins research model. Here he followed and validated rather than led. Although Harvard had created a graduate department in 1872 and awarded its first PhD in 1873, Eliot continued to embrace the primacy of teaching over research and to reject a research mission for his university; he maintained, as stated in his inaugural, that Harvard would not provide funds "to secure men of learning the leisure and means to prosecute original researches" (Eliot, 1869, 54). Harvard's continuing loss of faculty to Johns Hopkins in the 1880s changed his mind and altered the university's path quickly. By 1890, Eliot had established a graduate school of arts and sciences, which would administer an ever-expanding number of graduate programs but also advance the university's scholarly activities, which extended across the old and new fields, both pure and applied, and provide funding for (wait for it) "original researches." Within a decade, two-thirds of the Harvard faculty had PhDs.

During the final phase of Eliot's career at Harvard, he made whole the new American university, as he had prophesied forty years earlier, knitting together the models White, Gilman, and Rogers had created. He, more than any of the others, became the prophet of the new American university, given his longevity, accomplishments, gravitas, and the stature of his perch. During the Theodore Roosevelt presidency, Eliot's secretary was heard to say, "President Eliot is in Washington meeting with Mr. Roosevelt."

As the Industrial Revolution propelled the new American university reforms across the nation's colleges and universities, institutions adopted countless permutations and endless variations of policy and practice. Eliot wanted standardization, to create order out of the chaos, by establishing a common vocabulary and quality standards for higher education. Toward this end, he chaired the 1892 Committee of Ten, which set the nation's secondary school curriculum and admission standards for college as well as served in 1905 as the first chair of the Carnegie Foundation for the Advancement of Teaching board, which determined the minimum quality requirements for colleges and created the Carnegie Unit, the near universal academic course accounting system of the industrial era. He was a leader in establishing accreditation in 1885, the self-policing mechanism by which the academy judges the adequacy of institutional quality, and in launching the College Board in 1899 to establish a common standard to assess all students applying to college beyond their family income, race, religion, and the name of the secondary school they attended.

Eliot retired from Harvard in 1909 and died seventeen years later. His career extended across the experiments, the models, the diffusion, and the standardization of the American university.

4
· · · · · · ·

Standardization, Consolidation, and Scaling

What Eliot created at Harvard can best be described as a mixture, an incremental layering of reforms, combining them together, connecting, deepening, and broadening the changes he introduced to a college built for another era but never really integrating them or attaining a unified whole. He built an airplane from a horse cart while flying it.

In contrast, at the University of Chicago, William Rainey Harper created a compound with all the elements organically linked and bonded. Born a generation after Eliot in 1856 and young enough to be his son, Harper, who came to the presidency at the same age as Eliot, had the opportunity to build a new university, to construct the American university from scratch. There was nothing for him to change, not people, programs, or organization. The prototypes had been tested; the foundation had been laid. He built on that. For the purposes of this account, Harper played the role of consolidator.

William Rainey Harper was a prodigy, a scholar, a charismatic teacher, a renowned public speaker, an entrepreneur, and a religious leader. The son of a strict Presbyterian, small-town Ohio shopkeeper, Harper graduated from Muskingum College at the age of 14 where he fell in love with ancient languages, particularly Hebrew. Afterward, there were PhD studies, completed in two years at Yale before he turned 19, where Harper wrote a page-turner of a thesis entitled "A Comparative Study of Prepositions in Latin, Greek, Sanskrit and Gothic." This was followed by stints as a school principal and professor teaching ancient languages and Old Testament at two Baptist colleges, Denison and Morgan Park Seminary, where Harper joined the Baptist church. At the age of 23, he returned to Yale as a full professor of Semitic languages, where the prolific scholar taught Arabic, Aramaic, Assyrian, Hebrew, and Syrian.

In addition, the Yale professor created Hebrew and Bible correspondence courses that enrolled thousands. He taught brilliantly at Chautauqua, a national adult education program of lectures, music, entertainers, and preachers, which became popular across rural America in the late nineteenth and early twentieth centuries. He distributed thousands of pages of books, journals, and pamphlets annually to a legion of followers—students, media, the public, and a network of ministers.

• •

Harper was a superb salesman of the Baptist faith, but he was at bottom, an academic—"a skeptic in search of truth"—who questioned Biblical text and used scientific method to discover the answers (Boyer, 2015, 80–81).

In 1887, a time when 62 percent of undergraduates nationally were still enrolled in classical studies (National Center for Education Statistics, 1993, 64), the University of Chicago, a small Baptist college, closed its doors. John D. Rockefeller invited Professor Harper to help plan a new University of Chicago and then to become its first president. During his fifteen-year tenure, Harper created an academic city on a hill, a university of a scale never before witnessed in the United States, what would come to be considered the quintessential new American university.

Chicago offered coeducational undergraduate and graduate programs in the arts and sciences and professions including divinity, law, medicine, engineering, pedagogy, and the arts. It provided a home to new subjects such as Egyptology and sociology. It engaged in teaching and original research. Scholarly journals were created, and a university press disseminated the research of the University of Chicago faculty. It established an extension division, offering evening courses and public lectures locally and correspondence courses nationally, to educate adults across America. Harper envisioned a rich campus life with intercollegiate sports, sororities and fraternities, clubs, activities, and speakers, a collegiate version of Chautauqua. All of this would occur on a forty-building campus of towers and spires with landscaping designed by Frederick Law Olmsted.

Harper always said publicly that undergraduate and graduate education, teaching, and research were of equal importance to the university, but his heart was in the graduate school and original research. Harper aggressively recruited Chicago's faculty—seeking the nation's most distinguished senior scholars, several of whom had been college presidents prior to coming to Chicago as well as the most promising young talent. He raided faculty from the top universities. At Clark, a graduate school modeled on Johns Hopkins, Harper left with almost the entire faculty and its president, G. Stanley Hall, perhaps America's most eminent psychologist. He lured faculty to the Midwest by offering the highest professorial annual salaries in the country, up to $7,000, which is more than $180,000 today. He promised faculty complete freedom of speech, gave them the autonomy to establish the new disciplines and specializations they hungered for, and told them they would only teach graduate students, which proved less than accurate as the under-

graduate population at Chicago far outnumbered the graduate
students.

. .

Indeed, the first class in 1892–93 numbering 540 (plus 204
divinity students intended to demonstrate to Baptists the
university's continuing commitment to its faith and history),
consisted of 323 undergraduates and 217 graduate students,
both of whom the faculty needed to teach. The ratio of undergraduates to graduates continued to rise. The undergrads were
largely local; most lived at home or off-campus, while the graduate students were more regional, Midwestern with a smattering of students from other parts of the country.

The four-year undergraduate program was divided into upper and lower divisions, called the junior college and the university college. The junior college was a mix of subcollegiate
and collegiate studies, which was necessary because of the
inadequacy of preparation at most schools. Lower division students studied a prescribed distribution of general education
courses, which over time became increasingly structured, and
took electives. The upper division, intended as the real start
of university studies, was initially largely elective but became
more and more specialized, demanding increasing amounts of
coursework in a major subject.

Harper quickly wanted to jettison the junior college so Chicago could become a true university. He proposed that secondary education in America be extended to six years, including
the final two years of the common school and the first two years
of college. It was a proposal that went nowhere. Taking another
tack, he suggested transforming the nation's small colleges.
Feeling that many amounted to no more than glorified academies, Harper proposed most actually becoming academies or
junior colleges, another nonstarter. However, in 1902, working
with the superintendent of the nearby Joliet city public schools,

they together established the first public junior college in the nation. While Harper never managed to dispatch the junior college at the University of Chicago, he was the architect of a new institution in higher education, the junior college, the precursor to the many community colleges now enrolling more than half of the country's first-time freshmen.

At the university, the best he could do was change the enrollment balance between the junior and university colleges by encouraging transfer students to attend. By the end of his presidency, 60 percent of the baccalaureate recipients had attended another school before Chicago.

The graduate school focused on doctoral education, though the earned master's degree was a staple. Harper wanted every academic department to offer a doctorate and to establish an academic journal. Between 1892 and 1910, the university awarded 573 doctorates, principally in the sciences but across the disciplines and professions, making Chicago one of the largest producers of PhDs in the country. In the years that followed, the number soared, which was actually problematic since there weren't enough professorial jobs to absorb them. Many graduates became teachers in the schools or went into university administration.

The principal means of instruction at Chicago were the lecture, seminar, lab, and colloquium. The recitation was relegated to history. Even textbooks were looked down upon.

The university adopted a year-round, quarter calendar consisting of four twelve-week terms with a one-week break between each. In contrast, the norm in higher education was two semesters annually with a summer hiatus, a vestige of the agrarian era when the break was needed for planting and harvesting on the farm. In the quarter system, faculty would teach three-quarters a year and spend the fourth, for which they were paid, on research which the university supported. Their teaching load was light, only two courses per term. For students, the quarter system meant they could complete an undergraduate degree at their own pace, in three years if they studied without a break. The twelve-week terms were further divided into six-week segments, which permitted students to enroll at Chicago eight times a year. The quarter system made sense economically for the university; it permitted the University of Chicago to operate twelve months a year, allowing higher enrollments without overcrowding or boosting class size, which was initially limited to thirty but was usually smaller. Class attendance was mandatory.

Perhaps the most dramatic change was in the structure and scale of the University of Chicago in comparison with its classical college ancestor. The university had come to look like a corporation. Its twenty-one-member board, though two-thirds were required to be Baptist, was dominated by corporate leaders, including John D. Rockefeller, who was Baptist. Lay leadership overshadowed religious, money changers loomed larger than priests, and philanthropy mattered more than piety. It was a board that gave tens of millions of dollars; Rockefeller alone gave $24 million. However, the board did a dreadful job of reigning in Harper's continual overspending and deficits, behaviors they never would have allowed in their own companies. His philosophy was to buy what he thought the university needed and ask donors—industrial titans, Baptists, and local boosters—to make up the difference. The great University of Chicago was bought not made as would be true for other great universities built during the era—Stanford, Duke, Rice, and Vanderbilt.

•   •

The president was no longer a minister, but the manager of a corporation with more than a million-dollar budget. He was a fundraiser, an administrator, the apex of a bureaucracy, a public figure, the external face of the university, the recruiter and developer of talent, the visionary and planner of the university, the academic leader of the faculty, a scholar and teacher, the guardian of the students, the person responsible for making the trains run on time, the fiscal supervisor, plant manager, and the head of campus services.

By 1909, Chicago was a sprawling enterprise, enrolling more than five thousand students and employing nearly three hundred faculty whose jobs were sorted into six different ranks (Slosson, 1910, x). The organization was divided into schools, colleges, divisions, departments, institutes, centers, administrative offices, and auxiliary enterprises, headed by deans, chairs, directors, chiefs, and people with a host of other titles.

The students prepared for industrial era jobs in business, law, medicine, and teaching. Chicago's second president, Harry Pratt Judson, wrote a book in 1896 entitled *The Higher Education as a Training for Business*, explaining why college was excellent preparation for business careers.

The economist Thorstein Veblen, a marginal figure at the University of Chicago who served as a fellow and assistant professor during the Harper years, lamented the loss of a past now forever gone to higher education and lambasted the system that replaced it. In his book *Higher Learning in America*, Veblen decried the new American university's vocationalism, utilitarianism, bureaucracy, commercialization, specialization, accounting, and classification systems. He attacked the power of money, the rise of free electives, a credit system that he called units of erudition, subjugation of faculty, presidents who had become captains of erudition, boards dominated by businessmen, and the resulting trivialization of learning. He was howling into the wind.

Harper died prematurely of cancer at the age of 49. He spent the night before his death in the hospital writing a plan for the next phase of the University of Chicago's future. In the course of a sadly short career, he built a truly great university and established the national model of the new American university that would power the Industrial Age.

Standardization

The industrial era demanded a more highly educated and specialized workforce—scientists, engineers, businessmen, doctors, lawyers, and teachers. Higher education boomed.

By 1910, four years after Harper died, there were nearly a thousand colleges and universities in America; 38 offered doctoral degrees. They enrolled more than a third of a million students, including 9,300 graduate students. Nearly 5 percent of the college-aged population attended these institutions and over 36,000 staff found employment in them. That year, they awarded 37,144 baccalaureate degrees, 2,113 master's degrees, and 443 doctoral degrees (Levine, 1987, 12; National Center for Education Statistics, 1993, 75).

Colleges were on their way to becoming universities that looked and acted more like commercial enterprises than the classical colleges from which they descended. They commonly offered degree programs in the sciences, the other newly emerging academic disciplines and the professions. Graduate education was on the rise. The times demanded it. Great universities modeled it and validated it.

The problem was that the nation's colleges and universities all did these things differently. Higher education's growth was anarchic, chaotic, and disordered as institutions added a seemingly endless number of new degrees, adopted a cornucopia of new programs of dramatically varying quality and design, hired new staff with little common experience or credentials, and admitted and graduated new students employing a kaleidoscopic range of standards. The shared homogeneity, the common understanding of what constituted collegiate education and the agreed-upon practices of the past faded, replaced by a free-for-all in which each institution made its own rules. The meaning of such fundamentals as what constituted a course or what studies should be required for a degree or what preparation was needed for a career became blurred and confused.

This seeming disarray set off a movement in the last decades of the nineteenth century to standardize higher education and develop common principles, policies, and practices. Four types of organizations were instrumental in bringing this about: (1) government, (2) professional associations, (3) accrediting associations, and (4) foundations. Together they produced what Edwin Slosson in 1910 called "the standard American university" (Slosson, 1910, 382).

The United States does not have a ministry of education that oversees education nationally. Rather, the Constitution assigns that responsibility to each of the states. As a consequence, though the states were key actors in formulating, adopting, and funding the new standards, the process was led by a web of voluntary professional associations that exploded in the 1880s and 1890s as the disciplines took root in the academy. Each discipline formed its own association, often at the impetus of the model universities, which defined their field, professionalized the faculty, and shaped the discipline's values and norms in teaching, research, and curriculum.

At the same time, colleges and universities banded together with peers in scores of combinations, creating a flood of new organizations commonly referred to by their acronyms. In 1887 alone, associations were established for state universities, land-grant colleges, Baptist colleges, and women's colleges. Thirty-one years later, an umbrella organization, the American Council on Education, was created to hold it all together and advance a common higher education agenda. These associations set membership criteria defining expectations for institutions of their type and offered members opportunities to explore common problems, develop common solutions, and lobby for their cause.

Accrediting associations were born during this era as well. Between 1885 and 1895, these organizations, initiated to develop high school graduation and college admission standards, spread across much of the country—the Northeast, mid-Atlantic, South, and Midwest, eventually forming six regional accrediting associations, covering the fifty states. They evolved to become the self-policing arm of higher education—powerful institutional membership organizations setting the criteria for what constituted a college, assessing how well individual colleges met those criteria, and announcing to higher education and the public those that did.

The final actor was foundations, which provided funding and often the leverage required to standardize higher education. In addition to making large personal gifts to support new and existing universities, the industrial titans created a vehicle for dispensing their philanthropy, the charitable foundation. Andrew Carnegie's Foundation for the Advancement of Teaching and John D. Rockefeller's General Education Board, later absorbed by the Rockefeller Foundation, played outsized roles in standardizing higher education.

Together these four organizations standardized American higher education, creating a common accounting system across the nation's colleges and universities, rooted in the credit hour and establishing a higher, more rigorous shared quality floor for the programs they offered. Both the quantitative and qualitative aspects of higher education were standardized.

Setting Common Quantitative Standards

The breakup of the integrated classical curriculum into courses, the spread of the disciplines, and the rise of the student elective system, adopted in varying degrees throughout most of traditional higher education before the end of the nineteenth century, created an enormous problem for the nation's colleges and universities. In this new world, it was unclear what constituted a course, how an institution or its students should measure academic progress, or even what the requirements should be for graduation.

At first, institutions developed their own idiosyncratic practices. For instance, Harvard required eighteen courses to graduate, describing the course as a class that meets four or five times a week for a term. In contrast, the University of Michigan demanded twenty-four to twenty-six courses, defining a course as "five exercises a week during a semester whether in recitations, laboratory work or lectures" (Levine, 1978, 159). The only thing the two universities shared in common was using the word course. They differed in the number of courses required for graduation, the number of times a course needed to meet, and the length of their terms. No mention was made of how long each course session needed to be either.

The difficulty was exacerbated by the explosion of public secondary school enrollments. Although the first public high schools didn't appear until the 1830s and '40s, three hundred years after the first college was founded, by 1900 their enrollment was more than twice that of higher education (National Center for Education Statistics, 1993, 36). Colleges received a ballooning number of applications from students who attended a large number of different secondary schools that offered a variety of different programs of widely varying quality.

The process of standardizing higher education began with the schools. At first, standardization efforts were local. Starting in the 1870s, individual universities, notably Michigan, Wisconsin, and California, began visiting potential feeder schools and certifying their quality to determine which students to admit.

This was not a very efficient process, as secondary schools were growing in number faster than colleges could certify them, and the number of colleges certifying them, repeating the work of the others, mounted. Standardization moved to a collective, regional stage. In 1885, the New England Association of Colleges and Preparatory Schools was established to build a nexus between secondary and tertiary education, which didn't really exist since the high school had been created independently of both the common schools and the colleges. In fact, colleges and high schools initially competed for students. Two years later, a similar organization popped up in the mid-Atlantic states.

Then standardization went national. In 1892, believing the problem to be countrywide, President Eliot asked the National Education Association, a professional association for teachers, to appoint a Committee of Ten, outstanding educators from both schools and universities as well as the US Commissioner of Education, to determine what the high school curriculum should be and how the two systems should be articulated in terms of college admissions. This was the first national attempt to standardize the high school curriculum or to coordinate secondary and higher education, though many, many more would follow. After extensive research, the Committee of Ten recommended a single, national high school curriculum, mirroring the programs of the strongest schools in the country and designed to prepare all students for college.

With the goal of enacting that recommendation, Columbia president Nicholas Murray Butler, with support from Eliot, asked the Middle States Association, a regional accrediting association, to establish a College Entrance Examination Board to develop college admissions tests, based on the Committee of Ten recommendations. The first tests were administered in 1901.

Other initiatives to bring order went on simultaneously, focusing increasingly on using time as the basis for standardizing education. Toward this end, in 1895, the New York State Regents, the state's education governing board, proposed the "count," "ten weeks of work in one of three subjects taken five days a week," as the standard measure of academic instruction in schools. Two years later, Eliot countered with the "point," the study of one subject four to five sessions per week for a term. Twenty points would be required for college admission. The College Board concurred with Eliot's sentiments in 1899, but proposed instead the "unit," the equivalent of two of Eliot's points. In 1902, the North Central Association, another regional accreditor, redefined the "unit" as a course of no less than thirty-five weeks, meeting four to five times per week for no less than forty-five minutes (Levine, 1978, 160).

And so it went, until 1906 when the Carnegie Foundation for the Advancement of Teaching, funded by $10 million from Andrew Carnegie and chaired by Eliot, fixed the definition of a unit and set the standards that would establish common practices in the nation's schools and colleges. The foundation, created to provide pensions for professors, often impoverished after retirement, established criteria for the colleges that would be invited to participate. They needed to have at least six full-time faculty, department chairs with PhDs, a four-year liberal arts program, a secondary school completion requirement for admission, and a nondenominational orientation. The students they admitted had to have earned at least fourteen units of high school credit. Carnegie defined the unit as five recitations per week in "anyone of four courses carried five days a week during the secondary school year" (Levine, 1978, 160–161).

The Carnegie definition, anchored in the promise of a pension for faculty, stuck. The Carnegie unit, or credit, became the standard currency in higher education, not only for the students colleges admitted but for their own work. It became the basis for the industrial era academic accounting system, the equivalent of degrees for determining temperature or pounds for measuring weight. The Carnegie unit defined the meaning of a course; it provided a measure of student progress, and it set a standard for college graduation. At bottom, it standardized the American university.

Setting Common Quality Standards

The rapid adoption of new, nonclassical studies raised the very same issues. There was an extraordinary array of dramatically different approaches to medical, legal, engineering, business, teaching, and nursing education and absolutely no agreement on what constituted adequate quality in admissions, curriculum, faculty, facilities, program length, or graduation requirements. The same four groups that created the quantitative standardization of higher education did the same for quality. The transformation was speediest and most comprehensive in medical education, which in 1900 was a disaster.

Most medical schools were far worse than the one Eliot encountered in 1869 at Harvard in the quality of their faculties, students, facilities, and programs. These schools turned out rotten doctors—ill trained, undereducated, and incapable of serving their patients. Institutions such as Johns Hopkins and Harvard were unique.

However, the Carnegie Foundation changed that. It transformed medical education in North America—dramatically raising the quality of the nation's doctors, their preparation for the medical profession, and the outcomes of their work. It did this with a 1910 study, carried out by a young educator named Abraham Flexner, who had been recommended by Eliot. Flexner visited every medical school in the United

States and Canada, wrote a report that established standards for medical education, identified model medical schools that already demonstrated the standards at Hopkins and Harvard, offered recommendations for improving the quality of medical schools, and provided an assessment of every medical school in North America.

Medical Education in the United States and Canada, better known as the Flexner Report, the Carnegie study had the effect of closing the country's poorest medical schools, strengthening weaker schools, and investing in excellent schools. It resulted in higher standards for doctors and medical education by the American Medical Association, the professional association in the field; more rigorous state certification requirements; and an outpouring of private and public funding for medicine and medical education. John D. Rockefeller's General Education Board contributed nearly $100 million, increased admission standards for students entering medical school, and improved the quality of medical services in the country. The report was not the first to recognize the problem of poor medical education and it certainly could not ensure the adoption of the changes it proposed. The problems were well and widely known; Flexner merely documented them.

The Carnegie initiative succeeded for a number of reasons. Unlike Wayland's reforms at Brown, the timing was right. There was broad dissatisfaction with the quality of doctors, medical education, and medical services in the United States. It was also the right organization to sponsor the effort. The Carnegie Foundation for the Advancement of Teaching had the standing, prestige, board of trustees, benefactor, and relationship with universities to make the work visible, important, and credible.

The report was compelling. The research was comprehensive, clear, and undeniable. It identified demonstrable models of medical excellence to establish expectations and needed standards of practice at Harvard and the Johns Hopkins medical schools. And its recommendations were straightforward, grounded in research, and targeted at specific stakeholders.

Implementation plans were built into the initiative. Networks of key stakeholders were created at the start of the project to build awareness, ownership, and willingness to act. These included the profession through the American Medical Association, educators by means of identifying model medical schools, state government, the press, and funders.

The report was broadly disseminated. Fifteen thousand copies were distributed to the key actors, and the press campaign was unprecedented.

The key actors needed to carry out change were mobilized by the Carnegie Foundation—the American Medical Association, state government and licensing boards, and funders. The Flexner Report was actually a setup. It was the key actors from government and the American Medical Association who came to Carnegie. They asked for the study to give them the neutral documentation to act. The only person who was unaware of this was Flexner.

The Flexner initiative standardized medical education, established a floor, and dramatically raised its quality in the United States. In less visible, concerted, and profound fashion, the same thing occurred all across the American university. Its programs were lifted, professionalized, modernized, and remade to serve the needs of an industrial society through the efforts of a new generation of leaders at their helms, on their faculties, in their boardrooms, and in the newly created professional associations; accreditors; and foundations. In the next decade, the Carnegie Foundation would issue Flexner-like reports of engineering, legal, and teacher education; none had the transformative impact of the Flexner Report, but all pushed in the same direction. By 1920, American higher education had been effectively standardized.

Scaling and Integration

What Harper created at Chicago was a one-off, a magnificent university but just a single institution. What the industrial society required was many such institutions.

It needed what Harper had accomplished at Chicago, the organic linkage of the proven but disparate elements created by the pioneering universities. However, it required this on a far grander scale. The multiplicity of new higher education institutions—research universities, land-grant colleges, technical and scientific colleges, and junior colleges, which mushroomed after World War I, needed to be rationalized and connected.

•   •

This scaling and integration would complete the transformation of the agrarian college and establish the industrial era system of higher education. The architect Clark Kerr* was born in 1911, two years after Eliot, the last of the new generation of presidents, left office.

Kerr was a Pennsylvania farm boy who attended Swarthmore College, then headed by Frank Aydelotte, the president who remodeled the failing institution and turned it into a selective, rigorous, and innovative version of an Oxford College. After graduation, Kerr migrated to California, with the American Friends Service Committee Peace Caravan, where he worked on street corners, talking to passersby about issues such as protec-

---

*This account of Clark Kerr and the making of the industrial era higher education system is based largely on a chapter Arthur wrote entitled "Clark Kerr and the Carnegie Commission and Council" in Sheldon Rothblatt's 2012 edited volume, *Clark Kerr's World of Higher Education Reaches the 21st Century.*

tive tariffs. The hostile receptions he received stayed with him the rest of his life.

He went on to earn a master's degree at Stanford and a doctoral degree in labor economics from University of California, Berkeley. His was a career that mixed teaching, research, and practice. He taught at Antioch, University of Washington, and Berkeley and published prolifically, but he also became a labor negotiator who faced off against the labor leaders and mobsters who ran the West Coast docks.

Kerr's rise was meteoric. In 1945, he came to Berkeley to head the Institute for Industrial Relations, a pet project of Governor Earl Warren, who was presiding over a state facing serial shutdowns as the labor grievances, stifled during the war, boiled over after. Kerr became the busiest labor negotiator in the West.

The turning point in his career came in 1949. As the Cold War heated up domestically, the Regents of the University of California threatened to fire all professors who refused to sign a loyalty oath. The faculty blew up. Kerr, who was a signer of the oath and a junior member of the university tenure committee, showed himself to be an outspoken, forceful, and reasoned advocate for the faculty before the regents. In 1952, when Berkeley searched for its first chancellor, he was the faculty choice. The 41-year-old Kerr remained chancellor for six years, when he was elevated to the presidency of the University of California system.

He was fired in 1967, at the behest of California Governor Ronald Reagan, who had campaigned on a promise to clean up the mess at Berkeley, which referred to the extended student demonstrations over free speech that had wracked the campus. Kerr was immediately appointed to chair the Carnegie Corporation's Commission on Higher Education and then its successor, the Carnegie Council on Policy Studies in Higher Education, which carried out a comprehensive and exhaustive study of the state of American higher education and the key issues facing the nation's colleges and universities.

In the course of his career, Kerr renamed the research university, the multiversity, offering a real rather than an idealized vision of what the institution had become, a decentralized academic superstore engaged in teaching, research, and service. He modernized the research university, making research its dominant feature. He mass-produced the research university, turning six campuses, only two of which could legitimately be described as research universities, into nine elite University of California campuses. He integrated the research university into a statewide higher education system, leading the development of a California Master Plan, which completed the industrial era transformation of American higher education in California. And then Kerr studied and documented what he and his predecessors had created, offering policy makers and academics recommendations on how to improve it.

Between 1957 and 1981, Clark Kerr modernized, scaled, integrated, refined, and championed America's industrial era system of higher education. He was the right person, in the right place, at the right time to do this.

Enrollments skyrocketed. The 1944 Serviceman's Readjustment Act, or G.I. Bill, intended to avoid massive unemployment following World War I, paid for 2.25 million former servicemen and women to attend college. Enrollment had only been 1.5 million before the war.

President Truman's 1947 Commission on Higher Education for Democracy called for much larger numbers, a doubling of enrollments by 1960. It proposed that a minimum of two years of free college be available to all Americans. Community colleges, an updated version of the junior college, should be developed. Upper division and graduate education should be expanded. Financial aid should be increased. The historic barriers to higher education—race, income, geography, gender, and religion—should be eradicated.

California was the epicenter for these changes and the president of the University of California was the leader. The state was booming economically, and its population was approaching and would shortly surpass New York's, becoming the largest state in the union. It had the disjointed and uneven rudiments of a statewide higher education system, and there was enormous pressure to expand it to meet the demands of the labor market and to serve a tidal wave of new students that every study projected would be coming. But the growth needed to be better planned and organized, more rational and less political than it had been in the past.

This led Kerr to carry out a raft of changes, but two were critical to completing higher education's industrial transformation. The first was cloning and scaling up the research university, making it accessible to an entire state and demonstrating that quality universities could be mass produced. At the end of World War II, the research university was still young and remained largely hot houses, particularly in the public sector. It had only been sixty-nine years since Johns Hopkins was founded. When Kerr became president, he inherited a six "university" system, composed of a grab bag of institutions varying widely in type and quality—Berkeley, UCLA, an agriculture school, a teachers college, a medical school, and an assortment of appendages, such as a marine biology station and an astronomy lab. Kerr strengthened and expanded each and when necessary remade them in the model of a research university. He added three new campuses at Irvine, San Diego, and Santa Cruz. Kerr built the modern University of California. In this sense, he did for the research university what Henry Ford did for cars. He mass-produced high-quality, low-cost education for a state and a nation that hungered for both.

Sociologist David Riesman once described higher education as a snakelike academic procession with the most prestigious institutions at its head and the lowest status colleges at the tail. The elite institutions led and the rest of higher education followed, a truism that was truer in the 1950s when Riesman said it. Kerr showed the best institutions could be reproduced in almost assembly fashion, and therefore, the rest could be, too. Kerr demonstrated that higher education was scalable.

Second, Kerr led the successful effort to produce a California Master Plan for higher education, which connected but established distinct and complementary missions for the public universities, four-year colleges, and two-year schools. It was a plan that at once sought to provide universal access to higher education for all Californians, establish diversity in the institutional choices available to them, ensure excellence in the higher education system, and create a rational plan and method for allocating higher education funding and missions. As it emerged from intense and lengthy negotiations, the master plan established three distinctive higher education sectors. One was the elite sector. Kerr's University of California would focus on research, grant doctoral degrees, and enroll the top 12.5 percent of high school graduates. The second was a mass access sector: the California State University System, which was charged with emphasizing undergraduate education, some professional studies, and teaching, admitting the top third of secondary graduates and providing limited master's-level graduate education. The third element was a universal access sector: the community colleges, offering transfer and vocational programs and providing an opportunity for all high school graduates to enter tertiary education. It was a plan that found a place for the university, the land-grant college, the scientific school, and the junior college and built on the strengths each offered.

The master plan, which Kerr negotiated, was in a very real

sense a peace treaty among California's colleges and universities, randomly located around the state often for political
reasons. They were stampeding toward a single homogeneous
model of higher education, epitomized by the University of California. Two-year colleges wanted to become four-year schools,
and four-year colleges wanted to be universities. Instead, California produced a pioneering model of higher education for
the industrial era built on the pillars of access, excellence, and
diversity. The eyes of the nation were on California, then as
now, and most other states adopted similar models.

The master plan was Kerr's proudest accomplishment and
earned him the cover of *Time* magazine's October 17, 1960,
issue. He arrived at the Carnegie Commission as the most-
admired and influential higher education leader in America.
When Kerr retired in 1981, the twenty-five classical colleges
enrolling one thousand students in 1800 had turned into
more than three thousand colleges and universities attended
by nearly twelve million students, 40 percent of the age group,
that annually awarded nearly a million bachelor's degrees,
over thirty thousand doctorates, almost three hundred thousand master's degrees, and more than four hundred thousand
associate degrees. For thirteen years, Kerr and the Carnegie
Commission and Carnegie Council successor placed under a
microscope the higher education system that he, Eliot, Gilman,
Harper, Rogers, and White had played such a large role in creating and asked how it could be made better. They studied the
effectiveness, efficiency, quality, accessibility, integrity, mission,
resources, performance, and outcomes of the system and the
institutions that composed it. The Carnegie Commission and
Council issued 142 books and reports proposing ways to refine
and improve the industrial era system of higher education.

5
. . . .

Transformation

What can we glean from the past that might be useful in think-ing about the future? The look backward focused on four facets of higher education's transformation: (1) the context or social conditions that drove the change, (2) the process by which the transformation occurred, (3) the people and organizations that both spurred and opposed change, (4) and the substance of the change, the issues, ideas, and content that constituted the trans-formation. Let's examine each in turn.

Context

The contexts then and now are very similar—that is, a nation undergoing profound economic, demographic, technological, and world change. In both cases, the society changed more quickly—demographically, economically, and technologically— than its social institutions. Because they trailed behind, the social institutions came to be perceived as out of date and less effective than they once were. As a result, they were pressured by their publics and their own financial woes to change. In the case of higher education, the most powerful forces for change were government, industry, and declining enrollments.

The changes in higher education required to serve the emerging industrial economy demanded not the reform of the nation's colleges but their wholesale transformation, including the invention of entirely new kinds of institutions—universities, scientific and technical colleges, and junior colleges. The disparity between today's emerging global, digital, knowledge society and the industrial era system of higher education is at least equally as large. The implication is that American higher education is once again headed for a transformation.

What is different today is that there is greater pressure on higher education to change. During the Industrial Revolution, higher education's role was to support the change, a fact that became obvious only after the Civil War when the professional and technical requirements of the industrial labor force emerged. In the antebellum period, there were only feints in this direction with the experiments with modern and technical subjects and new sources of their funding.

Today, higher education has become the engine that drives the global, digital, knowledge economy. The difference, as noted earlier, is that the information economy is fueled by knowledge and minds rather than by natural resources and physical labor of the industrial era. It's an economy that feeds on research and demands the most highly educated labor force in human history. Massachusetts recently became the first state in the nation in which the majority of its workforce is college educated.

Another difference is that the transformation of higher education during the Industrial Revolution required a century and a half from the early experiments to the integration of the system in 1960. The current change is likely to occur far more quickly for several reasons. First, the need for change is far more urgent today, given the knowledge economy's dependence on higher education, which is encouraging greater activism from government and funders.

Second, the speed of communication has increased dramatically, which is likely to accelerate the time frame for experimentation, diffusion, and standardization. It is also likely to increase the pressure on colleges and universities to change given twenty-four seven media coverage and an ocean of data now available to inform consumers, policy makers, and the public.

Third, the scale of the changes implemented today is geometrically larger than those of the Industrial Revolution. In the area of instruction, the industrial era change involved a switch from recitation and the traditional pedagogies to lectures, seminars, and laboratories. These changes occurred on a single campus and involved at most several hundred students. Today, we see instructional innovations such as massive open online courses (MOOCs) that dwarf these numbers. A single MOOC can enroll more than 100,000 students across the globe, and in less than a decade, tens of millions of students have enrolled in MOOCs offered by more than seven hundred colleges and universities.

The amount of time the transformation will take is unknown and a matter of intense speculation. Two members of the Woodrow Wilson National Fellowship Foundation Board of Trustees, who have been leaders in the educational technology world, debated this issue at nearly every meeting. One said the change would be quick, similar to the fall of the Soviet Union. The other said it would take decades, citing the pace at which higher education has adopted course management systems and new forms of certification such as microcredentials. The decider has ultimately proved to be the pandemic, discussed later in this volume, which is serving as an accelerator of the transformation of higher education, speeding changes that would have occurred over years into weeks and months.

The Process of Change

The process of higher education change during the Industrial Revolution involved seven overlapping stages: (1) demand for change, (2) denial of the need to change, (3) experimentation and reform initiatives with a focus on attempting to repair the existing model of higher education, (4) the establishment of new models of higher education at the periphery rather than mainstream of the enterprise that sought to replace the existing model rather than repair it, (5) diffusion of the new models with a prestigious institution at the center leading the effort and other mainstream institutions adopting the changes in their own fashions, (6) standardizing the cornucopia of varying practices and policies that diffusion spawned, and (7) scaling up and integrating the various pieces of standardized practice and policy to create the industrial era system of higher education.

It seems likely that the steps will be fundamentally the same in the current transformation of higher education. The process of change was not unique to higher education during the Industrial Revolution; each of the nation's social institutions underwent a similar process.

We are currently in the early stages of the transformation. The present looks similar to the first half of the nineteenth century, including demands for change, the denial of the need to change, and a myriad of institutional reforms and experiments. The demand for change is once again being voiced by government, business, funders, families, and the media. The issues are similar—cost, failing to keep up with current needs, and a reluctance to change. What was referred to as elitism and a need for democratization in the Industrial Revolution has now become equity and access.

There has been no Yale Report, a powerful and authoritative manifesto defending the status quo that galvanizes the opponents of change. That may or may not come in the future. Like the earlier transformation, skirmishes over change today tend to be local and campus based, occurring between faculty, administration, and trustees over issues varying from the adoption of innovations such as online degrees, a debate which the pandemic made irrelevant; the closure of low enrollment traditional programs; and the size and composition of the faculty to partnerships with for-profit educators, institutional governance, and budget cuts.

Reform initiatives, largely piecemeal innovations aimed at modernizing institutions and often intended to make them more distinctive and competitive, are everywhere. In contrast to David Riesman's notion of the snakelike academic procession, the leadership for change is now based in the tail. Troubled institutions in demographic and financial distress are searching for silver-bullet innovations to save themselves. The most successful of these innovations will diffuse up the academic food chain, finally being adopted by the least prestigious units of the most prestigious universities, such as continuing education. We will take this up in greater detail later.

We are not yet at the post–Civil War stages of transformation. Models such as Cornell, Hopkins, and MIT are yet to emerge. It's too soon. Higher education is largely engaged in experimentation. The existence of models can only be ascertained with accuracy by historians after the characteristics of a transformation are clear and the sources of diffusion are known. The same is true of the institutions and leaders who bring the models to the mainstream.

Consolidation, standardization, scaling, and integration complete the transformation. As yet, there is nothing to consolidate, standardize, or scale.

People and Organizations That Spur and Oppose Change

The cast of characters is much the same today as in the postwar decades. Their positions have changed largely by degree. Government control tends to be greater today because two-thirds of higher education institutions are public, and the federal government is more involved owing to the leverage that comes from Washington's higher education funding. Families and students, which have increasingly adopted a consumer attitude regarding higher education, continue to make their wishes known with their feet, but they are more vocal and litigious than in the past. The influence of media has also increased. Perhaps the *U.S. News & World Report*'s annual rankings are the best example. Their ranking criteria have an extraordinary impact on institutional practices. Because *U.S. News* includes admissions yields and graduation rates in its calculations, the number of colleges with early admissions programs, assuring admittee attendance, shot up, and the number of colleges willing to take chances on promising but risky applicants declined.

The institutional mix has changed. In 1976, there were 55 degree-granting proprietary or for-profit schools. By 2019 that number had risen nearly fourteenfold to 742 (National Center for Education Statistics, 2019c). These institutions have proved to be far more innovative than traditional higher education, sometimes to the good, often to the bad. They may increase and provide traditional higher education a way to jump-start innovative approaches to content, curriculum, and instruction.

The voluntary associations (scholarly, institutional, and accrediting) find themselves in a different position. Accreditation is the most vivid example. It was created to bring order to the chaos of higher education in the late nineteenth century and to standardize its policies and practices. Today, accreditation is under attack from government. The charge is that by using uniform rules designed to ensure conformity, accreditation is shaping and certifying colleges for the industrial era. It has become a barrier to change. Instead, government is demanding that accreditors modernize their quality standards, encourage innovation, and speed up the accrediting process.

Accreditation finds itself engaged in the very set of activities it performed successfully for more than a century and is being criticized for doing so. Accreditors are in much the same position as the colleges they regulate; they have to refit themselves for a new era or risk being replaced, and they are scrambling to do so. Later in the transformation when standardization is again required, they may well be asked to play compliance officer again.

The situation is no different for other voluntary associations. There are more defenders of what they have built in the past than agents of advancement for the future. However, because they represent their scholarly and institutional communities, there is little pressure to change outside of the professions.

Foundations continue to be powerful forces for change, even more powerful than in the past. Once again, it's the foundations of the titans, this time digital entrepreneurs with names like Gates, Chan-Zuckerberg, and Dell that are driving change in higher education. There are also relatively new foundations such as ECMC, Lumina, and Strada leading change. Today's foundations are more strategic than their predecessors and tend to engage in venture philanthropy, treating their giving much as they would their for-profit investing. They tend to focus on a small number of issues, emphasizing high-impact, high-leverage, big projects with the promise of scale. Lumina, for example, has targeted and made substantial investments in key, cutting-edge areas fundamental to twenty-first-century higher education including nondegree credentialing, competency-based education, nontraditional providers, and innovative partnerships. Foundations have generally adopted the Flexner approach of building coalitions and collaborations with the key stakeholders required to shape and implement change. Government has been a frequent partner, and staff migrations back and forth have been common.

Many of the same institutional actors will be involved in transforming higher education now as in the past. The external actors—government, families, media, and funders—have gained in influence. In at least the short run, the voluntary, nonprofit sector has become more of a deterrent to change than a driver. Foundations are the most creative of the actors, and they are at the moment the only sector in which a generational shift in leadership is already visible. Higher education continues in its schizophrenic role of both opposing and experimenting with change in the early stages of the transformation.

The Substance of the Changes

The look backward tells us American higher education is headed for transformation. We know the industrial era transformation was not like an avalanche that wiped out everything in its path. There are still vestiges of the colonial colleges; America's four-year, residential, liberal arts colleges are its progeny. But nothing emerged from the transformation unscathed. The liberal arts college changed its organization, staffing, students, curriculum, methods of instruction, and assessment. But it remained residential; it continued to offer a four-year undergraduate program, and it still awards a bachelor's degree.

For higher education institutions, the previous transformation produced both adaptive and disruptive solutions; that is, some colleges were able to meet the challenges of industrialization by reforming their existing operations. At the same, new and dramatically different institutions were created to meet the demands of the emerging national, analog, industrial economy. The current transformation is likely to be similar.

The transformation created new forms of higher education—universities, technical and scientific schools, and junior, now community, colleges—which quickly dwarfed the remnants of the old agrarian system. What remained was modernized rather than discarded. This seems likely to be repeated.

This is as far as we can go. A look backward helps us see the pattern of change, but it doesn't help us to see the substance. It sheds no light on the curriculum, instruction, assessments, credentials, facilities, students, or staffing ahead. Those will not be products of the past but of the emerging future. They will be determined by the needs of a knowledge economy, not the industrial economy the current system of higher education was created for and this look backward focused on. The look backward informs us only about the process by which the current transformation is likely occur, who the actors are likely to be, and where we now stand in the process. To better understand the nature of the changes we might expect in the future, we need to look both forward and sideways.

Part 2
LOOKING FORWARD

We name periods of profound change only in retrospect. It's
the historian's job. Until a name sticks, all sorts of possibilities
are attempted capturing one aspect or another of the ongoing
change. The period that came to be called the Industrial Revolution, a name popularized by British historian Arnold Toynbee in his 1884 volume *Lectures on the Industrial Revolution
in England*, was also called the Communications Revolution,
the Transportation Revolution, the Manufacturing Revolution,
the Agricultural Revolution, the Urban Revolution, the Market
Revolution, and on and on.

For those of us living through such periods, there is no
name that tells us what we are experiencing. Instead, these
are times of almost random, continuous, and disconnected
change. A world we have known is giving way to a disordered,
transient, unfamiliar, even alien world. Much that we have
taken for granted is in flux—how we live our daily lives, the
nature of family, work, and the commonweal. The social
institutions we depend on—education, government, health,
media, and finance—created for the passing era, no longer
work as well as they once did. They appear to be broken. Long-
held expectations, values, and dreams are challenged and, for
those hit hardest by change, shattered. The future is inchoate

and unknowable, a target for projecting both our greatest hopes and deepest fears.

This section of the book, "Looking Forward," is written from the perspective of someone living through the change. It necessarily lacks the historical perspective and certainty of "Looking Backward." Instead, it attempts to discern the future of higher education by focusing on three forces profoundly changing America: (1) demography, (2) the economy, and (3) technology. A fourth, globalization, is subsumed in the others. This section examines current trends in each area, projects them forward, and discusses their potential impact on higher education.

Chapter six focuses on the nature and impact of major demographic changes for higher education. Chapter seven discusses the advent and consequences of the knowledge economy for colleges and universities. Chapter eight examines the revolution in digital technology and its effects on higher education. Chapter nine completes the look forward, offering conclusions on what the study of the three forces tells us about the future of higher education today and the primary means by which higher education is likely to respond to those forces—adaptation.

Five caveats are important to note. First, the three forces are not comprehensive. The COVID-19 pandemic, which had the impact of accelerating the higher education changes discussed in this book, made that clear. Other potential drivers, such as climate change, could have a profound impact on the future, though perhaps less immediately or at least less predictably on higher education.

Second, the three forces are not discrete entities; they do not operate separately or independently. They overlap, and it can be difficult to understand where one ends and the next begins. For example, the combination of new technologies, the rise of the knowledge economy, and globalization have accelerated the decline of manufacturing in America rather than any one of the forces alone.

Third, the three forces can act in concert, in opposition, or independently. An example is their impact on government investment in education. The economy and globalization promote it; demographics discourages it. The knowledge economy, demanding a more educated population than its industrial predecessor, and globalization, which permits jobs to migrate around the world, fueling international competition to attract employers, encourages investment in education. In contrast, the aging of the population discourages education spending. An older population drives up health care and senior care costs, which compete with education funding in state budgets.

Fourth, the term *force* generally refers to pushing or pulling an object in a single direction. However, this is not the case with any of the three forces discussed. Each is actually an umbrella for a range of different phenomena that have varied impacts on society. For instance, demographics includes population characteristics such a fertility, race and ethnicity, migration, and mortality. These vary by region of the country and, in fact, have opposite impacts in different regions. For instance, declining college-aged populations in the Northeast mean excess higher education capacity in that region—too many colleges and too few students. In contrast, the increasing college-aged population in the West means insufficient higher education capacity—too few colleges and too many students.

Fifth, the three forces operate at least perceptually on different time frames and at different speeds. Demographic change and its consequences are experienced over decades, while the impact of new technologies is now felt much more immediately.

To address the division between those who say higher education will meet the demands of the emerging global, digital, knowledge economy by adaptation and those who believe the future will bring disruption, "Looking Forward" concludes that colleges and universities will be able to meet the challenges of demographic and economic change, principally by adaptation. However, the jury is still out on digital technology. Let's consider each in turn.

6
· · · · · · ·

A Demographic Sea Change

The US population is changing racially, moving, aging, and coming from abroad.

A New Majority

The nation has historically been overwhelmingly white, but a sea change is underway. By 2045, whites will make up a minority of Americans (49.8%). Hispanics will constitute nearly a quarter (24.6%) of the population. Blacks and Asians together will represent another fifth (21%) of the nation.

The pace of change is driven by burgeoning numbers of young people. By 2060, Hispanics will make up nearly a third (32%) of the US population under the age of 19. Whites will be only a few percentage points higher (36.5%). Asians and blacks will constitute slightly more than a fifth (22%) of this population (table 1).

The dimension of the shift is already apparent in our schools. Between 2012 and 2028, the number of Hispanics graduating

Table 1. Population of United States by Race and
Age, 2019, 2045, 2060

	All ages (%)		Under 18 (%)	
	2019	2045	2019	2060
Asian	5.8	7.9	5.0	7.8
Black	12.5	13.1	13.7	14.2
Hispanic	18.5	24.6	25.6	31.9
White	60.1	49.7	50.2	36.4
Other	3.1	4.7	5.5	9.7

Source: Authors' calculations based on US Census (2020) and
Frey (2018).

from high school will skyrocket, rising 52 percent. Multiracial
graduates will increase at an even greater rate (72%). In contrast,
Asians / Pacific Islanders will expand somewhat more modestly
(25%) and whites (−14%), blacks (−1%), and Native American
(−13%) graduates will decline (Hussar & Bailey, 2019, 17).

•   •

National statistics conceal at least as much as they reveal. Race
is another umbrella term that incorporates a range of sub-
groups with widely varying characteristics. Hispanics include
Cubans who have a 46 percent college attendance rate for the
18- to 24-year-old group as well as Guatemalans with a 28 percent participation rate. Similarly, at the poles for Asians are
the Chinese with a 77 percent college attendance rate and the
Burmese at 42 percent. The statistics offered in this chapter are
averages for each ethnic/racial group (Snyder, Brey, & Dillow,
2019).

   In addition, different states and regions of the country vary
profoundly in the racial and ethnic composition of their residents. As a gross overgeneralization, Asians tend to be concentrated in the Pacific states (minus Oregon), blacks in the South,
Hispanics in the Southwest and Florida, and Native Americans

Table 2. States with the Highest Percentage of Asians, Blacks, Hispanics, and Native Americans, 2020

Asian (%)		Black (%)		Hispanic (%)		Native American (%)	
Hawaii	36.8	D.C.	46.1	New Mexico	48.5	Alaska	14.0
California	14.1	Mississippi	37.5	Texas	39.2	New Mexico	8.8
New Jersey	9.31	Louisiana	32.0	California	38.9	South Dakota	8.4
Washington	8.3	Georgia	31.0	Arizona	31.1	Oklahoma	7.2
New York	8.2	Maryland	29.3	Nevada	28.5	Montana	6.2
Nevada	7.9	South Carolina	26.8	Florida	25.2	North Dakota	5.1
Massachusetts	6.6	Alabama	26.4	Colorado	21.4	Arizona	3.9
Virginia	6.3	Delaware	21.6	New Jersey	19.9	Wyoming	2.2
Maryland	6.2	North Carolina	21.1	New York	18.9		
Alaska	6.2	Virginia	18.8	Illinois	17.0		
		Tennessee	16.7	Connecticut	15.7		
		Florida	15.4	Rhode Island	15.0		
		Arkansas	15.3	Utah	13.9		
		New York	14.3	Oregon	12.8		
		Illinois	14.0	Washington	12.5		
		Michigan	13.7	Idaho	12.4		
		New Jersey	12.7				
		Ohio	12.2				
		Texas	11.7				

Source: World Population Review (2020a–2020d).

in the West. There are also sizable populations of blacks and Hispanics in Illinois, New York, and New Jersey, among other states. Four states are already majority minority: California, Florida, New Mexico, and Texas. New York and New Jersey are only a few percentage points behind (table 2). Ten cities in nine states are majority black. Twenty-eight cities in four states are majority Hispanic. One city—Honolulu—is majority Asian (World Population Review, 2020a).

So, what does this mean for higher education?

The answer is, it depends. Different states are facing dramatically different futures. But they share two common challenges.

First, the nation's education system has not been successful with today's emerging majority, and the pandemic put these

Table 3. Postsecondary Attainment of Persons 25 or Older by Race, 2019

Race	Bachelor's Degree or Higher (%)
White	40.1
Black	26.3
Hispanic	18.8
Asian / Pacific Islander	57.1
American Indian / Alaska Native	16.8
Multiracial	34.1

Source: National Center for Education Statistics (2019b), table 104.10.

students further behind. While Asians have exceeded all other races in educational achievement, Hispanics as well as blacks and Native Americans lag well behind whites (table 3).

The second challenge, exacerbating the first, is the rising cost of college. In 2018–2019, the average annual cost—tuition, fees, room and board—of a public four-year college was $20,598 and $10,950 for a two-year college. For private institutions, the costs were $44,662 and $28,627, respectively (National Center for Education Statistics, 2019e). In the aggregate, public four-year institutions have seen a 31 percent increase above inflation over the past decade; for private institutions, it's 23 percent (National Center for Education Statistics, 2019e).

Soaring costs have diminished the capacity of students to attend college and raised student loan debt for those who do to the highest levels in US history. This is particularly bad for blacks and other underrepresented populations, who have substantially lower incomes, far greater student loan debt, and higher default rates than whites (table 4). The median income for black families is lower than the sticker price of a year at a private four-year college. The problem was exacerbated many fold by the pandemic. Three groups—low-income Americans, less-educated populations, and people of color—bore the brunt

Table 4. Median Household Income, Median College Debt Owed, and Default Rates by Race

	Median Household Income ($)	Median College Debt[a] ($)	Default Rate[b] (%)
American Indian or Alaska Native	45,476	10,909	36.1
Asian	93,759	7,019	11.2
Black or African American	43,862	17,406	48.2
Hispanic or Latino	55,658	7,788	33.7
White	69,823	8,013	20.3
Other	53,097	13,472	25.9

Source: American Community Survey (2019); US Department of Education (2017).
[a]Federal; principal and interest, twelve years after 2004 matriculation.
[b]Twelve years after 2004 matriculation.

of the massive unemployment, incapacity to purchase staples like food and housing, and disproportionate death rates. When schools and colleges went online in 2020, students from these groups were less likely to have the digital equipment or internet access essential to participate. Combined, the effect has been to set back college access for already underrepresented populations by years—perhaps by as much as two decades (Mitchell, 2020).

There will be extraordinary pressure on higher education to address both issues. Rising tuition rates and mushrooming debt loads have already produced a firestorm of anger from students and their families, spurring mounting concern from policy makers and the media. It was a prominent issue in both the 2016 and 2020 presidential elections and remains high on the policy agenda for media, governors, and legislators. Free college has become a rallying cry for the progressive wing of the Democratic Party. President Biden is taking steps to reduce the student debt burden. Further action can be expected to follow.

In the very short run, the cost of college, which now has a

larger political base than the underrepresentation of the new majority, is likely to drive the twin agenda. But the equity and access needs of the country are quickly gaining momentum owing to America's increasing recognition of structural racial inequality, massive COVID unemployment, shortage of skilled workers, and desperate need for economic development.

How the two issues are resolved and who takes the lead in addressing them—higher education, government, or the marketplace—would have very different impacts on the nation's colleges.

• .

It is difficult to imagine higher education taking the lead beyond exemplary institutions in areas with high concentrations of new majority populations or commitment to addressing equity disparities. The history of American higher education has been the story of an evolving institution incorporating a growing number and diversity of students, beginning with white, Protestant boys and expanding to include women, blacks, Catholics, Jews, older adults, the poor, and many others. The process has been slow, generally graceless, and sometimes required the intervention of the government. More often than not, new populations have had to push their way into college rather than being invited. Women are a good example. Given higher education's general unwillingness to accept women until well into the late nineteenth century, separate colleges for women were established. Protracted and bitter battles over co-education continued for much of the twentieth century while women's enrollments in mainstream higher education grew to the point that female attendance surpassed males by 1980. The diversification of higher education has been a process of initial exclusion, then the creation of separate institutions for each new population at the periphery of traditional higher education, and finally gradual, accelerating, and usually incomplete inclusion in the mainstream, beginning with the least selective and most hard-pressed institutions. Community colleges, the open admission sector of higher education, have become the most frequent route to college for the new majority (blacks, Hispanics, and Native Americans) (table 5).

Accommodating each new population has required changes in higher education, often carried out grudgingly and with glacial speed, in curriculum, staffing, campus culture, physical plant, finances and admissions, and retention practices.

Higher education as a whole is unlikely and frankly unable financially to go beyond adopting marginal remedies—limiting its tuition increases, growing its financial aid budgets, and increasing its discount rates, the difference between its official price and what students actually pay.

Sharp reductions in state and local funding for higher education since 1980, magnified by the pandemic, which gutted state budgets, have raised tuition prices since student fees are the primary source of additional revenues for most colleges and universities (Mitchell et al., 2017; Mortenson, 2012). But higher education's financial practices have also contributed to the problem.

Colleges and universities tend to operate on a cost-plus pricing model; that is, they determine their expenses before setting their prices. In this model, expenses determine revenue needs, and tuition is the principal source of additional revenues. This is the reverse of how most people and organizations plan budgets; they typically determine how much money they have to spend, and then they decide how to spend it. Revenues normally determine expenses.

This is particularly unfortunate because higher education generally grows by addition rather than by substitution; that is, the new augments what already exists rather than replacing it. The result is that new and vital programs are added to old and dated ones, continually driving up the cost of the enterprise.

In addition, higher education is one of the few industries

in which competition actually increases cost. Called "the arms race," colleges compete by attempting to surpass one another in staffing, plant, programs, and services, a practice that produces excessive and unproductive cost hikes. Imagine if airlines competed in this fashion. They might slash the number of seats on each plane, substitute plush and roomy lounge chairs, introduce three-star cuisine, and perhaps employ a live string quartet on each flight and, of course, jack up prices to pay for it.

Alternatively, government is far more likely to take the lead in making college more affordable and growing new majority representation. It could do this by increasing higher education funding, potentially reducing the share of college costs borne by students. However, in the aftermath of the pandemic and with the aging of the US population (to be discussed shortly), health care and social security costs will balloon, producing a generational competition between two of the highest ticket items in state budgets—education and health care. There is the possibility of short term relief as part of federal support to stimulate the economy and provide COVID relief.

Or government could increase student financial aid. This still requires increased government funding but changes the target from institutions to students, thereby further empowering consumers. The idea of making the first two years of college free with subsidies tied to community college prices is gaining momentum. It reflects the increased educational demands of the workplace and lack of jobs for those without some college and is consistent with the nation's historic expansion of the length of free public education as required by the economy. The high school, created in the nineteenth century, grew in response to industrialization, ultimately becoming mandatory. The community college was first established at the turn of the twentieth century and mushroomed thereafter. In 1947, President Truman's Commission on Higher Education recommended that nearly half the college age population have at least two years of college. Today, a majority of first-time college freshmen begin their higher education careers at two-year colleges. One can expect that, even if the free, lower division proposal does not gain traction immediately, it will become the norm in the future, focusing not simply on higher education but also on other forms of postsecondary education. There are already well over three hundred Promise Programs across the country, supported by cities, states, and regions, which make commitments to local high school graduates to support their college attendance and their numbers are growing.

Another approach would be for government, dissatisfied with higher education's inability to control costs, to regulate prices. It could do this by imposing tuition caps as requirements for institutional participation in financial aid and other governmental programs.

The final actor described in the introduction, the postsecondary marketplace, is a wild card. While diffuse and lacking the concerted impact of government, it could have a significant effect on postsecondary cost and new majority access.

Of the mélange of marketplace institutions, for-profit colleges have been the most active in targeting the emerging majority, and they have been enormously successful in doing so, thereby demonstrating the capacity of postsecondary education to attract, recruit, and enroll this population (National Center for Education Statistics, 2020a) (table 5).

However, for-profit performance has been abysmal. Graduation rates have been low, and loan default rates have been high. Dependent largely on federal student loans and veteran's aid for revenue, for-profit colleges' staffing tends to be concentrated in recruitment and financial aid with minimal postenrollment advising and placement. While there are strong postsecondary for-profits, far too many gobble up and spit out new majority

Table 5. Undergraduate Enrollment in Degree-Granting Institutions of Higher Education by Level, Control, and Race/Ethnicity, Fall 2018

	White (%)	Black (%)	Hispanic (%)	Asian (Non–Pacific Islander) (%)	Pacific Islander (%)	American Indian / Alaska Native (%)	Two or More Races (%)
Four Year							
Public	56	12	20	8	<1	1	4
Private nonprofit	64	13	13	6	<1	1	4
For-profit	44	29	18	4	1	1	4
Two Year							
Public	49	14	27	6	<1	1	4
Private nonprofit	39	41	11	3	<1	2	4
For-profit	35	28	26	4	1	1	4

Source: National Center for Education Statistics (2020a, 141).

students without credentials or career skills. Regulations to curb these practices were adopted during the Obama administration and scaled back during the Trump presidency.

Two noteworthy developments mentioned earlier are the merger of Kaplan Higher Education, criticized by the US Senate Higher Education, Labor and Pensions Committee, with Purdue University to create Purdue Global and the purchase of proprietary Ashford University by the University of Arizona. These mergers offer the potential to join quality standards of two research universities with the capacity of two for-profits to recruit and enroll the new majority. Other such partnerships between mainstream higher education and marketplace organizations such as coding boot camps are on the rise.

New institutions, such as the University of the People (UoPeople), have also appeared. This tuition-free, nonprofit university, which offers online undergraduate and graduate degree programs in the professions, enrolls more than fifty thousand students across the globe. While there is no charge for course taking or books, UoPeople does have fees for assessment in each class, $120 for undergraduate courses and $240 for graduate classes. The result is that the total cost of an associate degree completed over two years is $2,460 and $4,800 for a four-year baccalaureate degree. The revenue model is low expenses, high philanthropic dollars.

Another venue for free or low-cost higher education are organizations such as MOOCs at EdX, Coursera, and Udacity. At the moment, however, there is no evidence that they have succeeded in attracting the new majority.

The bottom line is that with the advent of the new majority, higher education is facing a very real and mounting challenge, which cannot be ignored. The dimension of that challenge varies by state and locality. The amount of change it will bring to higher education depends on which actor—higher education, government, or the marketplace—plays the dominant role and what approach it takes. Additional funding means little change. Price controls mean more change. The marketplace is an unknown, though it offers compelling evidence that colleges can recruit and enroll the new majority at much higher rates than they do currently and perhaps at lower prices. That said, what is clear so far is that the rise of the new majority will require adaptive change in higher education described earlier rather than disruptive change.

Boom or Bust

Because of domestic migration, immigration, and differential fertility rates, the population of the United States is shifting geographically. The Northeast and Midwest are declining, and the Sunbelt is booming. The US Census Bureau divides the nation into four regions—the Northeast, Midwest, South, and West. In 1960, a majority of Americans (54%) lived in the

Table 6. States with 10% or Greater
Decreases or Increases in High School
Graduates, 2012–2013 and 2026–2027

New Hampshire	–19%	North Dakota	+41%
Connecticut	–17%	Utah	+28%
Michigan	–16%	Texas	+25%
Vermont	–16%	Wyoming	+21%
Maine	–15%	Colorado	+20%
Pennsylvania	–13%	Delaware	+20%
		Georgia	+19%
		Florida	+19%
		South Carolina	+18%
		Arizona	+17%
		Nevada	+17%
		North Carolina	+16%
		Washington	+16%
		Nebraska	+16%
		Oklahoma	+15%
		South Dakota	+11%
		Idaho	+11%
		Maryland	+10%

Source: Hussar and Bailey (2018, 53).

Northeast (25%) and Midwest (29%). A minority (46%) resided in the South (30%) and the West (16%) (US Census Bureau, 1961). Today, the balance is reversed. Most Americans (62%) are now residents of the South (38%) and West (24%). And the population in the Northeast (17%) and Midwest (21%) has dropped off precipitously (US Census Bureau, 2019). And the disparity is continuing to grow.

Regional high school graduation numbers reflect the shift. Between 2012–2013 and 2026–2027, the number of graduates annually in the Northeast (–6%) and Midwest (–3%) will decline but will substantially increase in the South (16%) and West (5%). Twenty-four states will experience double-digit losses (6) or gains (18) (Hussar & Bailey, 2018) (table 6).

The effect will be to create a boom-bust environment for

Table 7. Percentage of Population, Four-Year Degree-Granting Institutions and Private Four-Year Colleges by Region, 2018–2019

	Population (%)	4-Year Degree-Granting Institutions (%)	4-Year Degree-Granting Private College (%)
Northeast	17	24	25
Midwest	21	25	26
South	38	32	30
West	24	20	19

Source: National Center for Education Statistics (2019g), table 317.20.

higher education with some states having too many colleges and too few students and others having too many students and too little higher education. The situation is compounded by the fact that the nation's colleges and universities are disproportionately located in the declining regions. While 38 percent of America's population resides in the Northeast and Midwest, 49 percent of the nation's four-year colleges and 51 percent of its private four-year colleges are located there. In contrast, while 62 percent of the population lives in the West and South, these regions have only 52 percent of four-year institutions and 49 percent of private four-year colleges (table 7).

This is a historical anomaly. The Northeast and Midwest began building colleges nearly two centuries before the territories west of the Mississippi, fueled by competition among religious sects to propagate the faith and train church leaders. If the Methodists established a college, the Presbyterians built a nearby competitor and so on. Quite a few of these private institutions failed, but enough survived to make for a very crowded higher education market in the shrinking states. By contrast, in the West and South, public higher education dominated and aside from notable, often sizable political considerations, were built on a scale roughly comparable with state populations and geography. In this sense, Eastern and Midwestern higher education was built to seller specifications, and the West was constructed more to consumer needs. The South is a hybrid. All of this matters because high school students tend to pick colleges close to home. Some travel across the country, but most attending public four-year schools live less than an hour's drive away (Wozniak, 2018). Among two-year college students, close proximity is the norm.

The future of college enrollments needs be considered pre- and post-pandemic. What the pandemic did was to accelerate the anticipated enrollment changes projected prior to the virus, to expand the number of institutions closing their doors, and to hasten the rapidity of their closures. It did so by immediately reducing college enrollments, slashing foreign student attendance, decreasing the number of already-enrolled students returning to campus, and reducing the size of incoming classes in the fall. The sky-high unemployment rates made attending college unaffordable for many. The sudden and unanticipated financial shock pushed institutions at the edge over more quickly than projected and significantly increased the number of institutions at risk (Korn, Belkin, & Chung, 2020).

Had there been no pandemic, the long-term outcomes for higher education would have been very similar, but the change would have occurred more slowly. In 2018, when the pandemic was still the stuff of science fiction, Carleton College economist Nathan Grawe (2018) predicted a 15 percent drop in college enrollments between 2025 and 2029, followed by another percentage point fall in the years after. In addition to the major changes by region, enormous differences were projected by higher education sector. Demand for elite, highly selective higher education could be expected to rise by 14 percent, while enrollments in regional institutions would decline by slightly less (−11%). Hardest hit will be small, low endowment, less selective private institutions, particularly liberal arts colleges, which are heavily concentrated in the Northeast and Midwest (Barshay, 2018; Grawe, 2018).

The declines were underway even before the pandemic. In 2017, Moody's Investment Service reported 61 percent of Midwestern colleges had experienced enrollment drops versus a nearly 1 percent increase in students nationwide (Seltzer, 2017). Moody's further predicted a tripling in college closures and a doubling of mergers (Lederman, 2017).

Historically, institutions of higher education have had an extraordinary capacity to survive; they have shrunk but have clung to life and seldom closed. Even before the pandemic, a conservative estimate in New England is that at least 30 percent of institutions were at risk of closure (confidential). A potential fatality is the historic liberal arts college. Its future, definitely in diminished numbers, is uncertain given both the closures/ mergers and vocationally oriented curriculum changes designed to increase their market appeal.

• •

Even for the majority of nonelite institutions in the Midwest and Northeast that escape this fate, the years ahead are going to be hard as they confront enrollment declines and financial woes. In this environment, the biggest winners are likely to be lawyers and management consultants.

Nonetheless, the culling ahead is likely to strengthen higher education in the Northeast and Midwest by eliminating the weakest institutions and redistributing their students to healthier peers. To ensure the closures, consolidations, and student transfers occur in a responsible fashion, states and accreditors will need to oversee the contraction, applying explicit standards of institutional viability. When this does not happen, there is a high probability of chaotic closures like that of Mount Ida College in Massachusetts, where the board announced the college was shutting down a month after faculty signed contracts and students were admitted for the fall.

The reverse will be true in the West and South. The major question is how states will respond to the rising tide of new students. Traditionally, they expanded existing institutions or built new ones. However, given the scale of the increases and the time, cost, and capacity limits of campuses, some are turning to innovative, digital solutions. The most notable is California's statewide online community college. Proposed by former Governor Jerry Brown, supported by the president of the community college system, and funded by the state legislature, this institution will be unique in mission, serving "stranded workers" in jobs likely to be lost to automation and the advance of knowledge. This new community college, awarding certificates and postsecondary credentials, will engage principally in upskilling and reskilling Californians for growth industries.

The population shift will produce adaptive change in Northeastern and Midwestern higher education. It will be felt by most institutions and result in increased institutional attrition and consolidation, but there is no evidence that it will change the traditional industrial era model of higher education.

In contrast, the growth in the South and West will certainly result in the expansion of existing campuses and perhaps even the building of new ones, but it is also likely to produce new models of higher education that deviate from current practice as in California. These efforts may offer the best possible window available for viewing the future of higher education in the making and could also potentially serve as a laboratory for developing disruptive innovation at scale.

In this sense, growth rather than decline is more likely to spur radical change in the industrial era model of higher education. The hard-pressed institutions in the East and Midwest are likely to serve as laboratories for experimentation as they desperately attempt innovative solutions to survive. In contrast, the most successful of those experiments are likely to be brought to scale in the West.

A Clash of Generations

Americans are aging. In 1960, 13 percent of the population was 65 years of age or older and 39 percent were 19 or younger (Centers for Disease Control and Prevention, n.d.). In 2035, for the first time in US history, the age 65 and older population (78 million) will surpass the number of Americans under age 19 (76.7 million) (US Census Bureau, 2018). Between 2020 and 2060, the 65 and older population will nearly double from fifty-six million to ninety-five million (Vespa, Medina, & Armstrong, 2018).

As with population migration, aging is also state specific and, with a few notable exceptions such as Florida, generally reflects the North-Midwest and West-South split. Utah has the youngest residents (median age 30.5 years), and Maine has the oldest (median age 44.3 years), with a remarkable decade and a half disparity between them (World Population Review, 2020e). So, the graying of the nation will have very differing effects from state to state.

What all states share in common is that the ballooning of the 65 and older population is being driven by the post–World War II baby boom generation, born between 1946 and 1964, who will all turn age 65 by 2029. They are a monster-sized generation, numbering 76 million and constituting nearly two out of every five Americans (39%). The postwar history of the country has in many ways mirrored their development. In their earliest years, America was focused on child-rearing, preventing childhood diseases, and building more schools and colleges. As the baby boomers moved into their teen years and adolescent rebellion, the country experienced the paroxysms of the 1960s and '70s. When the baby boomers married and had children, the quality of their kids' schools became a national priority, and a school reform movement was born in the 1980s and continued into the new century. During that period, every politician running for any office from town council to president of the United States needed to have an education platform to get elected. As the boomers' children completed school and college; as their parents aged, requiring more of their time and resources; and as boomers themselves entered retirement, the boomers' and the nation's focus shifted increasingly to senior needs, such as Social Security and Medicare.

Throughout their working lives, the baby boomers have been contributors to these programs. When they retire, rather than paying into government coffers for senior programs, they will be taking funds from those programs, and given the size of the boomer generation, the balance of contributors to recipients will sharply decline. This is clear in the nation's old age dependency ratio—the number of people 65 and over per hundred working age adults 15 to 64. In 1950, the ratio was thirteen seniors per one hundred working age Americans. In 2010, it rose to nineteen, and in 2050, it will nearly double to thirty-six (Pew Research Center, 2014, 49). The outflow of funds will be so great that the Social Security Trust Fund, which currently supports the program, will be depleted by 2034.

The growing costs of a burgeoning senior population exacerbated by their rising longevity and greater need for services such as health care, which increases dramatically in the final years of life, will result in a clash between older and younger Americans for funding. Today, the largest items in state budgets are elementary and secondary education (22%), public welfare (e.g., Medicaid, Supplemental Security Income, and assistance to needy families) (21%), higher education (10%), and health and hospitals (9%) (Urban Institute, 2018). In the federal domestic budget, government (6%), Medicare and health (6%), and education (6%) are the top three items. Social Security is seventh (3%).

Higher education is unlikely to win this competition. During the 2008 recession, higher education experienced larger budget cuts than its competitors. Between fiscal years 2008 and 2010, thirty-one states made cuts to health care, twenty-nine states cut services for the elderly and disabled, and thirty-four reduced spending for K–12 education; meanwhile, the highest number of states—43—made cuts to higher education (Johnson et al., 2011). The reasons remain. One is structural: while K–12 education and health care funding are protected by "constitutional funding mandates [and] linkages to federal matching dollars" (Zumeta & Kinne, 2011, 32), higher education is not.

The second is the capacity to raise money from consumers. Higher education is unique with regard to revenue generation. As Zumeta and Kinne (2011) note, "knowing its clients can be charged more in a pinch, states disproportionately cut its support in hard times" (32). The bottom line is that, as seniors ratchet up the costs of health care and Social Security, the resources to cover the increases won't come from growth in state and federal revenues. This gives states three choices. (1) They can reallocate budget funds, most easily from high ticket items, such as K–12 and higher education. (2) They can raise taxes. (3) Or they can reduce senior benefits. It's a zero-sum game in which either seniors or younger Americans lose. Reallocation would likely come at the expense of schools and colleges. Though seniors would share the burden of increased taxes, the costs will disproportionately fall on the shoulders of the working age population. Cutting benefits by increasing retirement ages will not affect current recipients but rather future recipients—younger Americans. More direct means of targeting current seniors, including reductions in senior benefits, imposition of means tests for senior participation, and increases in senior cost shares, could raise the burden on their families.

The inescapable conclusion is that the graying of America poses a huge challenge for the nation, extending far beyond questions of who pays and who benefits, but also to the size and composition of the labor force, which necessarily includes the third rail issue of immigration policy. Higher education could be affected, depending on the remedies government adopts. Adaptive change due to reduced budgets, increased demands for cost reductions by policy makers, rising government accountability requirements regarding college efficiency and effectiveness, and growing concern over the cost of college by the public are possibilities.

Colleges and universities are already contending with another age-related challenge. Levine and Dean (2012) found that traditional-aged students 18 to 22 years old differ markedly from their older classmates. Older adults are more likely to be women, attend college part time, come to campus just to go to classes, work longer hours, and have a host of off-campus responsibilities, including jobs, families, spouses/partners, noncollege friends, and an off-campus community life. Among students who are 25 or older, 51 percent are parents (Institute for Women's Policy Research, 2018; Marcus, 2019). Compared to their traditional-aged peers, they're far more likely to come from a low-income background (66% versus 36%) (Institute for Women's Policy Research, 2018; Marcus, 2019). They're also working longer hours while enrolled: 57 percent work more than twenty hours per week (Marcus 2019). College is generally not their primary concern but only a part of the mix. The balancing act is often too much to manage: the six-year completion rate for students who enroll at age 24 or older is 48 percent, compared to 64 percent for "traditional" students (Causey et al., 2020).

According to Levine and Dean's research, these students are seeking the same kind of relationship with their colleges that they have with their banks, supermarkets, and internet providers. They ask the same four things of each: (1) convenience, (2) service, (3) a quality product, and (4) low cost. With regard to college, what they are looking for is a convenient location, parking near classrooms, and courses offered at convenient times. They want excellent customer services in areas such as admissions, financial aid, and registration. They want high-quality instruction relevant to the real world by professors who are up to date in their fields and accessible to students. They want low tuition and fees. In addition, they want sensible pathways to completion. Older learners returning to college often find that degree completion is far from straightforward. More than 40 percent of previously earned academic credits aren't accepted, forcing these students to retake coursework they may have previously completed (Marcus, 2019).

These students do not want to pay for activities, services, and staff that they are not using, gyms and student unions they don't visit, events they don't attend, and electives they don't take. They are asking for a stripped-down version of higher education and are prime candidates for consumer-oriented, anyplace, anytime instruction.

Levine and Dean found them to be markedly different from younger, traditional, full-time, and residential students who want college to have all the bells and whistles in facilities, services, activities, events, sports, and a cornucopia of classes. In the years ahead, the traditional, 18- to 22-year-old, full-time, residential collegiate population will likely continue to decline and the older, part-time population will expand.

This is a situation that should have its greatest impact on individual institutions. It will require each college and university to decide how it will respond to competing demands. Will it try to offer programs for both populations, or will it focus on one? The results of those decisions could produce major changes in some institutions. Private, less selective, liberal arts colleges in the Midwest and Northeast, which have historically focused on traditional students, could look at demographics in their regions and decide their futures reside with older, part-time, working students. There is likely to be an explosion of niche programs, small specialized initiatives designed to reach out to specific segments of the population—single moms, seniors, returning students—as institutions attempt to keep their feet in both camps. However, the changes produced will be adaptive.

• •

The nation is undergoing a demographic sea change that will affect various states and regions of the country differently, both in degree and in kind. It will bring about contractions and expansions in institutions, students, and resources; however, there is little evidence that it will produce transformative changes or disruption in the industrial era model of higher education. Colleges and universities will be able to adapt to respond to changes they face.

7

· · · · · · ·

An Emerging Knowledge Economy

If, like Rip Van Winkle, you went to sleep in 1947 and woke up today, the economic landscape would be nearly unrecognizable, turned upside down. You would find the great cities, capitals of industrial America—Detroit, Cleveland, Buffalo, and Baltimore—to be ravaged by deindustrialization and struggling to reinvent themselves in a region of the country now called the Rust Belt. You would learn that small Western cities, once regarded as backwaters—Seattle, San Jose, Austin, and Portland—were inventing a new American economy, and their populations had grown eightfold and now totaled more than eight million.

You would see that industrial era jobs in fields such as manufacturing, construction, and mining had largely disappeared. In 1947, they constituted nearly half the workforce; by 2020, they had dropped to 15 percent* (Carnevale, Jayasundera, &

---

*Despite the sharp reductions, it should be noted that manufacturing output has actually increased owing to technology, increasing productivity, and a better-educated workforce (Desilver, 2017).

Gulish, 2016a, 4; authors' calculations based on Current Employment Statistics, 2020).

And you would find knowledge economy jobs in industries such as health care, consulting and business services, financial services, government services, and educational services to be booming. They represented 28 percent of employment in 1947 and rose to 52 percent of the workforce in 2020 (Carnevale et al., 2016a, 4; authors' calculations based on Current Employment Statistics, 2020).

Put simply, you would wake up to a topsy-turvy world in which industrial era jobs and industries had been displaced by their knowledge economy successors, and the requirements for getting a job had fundamentally changed.

The best lens for understanding what happened is the 2007 recession, which acted as an accelerator of the shift. It quickly shed millions of industrial jobs and rapidly replaced them with knowledge economy positions, telescoping changes that would have occurred over a much longer period of time. At the depth of the recession in 2010, 7.2 million jobs had been lost; 5.6 million were in low-skill industrial era jobs—1.6 million in office support, 1.5 million in construction, 1.2 million in manufacturing, and so on. By 2016, the US labor market had fully recovered from the lingering effects of the Great Recession, adding 11.6 million new jobs. The recovery was not equally distributed, however; job creation occurred overwhelmingly in knowledge economy work, including 1.6 million new jobs in business and management, 1.5 million in the health professions, and nearly a million in technology occupations (Carnevale, Jayasundera, & Gulish, 2016b).

The new jobs demanded more education than those they replaced; 99 percent required at least some college. Three out of four (73%) went to people who held baccalaureate degrees or higher. The number of jobs for people with graduate degrees

Table 8. Jobs Lost and Gained during the Recession by Education Level, 2007–2010

	2007–2010	2010–2016
High school or less	−5,600,000	80,000
Some college / associate degree	−1,750,000	3,080,000
Bachelor's degree	−66,000	4,656,000
Master's degree or higher	253,000	3,768,000
Total	−7,176,000	11,593,000

Source: Carnevale et al. (2016).

actually increased at the height of the recession. In contrast, for those with a high school education or less, there has essentially been no recovery. Of the 5.6 million jobs they lost, only 80,000 had been recovered (table 8).

The jobs also demanded a different set of skills: twenty-first-century skills. There is no shortage of publications on that subject; Amazon sells more than one thousand volumes on the topic. It's a topic that's garnered the attention of foundations such as Lumina, associations such as the American Association of Colleges and Universities, and think tanks that include the National Research Council.

Although twenty-first-century skills vary from author to author, they tend to cluster in two groups. One group focuses on skills essential to succeed in a time of profound and continuing change, including critical thinking, creativity, continuous learning, problem solving, adaptability, and the like. The other cluster focuses on the areas in which change is currently occurring, such as technology and media literacy skills, reflecting the nation's shift from an analog to digital technology; cross-cultural competence, rooted both in America's increasing population diversity and globalization; knowledge literacy and data management skills, essential for an information economy in which knowledge is exploding; and teamwork, collaboration, and communication competencies needed for knowledge economy workplaces that are growing more horizontal than vertical in organization.

The bottom line is that Americans need more education at higher levels than ever before. For the first time, there are more college graduates than high school graduates in the workforce. This is translating into demands by policy makers and employers for greater high school graduation rates and increased college attendance and completion. At the same time, states are increasing high school graduation standards, though increases in student college readiness are not yet apparent. This is an area in which COVID-19 set back the clock rather than advancing it.

For postsecondary education, including collegiate and technical noncollegiate programs, consumer demand can be expected to increase. The growth, however, will be insufficient to compensate for the demographic declines in the Northeast and Midwest, but it will exacerbate the undersupply of higher education in the South and West.

A complicating factor is that industrial era jobs that in the past required only a high school diploma or less increasingly demand specialized technical, subcollegiate, postsecondary training. The mix of education that students and employers will seek remains uncertain. Rather than attending college, some will choose shorter, more vocationally oriented programs, such as coding boot camps, health paraprofessional courses, and information technology assistant programs. Rising numbers of college grads are also enrolling in such programs at community colleges and other subcollegiate institutions after completing a baccalaureate. This may mark a shift in traditional enrollment patterns or alternatively an interim step before colleges adopt such programs themselves. Indeed, the number of partnerships between for-profit and nonprofit traditional institutions and nontraditional providers is on the rise as noted earlier.

College and university curricula and extracurricular activities can be expected to change to incorporate these new skills. Throughout US collegiate history, the extra-curriculum has filled in the gaps in the formal curriculum, such as the establishment of student literary societies during the Enlightenment, when college curricula had yet to adopt the works of authors such as Montesquieu, Rousseau, Kant, and Adam Smith. Once again, the extra-curriculum more than the curriculum via clubs, workshops, internships, and career services may be the vehicle for addressing student career needs.

From Fixed Time and Process to Fixed Outcomes

The shift from an industrial to a knowledge economy has revolutionary implications for higher education because industrial economies are rooted in fixed time and processes and knowledge economies are grounded in fixed outcomes. Fixed time and processes are an inevitable consequence of industrialization and the shift from handmade to machine-made goods. In contrast to the work of independent artisans, manufacturing by machines established an orderly sequential process of production, requiring the coordination of a number of laborers and workstations, each of which added to the product until it was completed. In this system, the clock became king, dictating when laborers came to work and when they departed, determining the amount of time necessary to produce the product workstation by workstation, and setting the arrival times for raw materials and the shipping schedule for completed products.

The quintessential technology of the era was the assembly line. In Charlie Chaplin's 1936 film *Modern Times*, the assembly line at a state-of-the-art factory was the centerpiece of a comic masterpiece satirizing industrialization. Sixteen years later, the

sitcom *I Love Lucy* did the same thing, making comedienne Lu-
cille Ball an assembly-line worker at a candy factory.

The humor in both resulted from a traditionally well-ordered
and well-timed process going badly awry, overwhelming two
incompetent workers, driving one mad and causing the other
to flee in shame. The reality is that the assembly line was one of
the most successful and most emulated technologies of the era.

Indeed, our schools, which were created for industrial
America, closely resemble the assembly line. The norm is that
schools enroll children at age 5, batch process them by age in
groups of twenty-five or so, teach them for thirteen years, nine
months a year and 180 days annually.

Colleges are similar. With variations, the baccalaureate is
traditionally a four-year course of study, commonly consisting
of eight fifteen-week semesters in which students take four or
five courses, meeting three times a week for fifty minutes per
session. After completing thirty-two to forty courses or the
credit equivalent successfully, students are awarded a bachelor's degree. Progress is measured by seat time, the amount of
time students spend in a classroom.

In both industrial era schools and colleges, the time and
process of education are fixed, and the outcomes are variable.
Knowledge economies are just the reverse. They depend on the
quantity, quality, and accessibility of knowledge rather than on
the means of producing that knowledge or the amount of time
its production requires.

In the knowledge economy, higher education can be expected to shift from standardizing time and process to adopting
uniform student outcomes. This represents a transformative
change of greater magnitude than any of the changes discussed
so far.

States are currently attempting to combine both the industrial and knowledge age approaches to education, grafting the knowledge economy emphasis on outcomes onto industrial era schools by setting standards or outcomes for graduation and mandating tests to assess their achievement. A variety of initiatives are also underway to hold teachers and schools accountable for the results. The goal is to fix the process, the time, and the outcomes of education.

This is an untenable situation. It isn't possible to standardize all three because students learn at different rates. If time is fixed, then outcomes will necessarily vary. If outcomes are fixed, students will require varied amounts of time to achieve them. States will ultimately need to choose between an industrial and knowledge era education system. In the end, the nation's schools and colleges will need to be refitted for the emerging society as they were during the Industrial Revolution. As was the case then, all of our social institutions, education included, can be expected to change at a slower pace than the nation.

The knowledge economy college does not yet exist. But this is what we can anticipate. The most fundamental change, which deceptively sounds like a rhetorical flourish, would be a shift in higher education's focus from teaching, the process by which we educate, to learning, the outcomes of that education, from a focus on the teacher to a focus on the learner.

If made, the academic heart of the college would no longer be the courses the faculty teach but the learning outcomes or competencies—skills, knowledge, and attitudes—students are required to demonstrate to earn a diploma. Unfortunately, the term *competency-based education*, which best describes this approach to learning, carries a lot of baggage. It has been relegated to fuzzy jargon, used to describe a grab bag of disparate collegiate practices, resulting in sharp divisions among educators regarding its desirability. Nonetheless, this discussion uses *competency* as a synonym for *learning outcome* and *competency-based education* as synonym for *outcome-based education*.

The time to achieve these outcomes would vary from student to student depending on how long it took each to achieve mastery. Because students learn different subjects at different rates, they would need varying amounts of time to master each competency. The program, which would have to be time independent, would accordingly need to be individualized. Technological advances, to be discussed shortly, makes individualized learning increasingly possible.

The process of mastering competencies would also vary from student to student. It wouldn't matter how the student achieved mastery. All that counts is that the student accomplished it. This means students can learn by taking courses, having experiences, engaging in self-study, playing games, or even precognizing. The process by which learning occurs is irrelevant.

This shift would require a new academic accounting system. Credits and Carnegie units, which are time-based, would become irrelevant. In a world without a clock, a new unit of currency and academic accounting system would need to be established, rooted in outcomes or competencies rather than credits. This would require common definitions for competencies—the equivalent of the *Diagnostic and Statistical Manual of Mental Disorders* in psychiatry, which offers a common language and standard criteria for classification of mental diseases. The *DSM* "contains descriptions, symptoms, and other criteria for diagnosing mental disorders. It provides a common language for clinicians to communicate about their patients and establishes consistent and reliable diagnoses that can be used in the research of mental disorders. It also provides a common language for researchers to study the criteria for potential future revisions and to aid in the development of medications and other interventions" (www.psychiatry.org).

It is likely that developing shared definitions will entail the same protracted, messy drama that characterized the invention, adoption, and standardization of the credit unit during the industrial era.

Assessment would need to change as well. The A–F grading system and the variations thereof are geared to fixed periods of study. They measure how students stack up against peers when they have studied the same subject for the same length of time. An A indicates they performed very well, and an F means they failed; B, C, and D are the gradients in between.

In competency-based education, the length of the course of study varies, and the focus shifts to the outcomes students are required to achieve. Assessment is basically pass-fail. Students either have mastered the competency or have not. A letter grade has no meaning in this system.

The character of assessment would need to change, too. In the outcome-based college, assessment would be primarily formative rather than summative, determining what remains for students to learn in order to master a competency. In this system, the final formative evaluation is actually summative, determining the student has indeed mastered the competency, and no additional work remains to be done.

Certification would also look very different. The familiar institutional transcript with the names of courses taken, the grades received, and the degrees awarded would give way to a lifelong transcript, enumerating the competencies mastered, the certifying authority, and date of certification.

The number of certifications—degrees and certificates—is likely to expand with the growth of microcredentials and badges signifying mastery of a competency or a bundle of related competencies in areas such as cybersecurity, Chinese language, human resources, or supply chain management.

At first, these certifications can be expected to vary widely from certifying organization to certifying organization, even when the credentials have the same name because government and professional regulation in this area is minimal. The awarding organization does not need to be a college: it could be an industry leader, such as Google or Microsoft, whose endorsement would mean more than that of most colleges. Over time, as common definitions of competencies grow, we can expect to see increased uniformity in the credentials associated with them.

This college will not appear overnight. All other models of higher education will not disappear when it does, which was also the case during the industrial transformation. Rather, these are the directions in which higher education can be expected to move in a knowledge economy. We are seeing a plenitude of experiments with outcomes-based education, individualization of education, time variable programming, new technologies, new forms of certification and assessment, and all the rest of the elements that will constitute knowledge age higher education.

The bottom line is that the knowledge economy promises to make new and substantial demands on colleges and universities, but there is no evidence that colleges will be unable to respond to them by adaptation and successive piecemeal changes.

8

. . . .

A Technological Revolution

Complicating these demographic and economic shifts or perhaps overwhelming them is the revolution in technology.

This revolution is ubiquitous, inextricably intertwined in our lives and with the social institutions that surround us. It has already touched seemingly every aspect of our being—personal, social, civic, and commercial. The technology revolution has influenced how we are born to how we die and just about everything in between: how we communicate, how we do business, shop, date, play, socialize, learn, travel, bank, worship, vote, and work. COVID-19 has been a superspreader of the revolution, constricting the nondigital aspects of our lives and dramatically expanding the digital.

That the impact to date has been so profound tells us little about what is coming. That remains uncertain and unknowable. What we do know with certainty is that the rate of change is getting faster and faster. Bloomberg opinion columnist Barry Ritholtz (2017) put it this way: the "pace of innovation and disruption is accelerating" rapidly. The result is that "creative destruction caused by technology is ... rampant," and the impact on markets, companies, and labor is profound (Ritholtz, 2017).

We recently spoke with the chief information officer at a leading research university who laughingly said he had been asked for a ten-year technology plan for his institution. He thought anything beyond three years was science fiction. In this sense, most of us are like the farmers and artisans of agrarian America who couldn't foresee the First Industrial Revolution or the canal builders and the entrepreneurs who grew prosperous on water and steam power who couldn't envision a Second Industrial Revolution built of steel, powered by oil and electricity, and connected by a transcontinental railroad.

We do, however, know some of the technologies that will be important in the years ahead, but their scope, impact, and timing is uncertain. Another question mark is what new technologies may emerge in the years ahead. (We are rooting for time travel.)

This chapter focuses on five digital technologies that we know will powerfully affect the future of society and higher education: (1) the internet, (2) mobile devices/computers, (3) big data, (4) artificial intelligence (AI), and (5) virtual reality/augmented reality (VR/AR). They are at very different stages of development and have very different roles in the technological revolution. The first two technologies are the foundation of the digital revolution, providing a sender, a receiver, and a connector, comparable to the telegraph and the wires that joined them. The other three—big data, AI, and VR/AR—build on that foundation, enhancing digital analysis, application, scope, and content.

Like the Industrial Revolution, the digital revolution can be expected to occur in two overlapping stages. The first is the advent of the internet and the diffusion of mobile devices and computers, which constitute the foundation of the digital revolution. They mark the creation of mechanisms to send, distribute, and receive digital content. For higher education, they constitute the rudiments of online education.

The second stage, building on the first, includes big data, AI, and VR/AR.

Let's turn to the five technologies.

The Internet and Mobile Computing: The Foundation

A friend told us about a conversation with his young daughter. He told her people didn't have computers when he was her age. The daughter asked, "How did they get on to the internet?"

Arthur learned why she posed this question when he asked a group of college students how they were adapting to the tidal wave of new digital technologies. One observed, it's not technology unless it happens after you are born. If the technology existed before you were born, it's a fact of life, a given. It would be like asking Arthur or Scott how they were adapting to the light bulb, refrigerator, or automobile. They never knew a world without them. They were always there like the sunrise, eating breakfast in the morning, or getting dressed for school.

For current undergraduates, 18 to 24 years old, the internet and digital devices have always been there. But for a nearly four-hundred-year-old higher education system, they are still relatively new. To overstate it a bit, the result is that digital natives are being taught by digital immigrants at predominantly analog colleges and universities. Levine and Dean (2012, 23) offered a typology of the differences between digital students and the institutions they attend, which very much reflects the differences between the industrial and knowledge era universities described earlier (table 9). It is a generation that will encourage the transition, preferring learning to being taught,

Table 9. Traditional Universities and Digital Natives

Traditional University	Digital Natives
Fixed time (e.g., semesters, office hours)	Variable time (24/7)
Location bound	Anytime, anyplace
Provider driven (university determined)	Consumer driven (student determined)
Passive learning (hands off)	Active learning (hands on)
Abstract	Concrete
Analog media	Digital media
Teaching (process)	Learning (outcome)
Individual	Collaborative (group)
Depth focus (hunting)	Breadth focus (gathering)

Source: Levine and Dean (2012, 23).

wanting education anywhere around the clock rather than at circumscribed times and locations, desiring customized rather than off-the-rack instruction, and seeking consumer-driven rather than provider-driven education.

Today, 96 percent of 18- to 29-year-old adults have smartphones (O'Dea, 2020). They are the go-to mobile device for college students socially and academically more so than personal computers or tablets (95% vs. 88% for US teens) (Anderson & Jiang, 2018). More than half (51%) use phones or other mobile devices to access their college's learning management system, 41 percent to carry out research, 40 percent to complete assignments, and a third to access class lectures (Zimmerman, 2018).

The impact of digital devices on campus goes far beyond the classroom. It has changed student communications and relationships with professors, administrators, peers, and parents, enlarging the college community for each student to include hundreds of online friends. Campuses report they no longer know how to contact students, who have multiple email accounts and cell phones rather than landlines. They also communicate via social apps, with the most popular being YouTube (used by 90% of individuals ages 18–24 in the United States),

Facebook (76%), Instagram (75%), and Snapchat (73%) (Perrin & Anderson, 2019). This comes with a growing expectation that professors and administrators should be available around the clock like Amazon. Mobile digital technology has changed the way students communicate, play, socialize, shop, protest, get news, participate in politics, spend their time, and use the campus. It's also changed standards of conduct creating new opportunities for incivility and academic dishonesty, both of which are on the rise (Levine & Dean, 2012, 22–23).

The change with the greatest capacity to reshape higher education is online education, which the ubiquity of mobile devices makes possible. Even prior to the pandemic, when higher education switched from face-to-face to online instruction, sizable numbers of college students were already studying online—35 percent were taking at least one online course and 17 percent are taking only online courses (National Center for Education Statics, 2019f). It remains to be seen how much of the online COVID-19 instruction will persist at traditional colleges and universities. Whether a lot or a little, online education promises to have a major impact on higher education.

Here's why. First, online enrollments are concentrated in a small number of institutions. Ten universities account for more than 10 percent of the enrollment and forty-seven universities account for nearly a quarter (22%) of online enrollments (Seaman, Allen, & Seaman, 2018). For instance, the University of Phoenix enrolls approximately 100,000 online students (Chappell, 2019), Western Governors has 119,618 students (Western Governors University, 2019), Southern New Hampshire University enrolls approximately 150,000 students (Southern New Hampshire University, 2021), and the University of Maryland Global Campus has 58,281 students (University of Maryland Global Campus, 2020). This could portend an Amazon-like phenomenon in which book sales became two separate businesses—brick-and-mortar and online bookstores. The same thing is possible in higher education. That is, the creation of two competing sectors—one digital and the other analog—attracting students with very different wants and needs.

Second, the demographic shifts described earlier also support the split. Western and Southern higher education needs to increase capacity; building new plant is too expensive and insufficient in size to accommodate the coming enrollment boom. Expanding online learning, as California is doing by creating its virtual community college, is more economical, more flexible in responding to geographic need, and more scalable.

In the Midwest and Northeast, the declining college age population is likely to spawn competition between online and campus-based education. This will be accelerated by a growing demand for online courses at three-quarters (80%) of the nation's colleges and universities (Best Colleges, 2019, 22), particularly among traditionally aged college students (18–24) who are the bread and butter of four-year brick-and-mortar colleges in the region. In 2012–2013, 20 percent of these students participated in online education; by 2018–2019, that proportion had more than doubled to 41 percent (Best Colleges, 2018, 7; Sallie Mae, 2019). In 2020, an anomaly, that number approached 100 percent. However, it means for ill or good most college students have experienced substantial online instruction.

Third, the reasons students enroll in online programs also suggest major growth in the years ahead. Reskilling and upskilling, which are going to explode in demand, are the primary rationales. Over two-thirds of online students (69%) say that they enrolled in order to launch, accelerate, or switch their careers (Best Colleges, 2019, 6).

Fourth is the advent of MOOCs, online classes on steroids, with universal access and unlimited enrollments. First introduced in 2006, the major MOOC providers now have enrollments in the millions: Coursera (78 million) (January 2021, with former CEO), edX (24 million) (Shah, 2019b), XuetangX (24 million), and Udacity (11.5 million) (ICEF Monitor, 2020). What makes MOOCs a potential challenge to traditional higher education is that they are increasingly awarding certifications. MIT offers a number of micro-master's degrees, beginning with supply change economics, which if successfully completed allows a student to matriculate at MIT to complete a full master's in the field. The micro-master's is also increasingly becoming a stand-alone credential for employers. Going a step further, in January 2020, Coursera announced a partnership with the University of North Texas that would allow the platform to offer its first online bachelor's degree from a US university (Bauer-Wolf 2020). The new bachelor of applied arts and sciences degree program, targeting nontraditional students and providing multiple degree paths, is now up and running.

These online programs are in their earliest stages of development. When we look back at the current versions in the years ahead, they will seem primitive. Owing to increasing student demand, shifting demographics, and the need for upskilling and reskilling in the workplace, online education can be expected to expand significantly. There is the possibility of higher education splitting into two industries—online and brick-and-mortar postsecondary education. MOOCs, offering a growing array of certificates and degrees, are at best an unknown but have the potential to become a low-cost competitor to traditional higher education.

Big Data

Each day, 2.5 quintillion (15 zeros) bytes of data are produced (Petrov, 2020). To get a sense of what that means, this includes both the structured (e.g., text) and unstructured (e.g., audio and video) data we produce. It grows at an explosive pace every minute of each and every day as 694,444 hours of content are viewed on Netflix, 231,840 Skype calls are made, 4.5 million YouTube videos are watched, and 511,200 tweets are posted. Even our vehicles contribute to this explosion of data, with each connected car generating four terabytes of data daily (Raconteur, 2019). It includes data of a previously unprecedented scale and complexity from sources varying from space missions and satellites to genomes and meteorology. The simple fact is that 90 percent of all data have been generated in the past two years; as of 2020, there were forty times more bytes of data "than there are stars in the observable universe" (Domo, 2019, para. 1).

To be more precise, big data refers to data sets that have until recently been too big or too complex for traditional data processing. Advances in data retrieval, storage, processing, and analysis have changed that with broad-ranging implications, touching almost every aspect of human behavior and the world around us from what we buy and how to prevent diseases to how we avoid natural and human-made disasters.

In higher education, the most visible result so far has been adaptive learning. Georgia State University has been a leader in this area. Organizations such as Sophya, located in Cambridge, are now partnering with universities to create the equivalent of an educational GPS (global positioning system), providing each student in real time with the individualized resources necessary to master learning goals and offering universities metrics on the most effective practices in promoting learning.

This can profoundly change the nature of higher education assessment. The current model is generally retrospective and often high stakes, informing students at the end of a unit or a term whether they have successfully learned the subject they have been studying. If not, they need to repeat it.

Imagine if your GPS worked that way. Instead of getting

feedback as driving errors were made, the GPS might instead provide feedback on an hourly basis; at which time, it might inform the driver that the car had gone forty miles in the wrong direction, followed by the familiar recalculating. That would not be particularly helpful, but it is the way most assessment in higher education occurs.

Big data allows us to determine how students learn, what errors or misunderstandings they commonly make in mastering a subject, the most effective resources to get them back on track, and their progress toward achieving learning outcomes. In the years to come, end-of-term tests are likely to be replaced by assessments with in-course corrections. In this environment, textbooks, which are a one-size-fits-all form of instruction, can be expected to give way to customized learning materials tied to the specific outcomes a student is trying to achieve and rooted in the progress the student has made in achieving it. This would mark the shift from summative to formative assessment described earlier as well as a change in the focus of education from teaching to learning.

Artificial Intelligence

There is an old joke that the factory of the future is likely to be a machine, a person, and a dog. The dog would be there to make sure the person didn't touch the machine.

Artificial intelligence is self-driving cars; computers that play chess, write newspaper articles, read X-rays, and compose music; robots, drones, and digital assistants. But it is also many things that have become part of our daily lives—the GPS, ATM, and ticket vending machine. Artificial intelligence is the capacity of machines to perform tasks traditionally requiring human intelligence—reasoning, perception, problem solving, decision making, and learning. Machine learning is the ability of computers to progressively improve their performance from data rather than being specifically programmed. It's how Alexa and Siri improve their capacity to comprehend human language and how driverless cars gain sophistication in negotiating the roadways.

An inevitable consequence of artificial intelligence is automation, the process by which technology replaces people in tasks traditionally carried out by human beings. The dramatic decline in manufacturing jobs in the latter half of the twentieth century was actually correlated with an increase in manufacturing productivity, as more than four out five of those jobs were automated out of existence, which slashed labor costs and increased manufacturing flexibility, efficiency, consistency, and output (Hicks & Devaraj, 2015).

Today, automation is spreading beyond low-skilled jobs requiring a high school diploma or less. Research indicates that somewhere between 5 percent and 47 percent of all jobs will be lost to automation in the next ten to twenty years (Manyika et al., 2017; Frey & Osborne, 2013). The effects will not be equally distributed: Frey and Osborne's analysis also showed that the low end of the income spectrum is at much greater risk. Eighty-three percent of jobs with hourly wage under $20 will face pressure from automation, compared to 31 percent of jobs in the $20–$40 range, and only 4 percent for those in $40 and higher bracket. A McKinsey study went beyond job titles to examine tasks actually entailed in specific jobs. It concluded 51 percent of all working hours could be automated (Manyika et al., 2017). It found jobs entailing routine work at all levels of education and in all professions are likely candidates for automation. This includes cashiers, clerical support, and administrative assistants but also doctors, lawyers, and journalists.

At the moment, the jobs that are most likely to be resistant to automation, beyond those requiring expertise in the design and development of automation systems, involve nonroutine physical and manipulation skills, creative intelligence (e.g., creating and valuing), and social intelligence (e.g., negotiating, persuading, and caring) (Frey & Osborne, 2013). These overlap significantly with twenty-first-century skills discussed earlier.

So here is what we know. First, some industries and occupations are likely to be automated out of existence, such as truck driving and delivery services, which employs over 3.5 million workers (Bureau of Labor Statistics, 2020). Guesstimates of its demise vary from a decade to twenty-five years, but trucking does not exist in isolation, and the industries that support it, such as restaurants and hotels, will be affected as well.

Second, most Americans will see minor to major changes in their jobs owing to partial automation and the degree to which their work is routine. Low-paying jobs will be the most severely affected.

Third, even in industries unlikely to be affected materially by automation, the half-life of knowledge is getting shorter and shorter as quintillions of data bytes are produced daily.

The result is that most Americans will need lifelong upskilling and reskilling of their job skills and knowledge, which will require a very different kind of education than colleges have historically provided. This might be described as just-in-case education—two- and four-year degree programs, including general education, a major, and electives intended to provide students the skills and knowledge believed to be necessary for life.

Upskilling and reskilling will produce a burgeoning demand, likely larger than the current college population for just-in-time education, the education required to give students the skills and knowledge they need right now, as in: "teach me the newest programming language by Thursday."

Just-in-time education is dramatically different than just-in-

case education, varying widely in content and duration, anything from a few hours to several years. It ignores established
time standards, uniform course lengths, and traditional credit
measures. It deliberately and intentionally champions variation.

Just-in-time education requires a non-clock-based academic
accounting system. It is rooted in the outcomes that students
want to achieve rather than the duration of time spent learning
them.

Given that most of just-in-time education will not lead to traditional degrees, new forms of certification will also be needed
to recognize the completion of such programs. These are likely
to be the microcredentials and badges discussed earlier. As
agreement is reached on the definition of various outcomes
or competencies, the definitions of microcredentials can be
expected to become standardized as well, field by field, competency by competency.

Just-in-time education requires transcripts that record all
of the credentials earned in the course of a lifetime rather than
the experience at a single institution. Beyond these changes in
academic practice, which are monumental, just-in-time education raises several fundamental policy questions.

First is the question of who will provide it. Jane Addams once
said of social work that, to be successful, it must have one foot
in the library and the other foot in the street. The same thing is
true of our colleges. They too need one foot in the figurative library, humanity's accumulated knowledge, and one foot in the
street, the real world as it exists today. In times of rapid change,
higher education has done well to maintain its foothold in the
library but has lost its hold on the street, where the change is
occurring in real time. The result is that a period of catch-up is
required.

Just-in-time education is about what's happening in the

street. Each institution of higher education needs to decide whether it wishes to participate in just-in-time education, which demands not only an up-to-the-minute understanding of the skills and knowledge needed by the workforce and its employers, but also the capacity to create programs and credentials rooted in the competencies they require. Some of these competencies will be highly technical, typically provided by community colleges and other postsecondary providers; others will be more traditionally the work of four-year colleges in areas such as communication, leadership, and other twenty-first-century skills.

Regardless of the decision an institution makes, there is likely to be fierce competition for just-in-time students from the postsecondary marketplace. It will come down to whether a student would rather learn the latest computer language and earn a credential from Microsoft or the local regional university. This assumes both make the instruction equally convenient, the service equally good, the costs comparable, and employer acceptance equally high.

Another policy question is, Who will pay for just-in-time education? Will it be covered by employers, will it be supported by government financial aid programs, or will the student be responsible? Likely, some combination.

Finally, how will the imperative of just-in-time education affect traditional notions of higher education access and the changing demographics of the country? Existing policy was created before the need for continual upskilling and reskilling, though calls for such education have been heard for more than fifty years by bodies as eminent as President Johnson's National Commission on Technology, Automation and Economic Progress (1966). What will be necessary is a reenvisioning of college access to include convenient, affordable, and up-to-date education tied to market needs across the life span.

Just-in-time education is just the beginning for artificial intelligence. One can imagine a variety of learning and instructional applications, both cognitive and affective. We recently saw the prototype for a robot designed to serve as a caregiver, counselor, and support for older adults, employing the emotional intelligence that has been a stumbling block for AI. In 2018, MIT announced it would invest $1 billion in artificial intelligence research and development, and China issued a plan to become the world leader in AI by 2030. Their ambitious blueprint begins with a focus on big data and autonomous intelligence systems in 2020 and planned breakthroughs by 2025 in medicine, city infrastructure, manufacturing, agriculture, and national defense. Laws, regulations, security assessments, and control issues are also to be addressed (Robles, 2018).

Virtual and Augmented Reality

Virtual reality (VR), which is an interactive computer-generated experience taking place in a simulated environment and augmented reality (AR), a form of virtual reality that occurs in an existing environment, are in their infancy. The Facebook website contains a story. The reader is on a train having an intimate conversation with the person sitting next to him about their hobbies, relationships, and goals. There is a wrinkle. The reader is actually wearing a VR headset; the train is virtual, and the reader and his companion are represented by avatars (Facebook IQ, 2017). Welcome to virtual reality.

With a usership numbering a quarter of the globe, Facebook is making a huge investment in VR, believing it will transform social networking. They are aiming to get virtual reality headsets, the equipment required to engage in VR, into the hands of one billion people, which is an audacious goal given that sales are now in the low millions.

However, marketing research by Facebook has found public interest in using virtual reality for social, professional, and entertainment purposes. A majority of those surveyed said they would like to have VR for viewing hotels and vacation sites (65%), seeing products in shops without having to go to the stores (60%), recording moments in life to relive later (59%), hanging out with friends who are far away (59%), and communicating with distant colleagues (54%) (Facebook IQ, 2017).

The potential of VR is extraordinary; the current state of affairs is paltry. It tends to be used most frequently for gaming and entertainment, and it's barely touched higher education. Businesses such as Walmart are already using it to train workers to deal with difficult customers.

But imagine all the ways it could be used. An entire college campus or a virtual class attended by real students from across the country and around the world could be simulated. They would all feel as though they were sitting in the same virtual classroom. A student from Iowa could ask a classmate from Tokyo to have tea after class at a simulated or augmented cafeteria, coffee shop, or even Starbucks. A professor could assign the same two students a joint project to be presented to their classmates next session. This raises a very large question. If all of this is possible through virtual or augmented reality, why do we need the physical plant called a college? What is the value when a ballooning number of students are merely coming to campus to take classes, and universities in the West and South lack the capacity to accommodate the growing demand for higher education?

Virtual reality could be employed to recreate fifth-century Athens or medieval Paris or Philadelphia during the Constitutional Convention. Students could be transported to the convention rather than read or listen to a lecture about it. With the development of virtual reality, they could see it, touch it, and interact with the people and activities at these pivotal historical moments. We could create virtual Williamsburg or Philadelphia in 1776.

We could simulate labs, field trips, internships, and abbreviated versions of junior year abroad. For instance, Case Western Reserve is using HoloLens to supplement anatomy instruction, letting students interact in augmented reality with the human body.

Virtual and augmented reality offer a new learning frontier for higher education limited only by imagination and resources. In the years to come, one can imagine a time when colleges will have a VR/AR shop in their IT operations and as an element of their three-year plans.

Digital technology has the potential to be a game changer with the capacity to fundamentally transform higher education. At this point, it is only speculation because the nature and application of big data, artificial intelligence, and virtual/augmented reality are yet to be realized or significantly felt by the nation's colleges and universities. What we do know is that major online providers such as Arizona State University, Southern New Hampshire University, and Western Governors University are actively studying, experimenting, and creating pilots to strengthen and enrich online learning with these features.

9

. . . .

Adaptation

"Looking Forward" has examined the impact that three forces—demographic, economic, and technological change—are likely to have on American higher education in the years to come.

The demographic changes in the race, location, and age of the American population are major challenges with great political and financial implications for higher education. They will cause regional expansions and contractions in the scale of higher education. They threaten to disturb the current funding of colleges and universities. Some institutions will close.

But their impact on the existing industrial model of higher education has been and promises to be minimal, that is, the mission, design, organization, programs, and staffing of higher education. The only glimmers of disruption have been in the regions of the country experiencing major growth in higher education demand and their potential to respond by adopting new models of higher education such as California's virtual community college.

Institutions in the Midwest and Northeast desperate to in-

crease enrollments in the face of declining college-aged populations may serve as laboratories for innovation, carrying out
experiments of the type described in "Looking Backward." They
could be the crucibles for testing the efficacy of a variety of new
and perhaps disruptive changes in higher education.

However, any disruptive models that will guide the future
are more likely to be developed in the growing regions of
the country—the West and South—under extreme pressure
to adopt larger-scale solutions to accommodate burgeoning
enrollment demand. At this time, such initiatives are merely
experiments without the traction or scale to disrupt traditional
practice.

The economic shift in the country from a national, analog,
industrial economy to a global, digital, knowledge economy
has brought profound changes in the economic landscape of
the nation geographically. It has also changed the labor and
job mix of the country, the requirements for employment, the
skills and knowledge needed by workers, and the types and frequency of education workers must have. For higher education,
the consequences to date have been minimal, necessitating
program revisions in the short run such as updating curricula
to ensure twenty-first-century skills are taught and increasing
institutional alignment with the street, aligning curricular and
extracurricular programming to the career education and marketplace needs of their students. In the longer run, far more
comprehensive and fundamental changes will be demanded
as the industrial era model of higher education gives way to
a knowledge economy successor. Several organizations are
taking the lead in building bridges between colleges, students,
and employers, such as AntrumU and EMSI, by translating
instruction, learning, and careers into a common currency—
skills.

There are options that mainstream colleges and universities

will need to consider, such as whether to embrace the growing demand for the just-in-time lifelong education required for up-skilling and reskilling, recognizing that, if they reject or fail in offering such programs, they will empower their postsecondary competitors.

Similarly, higher education will need to respond to rising criticism and declining public confidence, which will be dis-cussed more fully in chapter fifteen. When societies change quickly, their social institutions fall behind as is the case with the rise of the knowledge economy. The lag causes the insti-tutions to be criticized, scrutinized, and challenged regarding their efficiency and effectiveness. As long as they are perceived to be out of date, too exclusive, or too costly, they invite compet-itors to challenge them.

Higher education can respond to the changing economy by adaptation, adopting successive piecemeal reforms to address the challenges as they occur. Overall, the combination of job loss owing to automation and COVID-19 can be expected to increase participation in postsecondary education but not in numbers sufficient to compensate for the population gains and losses different regions of the country will experience.

The ultimate impact of the third force, the digital technol-ogy revolution, is far less certain. So far, only the first of its two stages is fully visible. In terms of the internet and mobile devices—the driving technologies of stage one—colleges and universities have been slow to act, but they have been respon-sible for innovations such as MOOCs. They proved they could move quickly when they had to, as evidenced in their response to COVID-19, migrating from face-to-face instruction to online education in days. Whether this will be sustained will take years to discern as institutions undercorrect and overcorrect to achieve what will be a moving balance. The conventional wis-dom is that in fall 2021 and beyond there will be less reliance on online instruction than in spring 2020 but more than in fall 2019. That's a very large interval. Whatever happens, the conclusion is that higher education has adapted to stage one.

Stage two—big data, AI, and VR/AR—is largely a blank page for higher education. To date, colleges and universities have employed them as supplements to traditional practices, which is likely more a commentary on colleges and the state of development of the three technologies than on their ultimate impact.

But it is not difficult to imagine a disruptive scenario: a new knowledge age university at the periphery of higher education, replacing the traditional model or diffusing into the mainstream, fundamentally changing the industrial era university. It would be powered by digital technology and driven by changing consumer appetites regarding the kind of education wanted. It would be supported by the increasing capacity of digital technology to provide that education, the advancement of our understanding of how humans learn, and the growing need for lifelong reskilling and upskilling. This new university would be learner-centered and outcome-based. It would also be time independent, individualized in programming, and offer a host of certifications and credentials. Many of the pillars of industrial era higher education, such as Carnegie units, fifteen-week semesters, four-year degrees, and textbooks, would be lost in the transition. Campus-based colleges will continue, but it remains to be seen whether virtual higher education will become the norm.

If and until such a scenario materializes, the conclusion of "Looking Forward" is that higher education can meet the challenges of the coming demographic, economic, and first stage of the digital technology change by adaptation.

Part 3
LOOKING SIDEWAYS

Looking sideways is comparative. It is the study of industries that face comparable challenges to higher education but were forced to change more quickly. The goal is to understand how, why, and the extent to which those organizations changed and to learn the ways in which organizations did and did not change, the time frame by which change occurred, and the consequences of continuity and change. The point of looking sideways is to gain an understanding of the ways in which higher education may be pressed to change in the years ahead, perhaps even to catch a glimpse of Christmas future.

Looking sideways focuses on three knowledge organizations that, like higher education, are in the business of generating, preserving, and distributing knowledge: the music, motion picture, and newspaper industries. Chapter ten focuses on the music industry, followed by the movie industry in chapter eleven. Chapter twelve is a case study of the newspaper industry. Chapter thirteen discusses what higher education can learn from these three industries which each experienced disruptive change.

We chose these industries because they are central and basic to the knowledge economy—sound, video, and print.

These enterprises are confronting the same demographic,

economic, technological, and global realities as higher education, but they differ from colleges and universities in at least one crucial respect. The music, motion picture, and newspaper businesses are for-profit enterprises, and colleges and universities for the most part are nonprofits. For-profits tend to change more quickly through a process of replacement; that is, the new replaces the old when it becomes dated or unprofitable. In contrast, nonprofits tend to change more slowly by a process of iterative reform or repair.

It is this difference that makes looking sideways valuable. It offers the potential to view higher education's future—what could happen tomorrow. So, let's examine the three for-profits in turn and consider what lessons they offer for higher education.

10

· · · · · · ·

The Music Industry

In the early 1900s, New York City was the center of a thriving music publishing scene. Ground zero was a few blocks on Twenty-Eighth Street between Broadway and Sixth Avenue. It was a beehive of lyricists writing songs and songwriters composing music. To a person standing on the street, the result was a dreadful, unceasing racket said to be painful to the ear, as countless musicians played innumerable melodies twenty-four hours a day. A *New York Herald* reporter compared the noise to people pounding on tin pans. The image stuck and the name Tin Pan Alley was born (Lule, 2016; Tschmuck, 2012). With strong copyright laws in place by the early 1900s, composers, singers, and publishers found great success in producing sheet music. Indeed, publishing was at the core of the music industry and for good reason: for most people with the means to do so, listening to music "on demand" involved learning to play the song themselves (Wikström, 2014). If you heard a song that you liked, you purchased the sheet music and played it on your piano at home.

That is, until two new inventions, products of the Second

Industrial Revolution, disrupted the music publishing business. First came the gramophone, invented by Thomas Edison in 1877. This predecessor of the record player took a while to catch on. The sound quality was poor, and the cost was initially very high, $3,700 in current dollars. The device was clunky, fragile, and temperamental. However, by 1920, product quality was up, prices were down, and gramophones, Victrolas, or record players could be found in most American homes. Record sales boomed, going from four million copies per year in 1900 to thirty million in 1909, and to over one hundred million per year by 1920 (Medium, 2014).

There were conflicts along the way, including clashes between the old order and the new as publishers and recording companies engaged in long and costly legal battles over the right to record music. In the end, publishers were out, relegated to administering copyrights and collecting royalties, and record companies were in.

Within the new industry, there was competition between rival technologies regarding whether music should be recorded on cylinders or flat disks. By 1912, the flat disk, which morphed into records, triumphed. Three companies—Edison, Columbia, and Victor—came to dominate the record business, not only driving sales of recorded music but also cultivating and marketing musical talent.

As records and phonographs came of age, a potential rival technology emerged, the radio, which was adopted even more quickly than the record player. In 1894, Guglielmo Marconi, an Italian inventor, set out to create a new business—wireless telegraphy, capable of transmitting sound long distances to portable receivers. Less than two decades later, he opened the first radio factory. In 1920, news reports, sporting events, and live concerts were broadcast for the first time on commercial radio stations. By 1930, 60 percent of Americans owned radios and manufacturers were incapable of keeping up with demand (xroad, n.d.).

Once again lawsuits followed, this time between recording companies and radio stations over who controlled the music. In 1912, the federal government stepped in and began regulating the radio industry, ultimately deciding which radio stations would be granted operating licenses, assigning radio stations operating frequencies and power levels, and levying fines against violators. Over the next two decades, the federal role grew, mirroring the increasing complexity of the industry, and in 1934, the Federal Communications Commission, a regulatory and oversight body, was established.

By the late 1940s, after "mergers, bankruptcies, and acquisitions" (Wikström, 2014, 120), a new trio of record industry leaders emerged: RCA Victor, EMI, and CBS Records and an industrial model was firmly in place. It was a consolidated or integrated enterprise in which the major labels controlled the entire music value chain, producing records, managing talent, and distributing content. They controlled the creative inputs, including composers, lyricists, and sound engineers. Artists and repertoire, or A and R, agents discovered music talent and signed them to an affiliated label. From there, the labels would manage everything from marketing to recording—with their own in-house engineers and equipment—to distribution (Graham, Burnes, Lewis, & Langer, 2004).

The record industry's initial hostility toward radio flipped 180 degrees. Radio came to be perceived not as a usurper but as an indispensable and essential partner. Having records played on the radio was a prerequisite for sales. This structure would remain largely unfettered until the late 1940s and 1950s, when substantive changes occurred in federal regulations.

In 1947, the Federal Communications Commission began to increase the number of broadcasting licenses it issued, ultimately doubling the number of radio stations. These new radio stations differed from their well-heeled counterparts, launched pre-1947, which generally had the resources to produce "elaborate live shows" (Tschmuck, 2012, 112), featuring top talent, orchestras, comedy, variety entertainment, and public affairs programming. The new radio stations lacked the funding to produce this kind of entertainment, leaving them with a big problem: What content could they broadcast?

The existing radio stations saw them as competitors, and the major labels were accordingly loath to work with them. The new stations were relegated to filling musical holes, playing genres of music the major labels ignored and targeting audiences labels failed to reach. A partnership sprang up between smaller, underfunded radio stations and independent ("indie") music labels associated with folk, rhythm and blues, country and western, and—most notably—rock 'n' roll. It was a symbiotic relationship: indie labels frequently gave these stations their records, counting on the benefits of radio exposure. At the same time, musical genres that had previously failed to achieve exposure suddenly became available to broad record-buying audiences. The partnership between upstart radio stations and nouveau indie labels set the stage for a revolution that would shake the entire music industry.

When it first emerged, rock 'n' roll was problematic for major record labels. De jure or de facto segregation was still in force in much of the country, so the majors avoided playing anything that sounded like "race music." Rock 'n' roll—grounded in blues and rhythm and blues traditions—was a risky proposition for an industry that "banked on continuity" (Tschmuck, 2012, 118) and profited from catering to mainstream tastes, providing a "tried-and-tested Tin Pan Alley sound" (Tschmuch, 2012, 104) that appealed to white, middle-class sensibilities. Even as rock 'n' roll became commercially successful, the majors largely continued marketing the same big-name singers.

When major labels did experiment with rock, they did so in ways that minimized risk. For example, when a rock 'n' roll track found success, the majors would commonly have white artists cover the song for the pop market. When Decca released a cover of "Shake, Rattle and Roll" in 1954, the sexually charged lyrics of the original track were sanitized for mass consumption. Even more aggressively, the majors commonly groomed new talent, white performers, teaching them "how to walk, how to talk, and how to act onstage" before they were ever permitted to perform publicly (Tschmuck, p. 119, as quoted in Gillett, 1971, 161).

In the rare cases that major labels signed rock artists, they waited, deliberated, and did so without any sense of urgency. Such was the case when, in 1955, RCA Victor signed Elvis Presley for $35,000, picking him up from the independent Sun Records (Wikström, 2014). The importance of this acquisition is hard to overstate. According to creative industries expert Patrik Wikström (2014), signing Presley was the primary reason RCA Victor was able to stay in the top music charts during the 1950s, at a time when other major labels struggled to remain relevant.

Rock 'n' roll caused a shakeup in the music industry. The leading players changed but the comprehensive integrated business model persisted. In 1948, several years before rock really took off, four labels (CBS-Columbia, RCA Victor, Capitol, and Decca) produced 81 percent of the tracks on the weekly top ten charts. Ten years later, this plummeted to 36 percent. As late as January 1955, *Variety* magazine reported that "the majors had released 42 of the 50 best-selling records of the previous year" (Tschmuck, 2012, 107), compared to eight from independent labels. However, only a year later, indie labels would succeed in placing eighteen records in the top fifty. By 1956, consolidation had weakened to the point that twenty-five record companies were represented in the top fifty chart. Six years later, the music industry reached its lowest level of market concentration of all time, with the eight largest labels capturing only 46 percent of the market (Tschmuck, 2012).

Of the major labels that had dominated the music industry prior to rock 'n' roll, only CBS and RCA survived the period. The failure to recognize and adapt to the staying power of rock 'n' roll was twofold. First, the majors believed rock was a passing, racially unacceptable, fad. Second, and perhaps more important, the major record labels were not set up to react to changes in consumer preferences. Industry leadership prized continuity over innovation and projected tomorrow on the basis of yesterday, which discouraged recognizing, much less betting on innovative artists or genres.

Commercially, rock 'n' roll developed and eventually thrived because of the support of independent record labels. The lesson was not lost on those major labels that survived the 1950s. In time, majors came to see indies not as threats but as potential sources of new talent. Some majors simply acquired independents, while others entered into formal partnerships with smaller labels, using them as incubators for prospective talent. The independents, which were both nimbler and more culturally responsive than the majors, came to serve as laboratories for new styles and musical genres. As music industry researcher Peter Tschmuck (2012) notes, "This outsourcing of music production and talent search to independent producers and labels allowed the majors to minimize the financial risk involved in trying to exploit new music styles. They simply shifted the initial risk to the independents and producers" (151).

By the 1960s, only a decade after they had rejected the rock 'n' roll revolution, major labels were signing artists such as Bob Dylan, Janis Joplin, the Rolling Stones, and Jimi Hendrix. By the 1970s, the independents constituted the equivalent of a farm team system for the majors, giving them low-risk and low-cost access to a large, diverse network of talent. As a result, new genres continued to emerge on a steady basis: punk rock, heavy metal, disco, grunge, and hip-hop would all realize widespread commercial success in the decades to come.

Digital Disruption

Technological change has been constant since the beginning of recorded music. Over time, records changed in size, composition, speed, content capacity, and quality. They ultimately gave way to cassettes and then to compact discs (CDs). MTV and videos became another vehicle for marketing artists to the public. What did not change is that record labels continued to be the gatekeepers of the music industry, maintaining control of talent, production, promotion, and distribution.

The first chink in the system was the emergence of recordable media (blank cassettes and CD-Rs). This diminished the music industry's capacity to control content; consumers gained the ability to capture music without needing to purchase albums legally and broke the industry's distribution monopoly while fanning the desire of consumers to choose the content they owned.

New technologies made consumer choice a reality. Beginning with pocket-sized transistor radios in 1954, music listening became mobile. Twenty-five years later with the advent of the cassette-playing Walkman, the consumer could also select the content. The Discman followed in 1984 and the cassette gave way to the CD.

Then came the game changer. Music went digital, and in 2001, the MP3 player, the best known of which was the iPod, hit the marketplace. It downloaded, stored, and played music the consumer selected, making music mobile, individualized, around the clock, and consumer driven.

It was a catastrophe for the music industry that began two years earlier, when an upstart online content sharing site called Napster, allowed users to freely share digital music tracks (Madden, 2009). Users of the site shared MP3 files and found that the convenience of freely accessing individual songs and downloading them locally outweighed inherent MP3 quality loss for all but the most devoted audiophiles (Rose, 2011).

Napster (and later, similar file-sharing services) upended the traditional distribution model (Wikström, 2014). A year after Napster went online, nearly one-quarter of adult internet users had downloaded music files, and over half had used Napster to do it (Wikström, 2014). The music industry responded aggressively, launching litigation not only against Napster but also against the individual file sharers (Wikström, 2014). The effect was mixed. While Napster was eventually forced out of business in July 2001, the damage was done. Economically, the effects of piracy would continue long after Napster disappeared, leading to massive losses for both music producers and retailers. One estimate asserts that US retailers lost nearly $1 billion in sales because of digital music piracy in 2005 alone, and this figure did not include the economic costs of lost jobs, salaries, and tax revenues (Siwek, 2005).

In the wake of Napster, there was no shortage of industry experts predicting that record labels would die and that musicians would soon sell directly to fans via the internet (Madden, 2009). After all, record labels, once vital to artist development and promotion, had become little more than intermediaries in an age of disintermediation.

This threat and the dire prognostications were "overblown" (Madden, 2009, 951), but in the first decade of the twenty-first century, it didn't look that way. In 1997, global recorded music revenues totaled nearly $40 billion; by 2010, they had dropped by half (Nicolaou, 2017). Indeed, the declining music industry spent the early years of the twenty-first century scrambling for a business model that would permit it to survive in the digital age. As CD, cassette, and record sales plummeted, no replacement revenue stream was readily apparent.

However, in 2005, a promising solution emerged. In partnership with the recording industry, Apple iTunes and others began selling digital downloads of individual tracks and albums. While initially successful, this was not the answer. It never generated revenue comparable to what had been lost as consumers moved away from CDs and other physical products (Nicolaou, 2017; Warr & Goode, 2011).

The true impact of Napster and similar sites, though, was not in the dollars lost to piracy; rather, it was the shift in consumer expectations. Listeners developed a taste for digital, on-demand, low-cost, or free access music. For music lovers, the grand vision was a celestial (or, alternatively, heavenly) jukebox. As early as 2000, experts predicted a future in which media consumers would be able to instantly access any piece of music ever recorded via the internet. It was not far off (Madden, 2009; Mann, 2000).

Since the 1960s, when technological advances first enabled greater amounts of content to fit onto vinyl, the music industry has been wedded to the album as the bundle of choice (Newman, 2014). Although many artists during this period released outstanding, thoughtful album-length works, the prevailing business model was to focus on crafting a hit single that would draw consumers to pay for the full album (Newman, 2014). At the turn of the century, by unbundling the album, breaking it into singles, Napster offered music consumers an alternative to the traditional requirement of needing to buy the whole album, demonstrating what music consumption could be if released from the constraints of the traditional bundle.

In more recent years, several related developments have effectively made the celestial jukebox a reality. Together, the improvement of wireless technology, the ubiquity of connected smart devices, and the development of digital streaming services has given consumers the access imagined at the turn of the century. In 1995, consumers interested in listening to a song on their own device would have needed to go to a music store to purchase a CD, which would contain other tracks that the consumer might or might not want. The consumer would then need a device to play the CD (probably portable, but no doubt prone to skipping and other inconveniences). Shortly after the turn of the century, services like Apple's iTunes Music Store began giving consumers a legal means of downloading unbundled tracks at ninety-nine cents each, even if that access was limited to a relatively small universe of songs and restricted to use on Apple devices (Ingraham, 2013). In 2020, that same consumer—for roughly the same price as a single CD each month—could subscribe to a service like Spotify or Apple Music for on-demand access to a universe of music. And these services are largely agnostic about which device the consumer uses. Personal computers, smart devices, car radios, and gaming systems are all allowed access to the celestial jukebox.

Today, subscription-based streaming services like Spotify and Apple predominate while traditional methods of consumption have continued to decline (aside from vinyl records, which have enjoyed a bump from audiophiles and nostalgists) (Gibson, 2015; Nielsen, 2020). Between 2018 and 2019, physical album sales continued a spectacular decline, falling by an additional 15 percent from $84.4 million to $73.5 million (Nielsen, 2020). Digital sales didn't fare any better: digital albums declined 24 percent from $52.3 million to $39.3 million, and digital track sales fell 25 percent from $401.4 million to $301.1 million (Nielsen, 2020). Yet music consumption overall rose from prior years, driven primarily by the explosive growth in on-demand audio streaming (Nielsen, 2020). Only a few years ago, in 2016, there were just over a quarter of a billion on-demand audio streams ($252.3 billion to be exact) (Nielsen, 2020). As of 2019, that figure had nearly tripled to 745.7 billion (Nielsen, 2020).

What Changed

Through most of the twentieth century, record labels held a firm grip on distribution, dictating the medium (e.g., the record, the cassette, the CD), the device (e.g., the gramophone, the Walkman), and the bundle (i.e., singles and albums). However, with the movement of music from the gramophone to the transistor radio to the Walkman to the iPod, to the mobile phone and beyond, just about every advance in music distribution has served to meet the consumer demand for more portable and accessible content. Napster opened the universe, offering a new paradigm for music consumption, one that heavily favored the listener at the expense of the label and unfortunately the content creators themselves.

The rise of on-demand streaming is now bringing growth to an industry that has suffered years of decline by adding new kinds of value to the consumer. First, streaming services offer access to a massive library of content, which includes both well-known and up-and-coming artists. Beyond dramatically expanding the musical universe available to consumers, the algorithmic capacity of the service to identify new artists the consumer might like given past selections enables new discoveries by listeners and the possibility of expanding their musical frontiers. For the industry, it also mitigates against the same old rut that so damaged the major labels with rock 'n' roll and provides a mechanism for keeping music alive and forward looking.

Second, streaming has changed how listeners consume music. Rather than having to purchase their music album by album or single by single, consumers now have access to the entire music library for a set subscription price. They have the power to choose what they listen to and the manner in which they want it bundled by creating their own playlists, the "mixtape[s] of the 21st century" (Johnson, 2016).

Third and perhaps most important, streaming services offer on-demand access to the library through portable devices, effectively realizing the longtime dream of the "celestial jukebox" (Warr & Goode, 2011). As an innovation, streaming is the latest in a long string of changes to music consumption. In a span of just over a century, music has migrated from the pages of sheet music to the record and from the record to the radio, the cassette, the CD, and the MP3 player. With each innovation, the portability and accessibility of musical content increased.*

Given the rise of streaming, the relative availability of home production tools, and the ubiquity of social media platforms today, the conversation has turned to the relevance of the record label in the digital age. The central processes to which labels once offered something of value (e.g., promotion, production, and distribution) no longer require the work of a large organization; instead, many of these processes can be handled from one's home.

In 2021, the music industry is very much in a state of flux. Artists, labels, and digital streaming services are all grappling with new roles, processes, and ways of reaching consumers. If anything is certain, however, it is that the models that fueled the industry through the twentieth century are now obsolete.

---

*This transition, however, has come at the expense of artists who receive only a tiny portion of the revenue generated. Even on Napster, the platform with the highest per-stream payouts, artists needed ninety thousand plays each month in order to earn $1,472—equivalent to the federal minimum wage (Sanchez, 2018).

11

· · · · · · ·

The Film Industry

The movie business, like music, was also a creation of the Second Industrial Revolution. It began with the invention of the motion picture camera and projector in the 1890s, variously attributed to Polish inventor Kazimierz Prószyński, the Edison lab, the Lumière brothers, and British photographer William Friese-Greene, with an exact date dependent on one's preference of inventor.

The history of the film industry is not very different from that of the music industry. It's a story of rival technologies; litigation; experiments in production, content, organization, distribution, and every other aspect of the business; and ultimately the emergence of an industrial era integrated business model.

In the beginning, at least in the United States, there was Thomas Edison who established a virtual monopoly in an as-yet nonexistent movie business, patenting seemingly everything required to make and distribute movies: filmmaking technology, film projecting equipment, and the films themselves. As the industry emerged, endless legal battles ensued as well as a sea of movie innovations designed, depending on one's perspective, either to skirt Edison's patents or to advance the field.

The audiences for films flowed from the exhibition or projection technology employed. Edison's lab created the kinetoscope, a cabinet-sized box with a viewer on top through which an individual could watch a moving picture, a strip of perforated celluloid film mechanically moved over a light bulb. Edison created kinetoscope parlors where the public could see the films one person at a time, and the kinetoscope toured with circuses, carnivals, and vaudeville shows. It came to storefronts and auditoriums all around the country.

In France, the Lumière brothers took a different approach, projecting moving pictures onto a screen for many to see simultaneously with a device called a Cinématographe. Mass viewership became the norm. In 1905, the first permanent US motion picture theater, the Nickelodeon, opened its doors in Pittsburgh, offering about a half hour of short films that changed weekly. Americans fell in love with the movies. One can only imagine how astounding it must have been to see photographs move for the first time. Theaters mushroomed across the nation.

The nature of films changed, increasing in duration from seconds to minutes to hours as the technology advanced. With greater length came greater complexity, the capacity of films to tell stories. Initially, films were recordings of everyday events—water shooting from a hose, a horse galloping, a baby eating, animals at the zoo. The first Edison film showed a man, none other than the inventor himself, walking toward and then bowing to the viewer. Longer films had plots and genres of films developed—drama, romance, comedy, adventure. In 1910, actors' names were included in the films for the first time.

Edison erected the first film studio in 1893, a building covered with tarpaper, called the Black Maria, as part of his New Jersey lab. Filmmakers congregated initially in Fort Lee, New Jersey, near the Edison studios. But year-round production required a more hospitable climate, so thirty studios, including Edison's own and Metro, which would become MGM (Metro-Goldwyn-Mayer), moved to Jacksonville, Florida. Then fifteen migrated to Southern California where filming conditions were even better, and Edison and his potential litigation were a continent away. Hollywood was born.

By the turn of the century, the number of companies making and distributing films had exploded. By 1910, there were approximately six thousand, seemingly all engaged in suing one another as well as competing for business in a very crowded marketplace. To bring some order to the business, the Motion Picture Patents Company—better known as the Trust—was created to set quotas on the number of films of various lengths each studio could produce. Four thousand film companies signed on, and the other two thousand sued and won an antitrust suit against the Trust in 1912.

A war of each against all ensued. When the smoke cleared in the early 1920s, five wealthy film companies emerged as the victors, called the majors, the leaders dominating the industry—20th Century Fox, MGM, Paramount, Warner Brothers, and RKO (Radio-Keith-Orpheum). Three more, called the Little Three, Columbia Pictures, United Artists, and Universal, formed a lesser galaxy. They controlled the production, distribution, and exhibition of movies as well as the talent that made it possible—actors, directors, writers—the people in front of the camera and all the people behind it (Schatz, 2008).

But the big five studios also owned theater chains, ensuring that they held firm control over every aspect of the enterprise, a span of control the record labels never had. The studios owned or controlled 17 percent of the nation's movie theaters, attended by 45 percent of moviegoers (Schatz, 2008). For independent theaters to exhibit their films, they were required to block book studio movies, that is, rent large packages of films, often two a week, 104 a year, composed of a mix of A-list movies with star performers and a considerably larger number of second-rate B-list movies, sight unseen. This guaranteed that studio B-list films would be profitable.

So powerful were the major studios that despite ignoring sound and continuing to produce silent films they maintained their hold on the industry. Jesse Lasky, a founder of Paramount, saw talkies as a fad, which had been kicking around for thirty years, and famously pointed to an oil painting in his office of trees blowing in the wind and asked whether it would be enhanced by a soundtrack of wind (Eyemen, 1997). The studios waited and watched the extraordinary success of talkies before entering the market. To put this into perspective, sound had generated as much wonder and excitement among the public as had pictures that moved. But the majors made the public wait and they were not replaced, nor had their control of the industry been usurped by the faster moving studios.

Indeed, the period from the late 1920s through 1948 is commonly called the "Golden Age of Hollywood." Not only did the big studios own the movie business, but their audiences continued to grow. Entertainment was one of the few low-cost pleasures widely available during the Depression when a higher proportion of Americans went to the movies than at any other time in history (Pautz, 2002).

Then the courts and a new technology remade the film landscape, bringing the golden age to a close. Eight independent producers, Hollywood legends, including Walt Disney, David O. Selznick, and Hal Roach, opposed studio ownership of movie theaters and took the issue to court. In May 1948, the

US Supreme Court affirmed their position declaring the joint ownership to be an antitrust violation. The court also barred block booking and blind bidding for the same reasons.

The twin rulings promised to dramatically reduce studio profits and diminished the number of films the studios produced annually since the guarantee of profitability for B films had been lost. It made the little three and other poverty row studios more competitive with the majors. It placed theater chains in a far better bargaining position with the studios for movies. Actors and other film professionals, previously all but owned by the studios, gained leverage over their employers since the number of studios that could employ them had grown; actors could also create their own independent production companies. Talent came to eclipse management. What had been called the studio system gave way to the star system. The studio monopoly was broken.

Another blow to the industry was the advent of television, which revolutionized home entertainment as much as radio had done for music. As with radio, aside from having to purchase a television, the content was free. The initial problems were the same for both—high cost per unit, poor quality, finicky technology, and lack of programming. However, adoption was relatively quick. In 1950, just under 4 million households owned a television; only five years later, that number had grown to 30.7 million households (Pautz, 2002).

In theory, television represented an existential threat to a film industry that had just recently lost direct control of its own exhibition resources. The 1950s were a time of experimentation, negotiation, and trial and error as the film industry sought to define its relationship with television. Ultimately, the film industry positioned itself as a content supplier to the television, selling their existing libraries of feature films as well as original series (Boddy, 1985). The industry was able to adapt to its new circumstances. While it needed to make significant changes to adjust to new competition and new modes of content distribution, it did so in such a way that preserved the existing industrial model.

In 1975, the movie and television industries received another technological jolt when Sony launched the Betamax videocassette-recording device. Like the music industry's experience with cassettes, the prospect of recordable media threatened content providers in the film industry. The initial reaction from the major film studios was aggressive. Universal and Disney, the two largest Hollywood studios at the time, filed suit against Sony, alleging that the recording device could be used by consumers to infringe on copyrights (Madrigal, 2012). The case, reminiscent of the battles between music publishers and record companies, eventually reached the Supreme Court, which in a 5–4 decision (citing Fred Rogers, an advocate for recording television programs) held that recording a television program constituted fair use, the legal doctrine that permits limited use of copyrighted materials without permission of the owner.

However, by the time the court ruled in 1984, home recording was already a fact of life. A second generation of video recorder, VHS, had already replaced Betamax, much as flat discs had replaced cylinders in the music business, and nearly half of all American households had analog videocassette recorders (VCR) (Demain, 2018). The VHS would be superseded by the Digital Versatile Disc (DVD) player. What the ruling represented, though, was a profound shift in movie content control. Within forty years, control had moved from studios to theaters to television to consumers. The movie industry actively and unsuccessfully resisted each of these shifts, eventually adapting when no other choice remained. In some instances, these adaptations proved lucrative, as was the case with the VCR and VHS tapes. Despite initial resistance, by 1989, home video was generating more revenue for studio-distributors than movie theaters (Schatz, 2008).

The budding home entertainment market was a new revenue stream, which expanded with the advent of video rental stores. Blockbuster Video, one of the most well-known rental services, was launched in 1985. At its peak, Blockbuster Video had nearly ten thousand stores and, in 2002, only eight years prior to declaring bankruptcy, was valued at roughly $5 billion (Downes & Nunes, 2013). Blockbuster's value as an intermediary was straightforward: with many physical locations, Blockbuster gave consumers a way of renting new releases (and old classics) and viewing them in their own homes (Kaplan, 2011). The concept of a rental was key to the Blockbuster model, in no small part because late fees for rentals returned after the due date were a significant source of revenue. In 2000 alone, late fees reportedly accounted for 16 percent of Blockbuster's total revenue, bringing in almost $800 million (Liedtke & Anderson, 2010).

Then came Netflix, another video rental company, which abandoned storefronts and physical locations, instead mailing its films to consumers in a DVD format. Launched in 1997, Netflix was convenient, cheap (as DVDs were relatively inexpensive to produce and ship), with no late fees (Downes & Nunes, 2013). The downside was that consumers needed to wait for their rental to arrive in the mail. At the time, Netflix did not appear to present a direct threat to Blockbuster. It was, in the words of former Blockbuster CEO John Antioco, a small "niche business"; when Antioco was approached in 2000 with an offer to buy Netflix for $50 million, he passed (Chong, 2015).

In all fairness, one could hardly be blamed for failing to see the potential of Netflix at the turn of the century. While the use of the US Postal Service for distribution, the shift to digital formats, and the absence of late fees were innovative, the core business model didn't differ substantially from that of the other rental services.

The Digital Disruption

In 2007, Netflix began an online streaming service (Downes & Nunes, 2013). At the time, less than half of US households had a broadband connection, so the technical infrastructure necessary for the company to succeed did not exist; it was a big bet (Downes & Nunes, 2013). The coming digital revolution worked in Netflix's favor: high-speed internet access boomed, and both the quality and speed of transmissions improved over time. The barrier that initially stopped Netflix from displacing Blockbuster—the wait between film selection and arrival— disappeared, making Netflix a cheaper, more convenient and higher-quality option than its brick-and-mortar competitors. By the time Blockbuster entered the digital download world, its retail stores—once its core assets—were major liabilities, dragging down revenues. In 2010, Blockbuster declared bankruptcy (Downes & Nunes, 2013).

As of 2020, Netflix had well over one hundred million subscribers and earned over $5.47 billion in revenue in the last quarter of 2019 alone (Rodriguez, 2020). It would be easy to chalk up the success of streaming services to mere convenience. Simply put, it is easier to watch a film in your own home than it is to head to the theater or drive to a rental store. In this way, the current tension between Hollywood and streaming services calls to mind the concerns of the film industry when the television first entered American living rooms. The difference is that, in the 1950s, the film industry had a way forward, a means of adaptation. If it could not continue to dominate distribution, it could at least maintain control of content production and profit from selling that content to television networks.

Today, however, Netflix is not only in the business of distribution but also production. Traditional film studios need to consider a multitude of factors when funding a motion picture (mass appeal, box office sales, etc.); Netflix, on the other hand, simply needs fresh content to keep subscribers engaged from one month to the next (Rodriguez, 2020). Even as Hollywood continues to play it safe by focusing on superhero franchises, reboots, and sequels, Netflix has become the distribution platform for both award-winning series (e.g., *Stranger Things*, *House of Cards*) as well as Netflix-exclusive films, a potentially mortal threat to the established film industry. The US box office continued to generate healthy revenues until the pandemic, mostly because of increasingly expensive cinema prices; looking strictly at tickets sold, cinema attendance has been on a long-term decline. In 2019, before COVID-19, North American attendance was reported as 1.24 billion, among its lowest points since 1995 (National Association of Theatre Owners, 2020).

What Changed

As with the music industry, a principal theme in the storied history of the film industry is the shift in control. In the early part of the twentieth century, film studios ensured their success by maintaining a firm hand on all aspects of the enterprise, controlling talent, production, distribution, and exhibition. Over the course of the century, the film industry surrendered this control bit by bit, especially with respect to distribution. From losing its theater chains to competing with television to attempting to kill off Betamax and VHS, the second half of the twentieth century ushered in a series of blows to the industrial model of the movie business. Later entrants to the movie business rooted in the industrial model—Blockbuster perhaps being the most notable—would suffer from the same failure to innovate fast that film studios experienced.

The same consumer demands that led to the rise of streaming in the music industry have fed similar changes in film and TV. For one, mobile access to a massive library of content makes services such as Netflix appealing to the everyday consumer. But there is more to it than simple convenience. Another major driver of Netflix's success comes from intelligent use of big data. Within the Netflix library, genre-related tags such as action/adventure, romance, and comedy barely scratch the surface of how the platform captures user preferences. Netflix, in fact, has tens of thousands of microgenres feeding algorithms that drive content delivery on a personalized basis (Rodriguez, 2020). These same data points also drive the content that makes its way to the platform in the first place. Consider that Netflix outbid both HBO and AMC for first rights to *House of Cards*, committing to two seasons before previewing a single scene (Baldwin, 2012). Why take such a gamble? It's not because of intuition but data. Based on information captured from customers' viewing histories and ratings, Netflix executives saw the series as a sure bet—and they were right (Petraetis, 2017).

Today, popular media is rife with references to the Hollywood versus Netflix battle. Ultimately, though, the story is not about one studio or a single company (after all, other companies such as Amazon, Apple, and Disney are also streaming); instead, it is about a changing model of creating and distributing visual entertainment. Over the past century, the film industry has fought repeatedly to protect the industrial model, attempting to adapt only when regulation (e.g., Supreme Court rulings in 1948 and 1984) or consumer behavior (e.g., mass adoption of television) forced it to. The struggle facing Hollywood today is that the industrial model no longer works. Disruptive change has come, offering new kinds of value that cannot be easily reconciled with the long-standing business model.

12

. . . .

The Newspaper Industry

The newspaper industry is unique among the sectors covered in this chapter. First, it is much older than the music and movie businesses—nearly three centuries older. The first newspaper was published in Strasbourg, Germany, in 1605. An American version, *Publick Occurrences Both Forreign and Domestick*, a three-page Boston monthly, which published British and local news, didn't appear for another eighty-five years. It was shut down after one issue by the colonial governor for publishing the equivalent of fake news—"doubtful and uncertain Reports" (National Humanities Center, 2006, 6).

The newspaper business reached its numerical apex even before the film and music industries took off. In 1760, before Samuel Slater built the first factory in America, there were twenty newspapers in the colonies. A century later (1870), before the invention of the gramophone, radio, and motion picture camera, there were six hundred newspapers in the country. In 1910, before the advent of the first radio station and the birth of talking films, there were two thousand six hundred newspapers in the United States, the largest number ever in American history.

Second, in contrast to movies and music, the audience for

newspapers is local rather than national or international. Ninety percent of their circulation occurs within one hundred kilometers of a newspaper's hometown in the same manner as higher education. There are only three national newspapers in the United States: *USA Today*, the *Wall Street Journal*, and the *New York Times*. The *Washington Post* and *Los Angeles Times* have a claim to membership in this group. This makes newspapers more sensitive to local demographic changes such as population movement and English language fluency than the music and film industries.

Third, the industrial model for the newspaper business is a product of the First Industrial Revolution rather than the second.

Fourth, the revenue model for newspapers is not based on selling content to consumers or exhibitors as in the film and music industries but on funding from advertisers who want to sell goods and services to those consumers.

Fifth, unlike music and movies, the newspaper business wasn't built by a small number of corporations controlling the industry. Instead, it began in colonial printing shops, where printers established a new business line. The First Industrial Revolution brought hundreds of new newspapers and a generation of founders: James Gordon Bennett and the *New York Herald* (1835), Horace Greeley and the *New York Tribune* (1840), and Henry Jarvis Raymond and the *New York Daily Times* (1851). They were succeeded during the Second Industrial Revolution by legendary giants who purchased their newspapers, most notably Joseph Pulitzer, who bought the *New York World* from robber baron Jay Gould in 1883, and William Randolph Hearst, who purchased the failing *New York Journal* in 1895, together creating what came to be called yellow journalism. The great newspaper families emerged from coast to coast in the same time frame, such as the Otis/Chandlers at the *Los An-*

geles Times in 1882 and the Sulzbergers at the *New York Times* in 1896.

The *New York Journal* was Hearst's second newspaper; he went on to build a diversified communications empire, which ultimately included twenty-eight newspapers, thereby establishing the first newspaper chain. Following in his footsteps were chains such as Gannett, Knight Ridder, Cox, McClatchy, the New York Times, Washington Post, and Times Mirror (Los Angeles Times) Companies. E. W. Scripps, founder of the *Cleveland Press* and subsequently owner of twenty-four other newspapers, added another element—the newspaper syndicate, a set of joint initiatives, including wire and feature services, which generated content, cut costs, permitted member newspapers to pick and choose the content they published, and allowed the differentiation of newspapers within chains.

As the industry declined in the late twentieth and early twenty-first centuries, ownership of newspapers grew more concentrated, reminiscent of the movie and music businesses. In 1983, 90 percent of US media companies were owned by fifty corporations. Today, that 90 percent—newspapers, television, radio, film, music, cable, internet, and more—are owned by six companies—AT&T, Comcast, Disney, CBS, Viacom, and Fox.

An Industrial Model

Three developments determined the industrial era business model of the newspaper: (1) technology, (2) pricing, and (3) advertising. The evolution of the printing press was a cornerstone in building the industry. The earliest newspapers were printed on updated versions of Gutenberg's fifteenth-century movable type press. However, the iron and steam of the First Industrial Revolution were game changers. In 1800, the cast iron press reduced the amount of pressure required to operate a printing press by 90 percent, which permitted printing on both sides of a sheet of paper and the doubling of the size of a newspaper page. Fourteen years later, powering that press by steam multiplied the number of pages that could be printed to 1,100 an hour. At midcentury (1843), the invention of the rotary press increased production to a million copies a day and the development of technology to make paper from wood chips rather than rags (1840) slashed the cost of newsprint. Later, the advent of the Linotype machine in the mid-1880s permitted the setting of whole lines of type rather than having to do so letter by letter, which allowed newspapers to expand beyond eight pages. This combination dramatically reduced the labor cost of newspaper publishing and raised the level of potential circulation to previously unimaginable levels.

What has come to be called the "penny press" in turn set the financial model for the newspaper industry. In 1833, in order to bail out his failing printing business, Benjamin Day founded the *New York Sun*. This is not as odd as it may appear since as noted most newspaper publishers were printers. However, Day went after a different market for his newspaper. At the time, newspapers, typically charging six cents a copy, had a small and rather elite clientele. Day slashed the price to a penny with the hope of dramatically growing circulation and was remarkably successful, selling five thousand copies daily within a few months, the highest number of any newspaper in the country. Within two years, volume had risen to fifteen thousand, and the price increased to two cents. Day also introduced newsboys, making it easier for the public to buy his papers at a convenient location without even having to enter a store.

Other newspapers followed suit in Boston, Philadelphia, Baltimore, and New York. Future papers of note were founded on the penny press model, including Horace Greeley's *New York*

Tribune (1841) and Henry Raymond's *New York Daily Times* (1851).

In 1830, average daily newspaper circulation nationally was 78,000. A decade later it had grown to 300,000 (Schudson, 1981) and kept rising to a peak of 63,826,000 in 1987 (Pew Research Center, 2019). The penny press democratized newspaper readership, expanding the consumer base to include those previously excluded groups such as laborers and immigrants. It was a quick and cheap way to read a new language and keep up with public affairs. The penny press also created a pricing policy that would prove far less than the cost of actually producing and distributing a newspaper. To survive, newspapers became dependent on another revenue source.

That's the third element of the industrial era model, advertisers. Newspapers printed ads from their earliest days; credit for the first is generally attributed to the *Boston News-Letter*, which in May 1705 published an advertisement for real estate on Oyster Bay, Long Island. There were newspapers in colonial America dedicated principally to ads and related items such as shipping news.

However, what changed with the penny press was that circulation numbers came to drive advertising dollars. It was simple math—the greater the circulation, the higher the number of potential consumers who saw an ad. In fact, in 1836, Émile de Girardin, editor of *La Presse* in Paris, lowered the price of his newspaper specifically to raise circulation and increase the price of advertising.

Newspaper business practices for advertising evolved as the nineteenth century progressed. Among the key innovators in this space was James Gordon Bennett, who published the *New York Herald* between 1835 and 1867. Similar to de Girardin's strategy, Bennett relentlessly pursued advertising dollars, increasing the cost to buy ads so that he could sell newspapers at a lower price. Further, Bennett took a novel approach to advertisements—not only did he shift ad runs from two weeks to a single day, he also put ads on the front page alongside major news (O'Barr, 2010). These strategies were designed to keep readers interested and engaged, and it's no surprise that we see many of these same techniques used in digital advertising today (i.e., visit the website of most major news organizations and you'll no doubt find advertisements embedded alongside major news stories, sometimes rather deceptively).

Annual advertising contracts and fixed yearly content gave way to daily ad renewals and updated messaging. Flat fees for ads were replaced by pricing based on circulation and the size of the advertisement. Postpublication billings became prepublication payments.

In 1879, advertising revenues made up an average of less than half (49%) of newspaper funding. Thirty years later with the rise of metropolitan retail stores, it was nearly two-thirds (64%) (Schudson, 1981). At the highest point of newspaper advertising revenue in 2005, advertising dollars ($49.4 billion) were 4.6 times as large as circulation revenues ($10.8 billion) (Pew Research Center, 2019).

And so the industrial model of the newspaper was born, rooted in high consumer volume, low product prices, and third-party funding from advertisers based on consumer volume.

Like the music and movie industries, radio and television posed serious challenges for newspapers but with more serious consequences. The initial newspaper reaction to radio was fear, but newspapers, although slower to broadcast breaking news, believed they had real advantages in offering more local news, greater depth of news coverage, and publishing pictures. They chose a novel solution. Newspapers bought radio stations, thinking of them basically as advertising, a brand extension and maybe a potential revenue source. The *Detroit News* was first with the purchase of radio station WWJ in 1920. By 1937, newspapers owned 194 of the nation's 689 radio stations (27%).

They attempted to do the same thing but even more successfully with television. Once again, the *Detroit News*, this time joined by the *Fort Worth Star Telegram* and the *St. Louis Post Dispatch* led the pack with television purchases in 1946. By 1953, newspapers owned 64 percent of US TV stations, or 88 of the country's 138 stations (Stamm, 2011).

The Federal Communications Commission stepped in once again, as it had in the music industry, to protect the diversity and free flow of ideas. After years of case-by-case battles over licenses and ownership, the FCC in 1975 limited media cross-ownership, setting numerical restrictions based on the size, type, and number of media in a market.

The resulting problem for newspapers was that radio and television were competitors, not the symbiotic partners the movie and music industries found them to be. Radio stations needed the content of record producers, and producers needed the exposure radio gave their records. Similarly, television provided an audience for movies, gaining ratings for television stations, which translated into ad revenues and a lucrative post-theater market for studios.

In contrast, television and radio didn't need the content of newspapers. They needed their readers. The principal source of revenue for all three industries was advertising, which made newspaper audiences more valuable than their content. Newspapers were losing that competition even before the FCC ruling. A 1974 Roper Poll found that 65 percent of Americans reported television to be one of their chief sources of news versus 47 percent for newspapers (Stamm, 2011). One of the early casualties of the rivalry was the afternoon newspaper, one of the three daily editions in the industry—morning, afternoon, and evening papers. It gave way to the greater frequency and immediacy of television and radio news.

Digital Disruption

Over the course of the 1970s, the US population grew by 11 percent, with a 22 percent increase in the number of households; during this time, daily newspaper circulation barely budged, growing by 0.2 percent (Butler & Kent, 1983). This stagnation, along with other factors, set the stage for a slow yet steady decline for the newspaper industry, beginning in the late 1980s.

The industry created any number of task forces, produced countless reports, and tried to break out of the spiral. In the late 1970s, there was an ambitious venture that began with putting newspapers on a computer screen via teletext and videotext. The ultimate vision was to create a new kind of medium:

> one that deployed databases on demand and interactive services melded to create a new kind of information experience. In this new world, newspaper executives envisioned information delivery not based on a story or narrative found in television, radio, or print, but on something akin to the encyclopedia. Radio and television had added sound and motion to the story form, but it remained linear, passive, and temporary. The new form of delivery would be interactive, passing an element of control to the user and thereby empowering the individual. (Herndon, 2012, 39–40)

However, by the mid-1980s, the industry's videotext initiatives were flagging. The timing was bad (i.e., the personal computer was not yet a common household fixture), and industry and consumers wanted different things (e.g., newspapers focused their energy on creating news for videotext systems, but users were far more interested in interactive features such as email). Plus, the technology was confusing for users and technical problems were legion (Meisler, 1986).

The failure of videotext could be dismissed as simply being an interesting historical footnote were it not for the fact that it would shape the industry's responses to the dramatic technological advances just around the corner. Newspapers read the failure "as a positive referendum on the future of printed newspapers" and during the 1980s and 1990s doubled down on the tried and true (Herndon, 2012). Newspapers would continue to experiment with new technologies throughout the 1990s and early 2000s, such as proprietary online services, but early tech failures made the industry risk averse and left it unable to protect or innovate within its core revenue model once the internet truly took off.

The bottom fell out after 2004. Between 2004 and 2018, one-fifth of all US newspapers closed (Carey, 2018). Circulation dropped by nearly half between 2005 and 2018, from 53.3 million to 28.5 million. Advertising revenue decreased by more than 70 percent over the same period, from $49.4 billion to $14.3 billion. And between 2006 and 2018, newsroom staff were cut by nearly half, from 74,410 to 37,900 (Pew Research Center, 2019).

As with the music and movie industries, the principal disruptor of the newspaper business was digital technology, though radio and television, augmented by cable and satellites, certainly exacerbated the situation.

Much of the lost newspaper ad revenue went to digital media. Very quickly, advertisers found that digital media would allow them to target specific demographics and reach global audiences instantaneously at a fraction of the cost of traditional advertising. Similarly, individuals who would have previously put classifieds in their local newspaper found a much more effective and more cost-efficient digital platform in craigslist.org. Between 2000 and 2007, craigslist captured $5 billion that would have normally been spent on classified newspaper ads (Seamans & Zhu, 2014). The industry's early fears of losing valuable classified dollars to new actors had come to pass. In the longer term, Google, Facebook, and Amazon have emerged as the big winners—in 2019, these three companies captured nearly 70 percent of digital ad spending (Perrin, 2019).

Six developments stand out in the digital disruption of the newspaper business—the invention of the internet; the advent of mobile digital devices; the rise of digital content producers, aggregators, and distributors; the arrival of blogs, podcasts, tweets, and other innovations in news packaging; the creation of social media; and changing consumer tastes.

First, came the internet and digital devices, described earlier as the first phase of the current two-stage digital technology revolution. They are the foundation providing a device for sending and receiving content and a digital highway connecting devices. It is the twenty-first-century update of Morse's telegraph.

Next, there was an explosion of news content generated by a multitude of digital start-ups and websites. Some were purely digital, and others were hybrids that combined print and digital content. They produced general content such as BuzzFeed, Slate, Vice, and Vox. They produced specialized or niche content such as Politico, Inside Higher Ed, The Packer (fruit and vegetables), and a throwback to the beginning of American newspapers, Maritime-Executive.com (shipping news). They aggregated content and curated it for individual users like Apple News and Flipboard. Or they did both like Yahoo! and

Huffington Post. Newly developed social media, particularly Facebook, Twitter, YouTube, and Instagram, provided the largest megaphone in human history as well as an echo chamber for blasting out their news to billions.

New forms of news communication emerged, including blogs, podcasts, and tweets. Video reporting beyond television surged. The result was a buffet of news choices for consumers in terms of where they got their news and the form in which they consumed it, varying from a friend's Facebook posts and presidential tweets to a story in the legacy (traditional) press or a cable news magazine. Generally, it was some combination.

But newspapers, which developed their own websites, appear to be the biggest losers. According to a 2018 study by the Pew Research Center, the most popular choice for getting news in the United States is television, and the least popular is newspapers. Half (49%) of Americans said they often got their news from TV, while only a sixth (16%) said the same of print newspapers. Between these poles were news websites (33%), radio (26%), and social media (20%). Of those news sources, Pew found declines from the previous two years in television and newspaper use, while websites, radio, and social media increased in importance and frequency of use (Shearer, 2018). This may actually overstate the importance of newspapers since a majority of newspaper readers find the stories they read via a search engine (one-third) or links in social media (one-third). Only a third come directly to the newspaper's home page.

An underlying but important change is in the way Americans think about news, particularly young people, who are the future of news consumption and for whom social media is their main source of news content. A study by Clark and Marchi (2017) found that for youth the authority of legacy newspapers such as the *New York Times* and *Washington Post* has dissipated, giving way to the stories and links on Facebook or Twitter communicated by friends and people or organizations they recognize and view as legitimate (Clark & Marchi, 2017). For them, news has become increasingly personal and the imprimatur of legacy newspapers is gone, along with the belief that news coverage can be objective and fact based.

There is no doubt that the day of the industrial era newspaper business is over. But what is coming is a matter of speculation. However, three recent efforts to transform troubled newspapers give a hint of what that future might bring.

The newspapers were purchased by three very wealthy entrepreneurs who made their fortunes outside the press. All three had the same goals for his newspaper—growing circulation, advertising revenue, and news quality, but they employed very different strategies to accomplish this, which is well documented in Dan Kennedy's book *The Return of the Moguls* (2018). What follows is a simplification of their initiatives, which all involved fundamental changes in the digital and hard copy versions of their newspapers, increasing the number of newsroom staff, rethinking the pricing of their newspapers, introducing new customer and advertiser revenue strategies, making operations more efficient, and improving technology.

Aaron Kushner, a serial entrepreneur, acquired the *Orange County Register* and focused on building a local print and paper newspaper. He doubled down on the idea that legacy newspapers had a future; his initiative failed.

John Henry, owner of the Boston Red Sox, purchased the *Boston Globe*. His goal was to create a top-of-the-line regional newspaper with a twofold strategy. First, increase the quality of the *Boston Globe* by eliminating unpopular sections, expanding popular features, and adding new content; hiring more reporters; and increasing investigative reporting. Second, raise newspaper prices as much as the market would bear, a reversal of the penny press philosophy and the tendency of newspapers to give away online content. Henry wanted to appeal to both an elite and mass audience, who he believed would be willing to pay more for quality content. The *Boston Globe* announced that it had become profitable in 2019.

Jeff Bezos, the founder of Amazon, bought the *Washington Post* seeking to make it a national digital newspaper. *The Return of the Moguls* offers an excellent account of the steps the new owner took to accomplish this. Beyond building newspaper quality, Bezos focused on technology. He improved the appearance, frequency of updates, and speed of the website and mobile applications. Bezos enhanced and diversified the *Post*'s digital content, variety, and distribution channels, making heavy use of social media and video. He employed analytics to personalize service, to target advertising audiences, and to maximize content appeal to consumers. Within two years of Bezos's purchase of the *Post*, the technology staff jumped more than tenfold and has continued to grow (Kennedy, 2018). The *Post* is now a profitable enterprise in which digital circulation dwarfs print.

These three initiatives point to a possible future for newspapers in which print continues to decline, the digital continues to grow, and consumers pay greater amounts for quality content.

What Changed?

Technology certainly changed, but so did just about everything else in the newspaper industry. The number of news providers ballooned, and the intensity of competition between them for consumers and advertising revenue grew red hot in what increasingly seemed a war of each against all, with a continually expanding all. In the past, for the most part, local newspapers ran ads for local businesses. It was such a sure enough bet that communications titan Rupert Murdoch once described the classified advertising section of newspapers as "rivers of gold" (Edgecliffe-Johnson, 2005). However, the 1975 FCC ruling intensified competition between newspapers and radio and television stations. The internet brought an explosion of new competitors for newspapers, including nonlegacy news websites and gigantic mega-sites such as Google, Facebook, and other social media. The analog and digital sides of newspapers also competed against each other for shrinking newspaper advertising dollars. And the rivers of gold dried up.

Advertisers changed. They turned away from newspapers in favor of cheaper, better-targeted, higher-volume, and more flexible venues.

Consumer tastes changed. They increasingly gravitated to the convenience and immediacy of twenty-four seven news access whether online, on television, or on the radio over a once- or twice-a-day newspaper. They preferred to choose the news they consumed and the form in which they consumed it. Unbundled content (individual stories, blogs, and podcasts) eclipsed bundled content (newspapers).

The very nature of news changed. News became personal, and the line between consumer and producer blurred. Everyone who posted a photo on Facebook, a video on YouTube, or a text on Twitter became a reporter of sorts. They made news content public and did something newspapers were never able do. They harvested and sold their massive amounts of consumer data to create an additional income stream beyond advertising.

In this sea of news and a widening ideological rift in the

nation, the authority of legacy newspapers waned. Particularly for young people, it was replaced by the news posted or recommended by the consumer's friends, colleagues, and known and trusted people and organizations. The traditional model of control, one in which the newspaper industry controlled every step in the chain from creation and production to distribution, fell apart (Herndon, 2012).

Newspapers also made three fundamental errors on the way to disruption.

First, they didn't know what business they were in. They believed they were in the newspaper business rather than the news industry. The result is that they devalued digital content, often giving it away free, and overvalued analog content, clinging to paper while digital providers mushroomed and thrived. Newspapers did not gobble up the new digital businesses in the same way they had radio and television. The closest they came is that Mark Zuckerberg accepted an offer from Donald Graham, chair of the Washington Post Company, to be an early much-needed investor in Facebook. When Zuckerberg got a better offer, Graham allowed him to renege.

Second, newspapers projected tomorrow to mirror yesterday. Whether through isolation, self-absorption, or overconfidence, they failed to see or even monitor the dramatic changes occurring in competitors, technology, and the marketplace. Early experiments, such as those with videotext and online proprietary services, had failed, leading the industry to adopt a protectionist stance—a doubling down of the status quo (Herndon, 2012). They took the failure of their early tech ventures as consumer approval of current analog practice.

Third, newspapers were myopic. Their vision was short term, focusing more on the next quarter than the years ahead, emphasizing quick fixes over long-term solutions. They cut costs rather than making investments in the future.

The inescapable conclusion is that Simon Jenkins, then editor of the *London Times,* was incorrect when he wrote in 1997: "For the time being its fanatical proponents need the sympathy and tolerance once extended to Esperantists and radio hams.... The Internet will strut an hour upon the stage and then take its place in the ranks of lesser media" (Jenkins, 1997).

13

· · · · · · ·

Disruption

When we began the research for "Looking Sideways," we had no idea the cases would be so similar. The accounts of the music, movie, and newspaper industries read like stories written by the same serial novelist. They have remarkably similar plots. Successful businesses were built during the Industrial Revolution. They faced and overcame adversity from competitors and regulators. They were undone by the digital technology revolution.

To be sure, there are notable differences in the three industries. Although all are products of the Industrial Revolution, they differ in their timing, with newspapers coming of age during the First Industrial Revolution and the movie and music industries in the second.

They differ in geographic focus. The music and film industries are national and international enterprises. Newspapers are primarily local, which not only shapes their content but also makes them more sensitive to demographic and economic fluctuations. Population loss in the Northeast, Mid-Atlantic, and Midwest is a threat to circulation in those regions, and the closure of nearby retail outlets and companies is deleterious to advertising. But, as with higher education, demographic and economic changes have forced some newspapers out of business, but they did not disrupt the newspaper industry's financial model; the newspaper business adapted.

They differ in their financial models. The movie and music industries have historically made their money by selling a product to buyers—films and records and more recently music tracks. By contrast, newspaper revenue has come principally from selling the buyers of their product to advertisers. By design, the price of a newspaper is less than the cost of producing it.

They differ in how they responded to perceived competitors. After the litigation failed, the music industry formed a symbiotic partnership with radio, and the film industry did the same with television. Newspapers, however, attempted to buy or establish their own radio and television stations until they were limited by regulators. The reason is that radio, television, and newspapers all gave their products away free or at low cost and depended on advertising dollars to make money. With news, they were all competing for the same pool of consumers. The mutual interest partnerships of the film and music industries didn't exist after government regulated ownership.

The commonalities in the accounts of the three industries loom far larger and more powerfully for higher education. They speak to the hows, whys, and extent to which those industries changed in the face of the same demographic, economic, and technological shifts facing the nation's colleges and universities. Thirteen commonalities stand out:

1. All three industries developed their business models during the Industrial Revolution, reflecting the

practices of the age, such as assembly-line production
processes and fixed time and location distribution.

2. They clung tenaciously to that model and to its
products—albums, physical movies, and newspapers—
until the model broke and even after.

3. All three industries used the same strategy to respond
to environmental change, seeking to make the minimum alterations in their business models necessary to
accommodate them in piecemeal fashion by means of
reform, repair, and adaptation.

4. All three attempted to employ that same strategy even
as their industries were being disrupted and they were
threatened with replacement. The organizational knee-
jerk response was maintenance by adaptation, rooted in
piecemeal over wholistic organizational change.

5. Demographic and economic changes did not alter the
business model in any of the three industries.

6. All three were disrupted by digital technology.

7. The three industries did not see the digital technology
threat coming, nor did they recognize the magnitude
of the change it would bring. Change happened behind
their backs while they were busy doing business as usual.

8. Short-term transitional organizations emerged that
extended the life of the industry's business model. The
best example is Blockbuster, which maintained studio
film production, analog formats, and industry control
of the enterprise. It changed only film distribution, by
creating neighborhood store film rentals, thus enlarging the potential audience for the industry, increasing
film longevity, and producing a new industry revenue
stream. Blockbuster failed when the industrial era film
industry business model failed.

9. The three industries flailed in the face of the ongoing technological revolution, adopted a flurry of puny remedies, and failed to find solutions. In essence, they half-heartedly threw a bunch of remedies at the wall and nothing stuck. They took their failure to be consumer approval of current practice.

10. The three industries engaged in self-defeating behaviors, such as expecting the future to mirror the past; thinking myopically, focusing on the short- rather than long-term future of the industry by, for instance, seeking to stay in the black financially through cost cutting rather than investing in the future; and neglecting the changing desires of consumers, the emergence and growing potential of competitors, and the advent and power of new digital technologies. This was particularly egregious in a world in which competitors used algorithms, artificial intelligence, and big data to service customers.

11. The reenvisioning of the three industries and the replacement solutions came from outside the industry rather than inside, from organizations like Google, Facebook, BuzzFeed, Netflix, and Spotify.

12. Beyond the emergence of digital technologies, consumer choice drove replacement. Consumers chose around-the-clock access over fixed-time access, mobile over stationary devices, user- rather than producer-determined content, personalized content over one size fits all, and unbundled rather than bundled content, as in a track over an album or a story over a whole newspaper.

13. The transformation of all three industries is still underway, and while the outcomes are uncertain, the future of each promises to be digital as their industrial era business models die.

The Implications for Higher Education

What we learn from looking at these three industries is that neither demographics nor the economy is likely to change the current industrial era model of higher education. They did not disrupt the music, film, or newspaper industries either.

The three industries were disrupted by digital technology. "Looking Forward" concluded that the digital revolution would occur in two stages—initially powered by mobile devices and the internet, followed by artificial intelligence, virtual and augmented reality, and big data. It found higher education would successfully respond to the first by adaptation, but the second stage was not sufficiently advanced to assess its impact on higher education. However, it would be magical thinking to believe that higher education in whole or part can escape the fate of the music, film, and newspaper industries.

The changes in these three industries did not follow the stages of the transformation of higher education during the Industrial Revolution. This appears to be a difference between change by replacement and change by reform and combinations of reform and replacement.

The three case studies are helpful on the issue of where disruptive innovation begins. As with higher education, as discussed in "Looking Backward," this happened outside the three existing industries. In higher education, this suggests that the postsecondary sector will drive both adaptive and disruptive change. The appearance of transitional organizations, such as the for-profit OPMs (online program management firms) that have partnered with colleges and universities to build and manage internet-based programs, is expanding.

Partnerships between higher education and for-profit education companies in programming, noted in the introduction, is a relatively new phenomenon. In the past, such partnerships generally were in the areas of auxiliary services, such as admissions, and backroom operations, such as finance and technology. But, today, there are a burgeoning number of academic partnerships intended to fill current programming gaps such as career education and enrich existing offerings. These partnerships serve higher education by responding to unmet consumer desires and aid for-profits by allowing them to take advantage of higher education's degree-granting authority.

Beyond disruption, the three cases demonstrate the profound impact that regulation can have on an industry. The courts and regulatory agencies severely challenged the existing business models in music, film, and newspapers. Whether it was the FCC substantially increasing the number of radio stations in the music industry, the Supreme Court barring studios from owning theaters and engaging in block booking in the film business, or the FCC restricting radio and television ownership by newspapers, regulations forced each industry to make major changes in how they did business, even though they managed to adapt.

The same potential exists today for higher education in a time of increasing demands for accountability by government, rising consumerism by students and families, and growing competition from other postsecondary providers. College pricing, student debt, and inequity in access and graduation rates are being widely criticized.

Finally, the three cases point to the type of change higher education is likely to experience. That is, the rise of anytime, anyplace, consumer-driven content and source agnostic, unbundled, personalized education paid for by subscription. This was the conclusion of "Looking Forward" as well.

Part 4
LOOKING AT THE PANORAMA

In The Hague, there is a museum named Panorama Mesdag, which has a 140-meter-long and 40-meter-high painting of the village of Scheveningen in the year 1881. The exhibit space is a round room. At its center is an observation gallery that gives the viewer the impression of standing on top of a very large sand dune with a 360-degree view of the sea, beach, and village below. The viewer sees the buildings, people, animals, boats, wagons, vegetation, and physical realities of daily life. It is breathtaking. Neither of us have ever seen anything like it.

Panoramas were a popular art form in the late eighteenth and nineteenth centuries; they were replaced by movies. The term *panorama* is derived from the Greek *pan*, meaning "all" and *horama* meaning "view." The most popular subjects were massive scenes, battles like Gettysburg, cities like Edinburgh, and landscapes like Scheveningen. The aim was to give the viewer a chance to see the whole when only small portions of the scene were humanly possible to view. The experience was frequently described as magical.

While our readers are unlikely to describe part four of this volume as magical, its goal is the same as the panoramas. It is to take the various and separate observations presented in the previous pages—the look backward, the look forward, and the look sideways—and paint a panorama of the future of higher education that incorporates all of them.

The headline for the story is that higher education will change profoundly to meet the demands of the global, digital, knowledge economy. It will indeed be transformed as were the music, film, and newspaper industries, and a major driver of that change will also be digital technology. All institutions will not change to the same degree, but all will change. Chapter fourteen discusses what will change, and chapter fifteen focuses on how and when change will occur. Chapter sixteen offers recommendations for higher education and policy makers.

14

· · · · · · ·

What Will Change?

The findings from "Looking Backward," "Looking Forward," and "Looking Sideways" point to five profound and jarring new realities, none of higher education's making, that will shape its future.

1. **Institutional control of higher education will decrease, and the power of higher education consumers will increase.**

When we speak of higher education today, we think of colleges and universities. Why wouldn't we? Everything else about higher education is ephemeral—knowledge evolves; faculty, students, and programs change. But colleges and universities are a constant. They are the institutions that create, sustain, and disseminate knowledge. They are the engine that drives the higher learning enterprise.

We tend to think about most industries, for-profit and non-profit, in terms of the institutions that comprise them—courts, hospitals, banks, schools, and the like. The first American corporation was established in 1790. The concept spread swiftly, and by 1860, there were more than twenty-five thousand in the United States (Sylla & Wright, 2012). Organizations became the centerpiece of economic life and thinking during the Industrial Revolution.

"Looking Sideways" is an account of three knowledge industries, which during the industrial era, were each dominated by a single institution—music labels, film studios, and newspapers. Over time, the specific labels, studios, and newspapers leading the industry changed. So did the regulations that governed them, the competition they faced, and the new technologies that emerged around them. But the key actor did not. It was always the same organization or institution—the recording label, the studio, or the newspaper. As with higher education today, those institutions defined the industry both in terms of its business model and the way we thought about the industry—Motown, Disney, and the *New York Times*.

But the advent of the global, digital, knowledge economy changed that. It multiplied the number of content producers and disseminators and gave consumers choice over the *what*, *where*, *when*, and *how* of the content they consumed. The historically dominant institution diminished in importance and control of the industry.

Here's the point. In the music, film, and newspaper industries, the industrial era was about institutions, the producers, and production of content. In contrast, the knowledge age focuses on the users of that content—the consumers—and consumption. The consumer became the dominant force in the industry, and institutional control declined. That same transition can be expected in higher education.

2. With near universal access to digital devices and the internet, students will seek from higher education the

same things they are getting from the music, movie, and newspaper industries.

As "Looking Backward" concluded, in all three industries, consumers chose around-the-clock over fixed-time access and anywhere mobile access over fixed locations. They selected consumer- rather than producer-determined content; individualized over uniform, or one-size-fits-all, content; and unbundled rather than bundled content, such as a track over an album or a story over a whole newspaper. They picked low cost over high with the exception of luxury goods. The same will likely be demanded of higher education.

College students favor these changes. In their research, Levine and Dean (2012) found in contrast to traditional higher education, digital natives preferred anytime, anyplace access to education rather than set locations and times, education driven by the consumer rather than the institution, and digital over analog media.

In addition, Levine and Dean (2012) found older adults, largely working women, attending college part time, sought affordable, unbundled, or stripped-down versions of college. When these students were asked what they wanted from college, they asked for convenience, service, quality, low cost, and to be charged for only the services and activities they used. They did not want to pay for facilities they didn't use, events they didn't attend, or electives they didn't take. They wanted to buy the equivalent of a track rather than an album or a particular article rather than the whole newspaper.

•   •

These preferences make sense in the context of an ongoing retreat by undergraduates from campus life, which fuels practices such as fixed locations and times for higher education. Levine and Dean (2012) reported that the proportion of students living in college housing had dropped continuously since at least 1969. Indeed, only 16 percent of undergraduates resided on campus prior to the pandemic (Kelchen, 2018). Less than a third of college students attended on-campus social events (33%), used the campus fitness center (33%), attended athletic events (25%), went to meetings of academic, student, or professional clubs (21%), or attended campus lectures, debates, or other academic events (19%) at least once a month. More than a third never did any of these things. This was true of a majority of students at community colleges where a high of 80 percent never attended academic or professional meetings and a low of 57 percent never attended social events (Levine & Dean, 2012). In the nationwide 2020 Community College Survey of Student Engagement, only 28 percent of respondents identified student organizations as being "very" important. Among community college students ages 25 or older, fewer than 20 percent ever used student organizations (Center for Community College Student Engagement, 2020).

Levine and Dean concluded that "campus life is the domain of traditionally aged, full-time students attending four-year colleges and working half time or less" (2012, 54), which as noted is a shrinking proportion of the collegiate population. They offered two caveats. Participation shot up for students working ten hours or less a week, and even among traditional students, most of the events they attended were not college sponsored.

Here is the point. Students' lives are increasingly filled by competing pressures and demands beyond college; more, for example, are working and they are working longer hours. Levine and Dean found a growing tendency, particularly among nontraditional students, to come to college only to attend classes, commuting in just before the start of class and commuting out immediately after. This encourages students to place a premium on convenience: anytime, anyplace accessibility; personalized education that fits their circumstances; and unbundling, only purchasing what they need or want to buy at affordable prices.

3. **New content producers and distributors will enter the higher education marketplace, driving up institutional competition and consumer choice and driving down prices.**

In the popular imagination, college is an idyllic campus where students go for four years to study and play after high school, attending full time, and living in dormitories. Most people, including many in higher education, are shocked to learn that fewer than a fifth of all college students are full-time, residential, and aged 18 to 22.

What does not readily come to mind when one thinks about college is the proliferation of new postsecondary institutions, organizations, and programs discussed in the introduction. In contrast to the imagined college, these initiatives are harbingers and trailblazers of the future of higher education in America. They challenge the existing model and expand consumer choice. Coursera offers an instructive example.

Coursera is an online learning platform company, a pioneer in MOOCs that was launched in 2012, and by 2019 was valued at something north of a billion dollars. Today, it offers seventy-eight million users more than four thousand courses and specialty studies, ranging across the fields offered by traditional universities from data science, engineering, and business to humanities, social sciences, and health.

But Coursera's view of education is more pragmatic and career oriented than traditional higher education, which is what both traditional and nontraditional students want from college. While offering a panoply of degree programs and courses in the liberal arts, such as music, classics, history, and economics, the website announces that in a 2019 survey, 87 percent of those who enrolled to develop professionally received a salary increase, a promotion, or the capacity to begin a new career.

Coursera also differs from traditional higher education in terms of who provides its content, which is an eye-popping list of more than two hundred of the world's leading universities and businesses. Its higher education partners are a veritable who's who of colleges and universities from around the world, including California Institute of Technology, Columbia, Duke, École Polytechnique, Hebrew University, Johns Hopkins, Moscow State University, Peking University, Princeton, University of California, University of Chicago, University of Michigan, University of North Carolina, and Yale, to name just a very few.

While an impressive roster, what is unique about Coursera is that it offers classes, specializations, and certificates from businesses and nonprofits outside higher education. The businesses are leaders in building and supporting the global, digital, knowledge economy and their practices and products are at the cutting edge in areas such as technology (e.g., Cisco, Google, IBM, Intel, and Microsoft), finance and management (e.g., Axa, Axis Bank, Fundacao Lemann, Goldman Sachs, and PWC), and merchandise and sales (Alibaba, Amazon, Danone, L'Oréal, and Procter & Gamble). The nonprofits, which are of equal renown, include the American Museum of Natural History, Exploratorium, Museum of Modern Art, National Geographic, World Bank, Yad Vashem, and many more.

To understand the potential impact of these new providers, we need to look at what they are actually offering. Two programs are illustrative.

The first is Google's Information Technology (IT) Certificate Program. Created to fill labor force needs in the field, the program consists of a five-course sequence on computer networking, operating systems, system administration, IT infrastructure, and IT security. Students rate each of these classes 4.7 or better on a five-point scale. It's a sub-baccalaureate program, in a field commonly offered at two- and four-year institutions, worth twelve college credits and awarding a Google badge, which is an accepted employment credential, aligned with professional licensure tests and standards. More than one hundred forty-seven thousand students have enrolled in the program, which Google advises can be completed in six months or less with five hours of study a week at a cost of $49 per month. The first month is free, and students make a commitment only a month at a time. During the pandemic, Google added two new certificate programs in data analytics and program management to the Coursera platform.

The second is a course offered by the Museum of Modern Art (MOMA) titled In the Studio: Postwar Abstract Painting. One of nine MOMA classes offered through Coursera, it is twenty-seven hours in length and priced at Coursera's $49 per month subscription fee. It has earned a 4.9 rating and currently enrolls more than forty-four thousand students. MOMA describes the course as an in-depth, hands-on look at the materials, techniques, and thinking of seven New York School artists, including Willem de Kooning, Yayoi Kusama, Agnes Martin, Barnett Newman, Jackson Pollock, Ad Reinhardt, and Mark Rothko. Through studio demonstrations and gallery walkthroughs, you'll form a deeper understanding of what a studio practice means and how ideas develop from close looking, and you'll gain a sensitivity to the physical qualities of paint. Readings and other resources will round out your understanding, providing broader cultural, intellectual, and historical context about the decades after World War II, when these artists were active.

• •

This description reads like a modern art course at just about any university. However, 55 percent of alumni who completed surveys attributed a tangible career benefit to the course.

The two courses could not be more different—one is purely vocational, and the other is straight up liberal arts. But they have five things in common. They are cheap, convenient, highly rated, heavily enrolled though their completion rates are unreported, and most important they are being offered by non–higher education providers.

The number and range of what are being offered is staggering. If we look beyond Coursera at what else their partners are doing, the Coursera programs are just the tip of the iceberg. For example, in addition to the two certificate programs Google offers through Coursera, it has seventy-eight more of its own and Microsoft has seventy-seven.

On the nonprofit side, the American Museum of Natural History has its own graduate school, which offers a PhD in comparative biology and a master of arts degree in teaching. It also provides six-week online courses on subjects such as the solar system, evolution, climate change, and water for $549 each with an extra fee for obtaining graduate credit. These courses also qualify for professional development credit for teachers.

The Public Broadcasting System has a wealth of professional development courses for teachers, lasting from an hour and a half to forty-five hours at all grade levels in subjects ranging from reading and math to leadership and instructional technology. It also certifies educators in eight areas of media literacy.

With Coursera, the looming issue for higher education is not just the explosion of content but the world-class standing of Coursera providers. Nonelite universities may be particularly at a disadvantage in competing with industry giants. Students will have the option of studying at and obtaining certification from Google, an international powerhouse with the latest technology and top human capital or the usually more expensive, local, regional university. They will have the choice of studying at the American Museum of Natural History or MOMA, two of the foremost museums in the world, or at a nearby college.

Another attribute of the new providers is that their programs by and large are online. They are accessible twenty-four seven. They do not adhere to the semester system or the academic clock. They offer a combination of competency- and course-based programs. The new providers are also more agile than traditional higher education. For instance, in March 2020, as colleges across the country were putting their classes online and closing their campuses, Coursera began offering courses on coronavirus and COVID-19. It also announced the Corona-virus Response Initiative, giving pandemic-impacted colleges and their students access to their courses for free. Within a month, two thousand six hundred programs had been used by institutions across the globe. A month later, Coursera unveiled CourseMatch, which automatically matches Coursera courses to their on-campus versions across the globe.

Few of the multitude of new providers will have the stature of Coursera's partners. Some will be analog; most will be digital. Nearly all will enroll fewer students than Coursera. They will vary in length, though predominantly offer around-the-clock access and not be location specific.

It is not at all clear what choices students will make between traditional and nontraditional providers. However, traditional higher education is undoubtedly facing mounting competition from a mushrooming number of new content providers, and students have dramatically more choices—often at lower cost—in how, when, and where they learn.

4. **The industrial era model of higher education, focusing on time, process, and teaching, will be eclipsed by a knowledge economy successor rooted in outcomes and learning.**

The shift from teaching to learning and from fixed time and process to fixed outcomes will occur for four reasons. The first is educational. The current model assumes all students learn the same things in the same period of time. In reality, if the time and process of education are held constant, student outcomes will vary widely. This is because different individuals learn the same subjects at different rates. Even the same individual learns different subjects at different rates.

We have the system of education we do with fixed time and processes, not because it is the best or most effective way to educate people but because of the time in which it was created. As described earlier, it is a product of the Industrial Revolution in which production was tied to the clock and processes of production were standardized. The industrial-era university mirrors these practices.

Educationally, it makes sense to focus on the outcomes we want students to achieve, what we want them to learn, not how long we want them to be taught. Imagine taking your clothes to a laundry. The proprietor doesn't ask you how long you want them washed. And for good reason. It's an absurd question. Your only concern is that the clothes be clean when you pick them up, irrespective of how long that takes. The outcome is what matters, not the process. The same is true of education.

The second reason is equity. In the current model of higher education, equity means enabling all students to have access to comparable facilities, professors, and programs for the same period of time. That is, equalizing the time and process of education. However, real equity would mean making it possible for all students to achieve the same outcomes, not assuring they will achieve those outcomes but giving them the differential resources they need to have the opportunity to achieve them. Equity is necessarily about access to equal outcomes, not access to equal process or time.

A third reason is that the current model requires all education experiences be translatable into units of time—courses, credit hours, seat time, and degrees. Time, as noted earlier, is the common currency or accounting system used to valuate, compare, standardize, and record educational experiences. For more than a century, this model worked well for the industrial-era university.

But it won't continue to work owing to the explosion of new content being produced by employers, museums, television stations, software companies, banks, retailers, and a host of other for-profits and nonprofits inside and outside higher education. They have generated a bazaar of time-based and non-time-based educational content—consisting of course- and competency-based programs; outcome- and process-based education; time-fixed and time-variable instruction; analog and digital formats; formal and informal learning; experiential-, machine-, peer-, self-, and classroom-based learning; individualized and uniform experiences; and degree-, microcredential-, and noncredential-granting education. Even among time-based programs, some are of such short duration, particularly the just-in-time offerings, as to be below the credit radar screen.

It's a grab bag of disparate curricular practices, which is growing increasingly heterogeneous and cannot be translated into uniform time or process measures. The one common denominator they all share is that they produce outcomes, whatever students learn as a consequence of the experience.

It is a difference that will make the historic time- and process-based academic currency and accounting system irrelevant and leave higher education with the need to find a replacement. In the short run, this will minimally require higher education to become bilingual—operate on two different standards—one, courses and credits, and the other, outcomes and learning. In the longer run, higher education will have no alternative but to embrace outcomes and learning as the knowledge economy accounting system successor. The currency is now being called competencies, though the name may change. "Looking Backward" pointed out that many names and definitions—units, points, credits—were applied before the Carnegie unit name and definition stuck in the early twentieth century. So while the nomenclature may evolve, what is certain is that the currency will be units of learning.

Fourth, the advancement of research on cognitive science, artificial intelligence, and learning science, the newest of the three fields, supports this. Learning science is the interdisciplinary study of how learning occurs in real-world settings—face to face and online—and how to facilitate it. Born at Northwestern University in 1991, learning science graduate programs are now operating at more than seventy-five major universities from coast to coast, from Stanford and University of Washington to New York University and University of North Carolina, Chapel Hill, with Arizona State, University of Wisconsin, and Carnegie-Mellon in-between.

5. The dominance of degrees and just-in-case education will diminish; nondegree certifications, and just-in-time education will increase in status and value.

American higher education has historically focused on degree-granting programs intended to prepare their students for careers and life beyond college. This has been described as *just-in-case education* because its focus is prospective, teaching students the skills and knowledge that institutions believe will be necessary for the future.

In contrast, *just-in-time education* is present oriented and more immediate, teaching students the skills and knowledge they need right now as in "teach me a foreign language or about pandemics or about a new technology right now." Just-in-time education comes in all shapes and sizes, largely diverging from traditional academic time standards, uniform course lengths, and common credit measures. It is driven by the outcomes a student wants to achieve. Only a small portion award degrees; most grant certificates, microcredentials, and badges.

In recent years, microcredentials and badges have been much discussed along with speculation about whether they will replace or erode degrees. The reality, however, is that non-degree certifications aren't new to higher education, only calling them badges and microcredentials is. Yale established the first certificate program more than two centuries ago in 1799 for students who took only scientific and English language classes (Geiger, 2015).

Since that time, certificate programs, generally sub-baccalaureate in technical fields and post-baccalaureate in the professions, have become commonplace. A study of four-year institutions more than forty years ago found that 21 percent of arts and sciences colleges and 28 percent of professional schools awarded certificates (Levine, 1978). They are even more common at two-year schools, which in 2018 granted 852,504 associate degrees and 579,822 certificates (Bustamante, 2019).

Certificates and degrees have existed side by side for more than two hundred years and seem destined to continue to do so in the future. However, degrees have always enjoyed a far higher status and been regarded as the far more valuable credential.

Several factors are likely to reset the balance between them. First, there is a growing perception that degrees are declining in value in the labor market, which may prove no more than a temporary blip. For instance, a number of marquee employers have announced they will no longer require college degrees for employment, including Google, Ernst and Young, Penguin Random House, Hilton, Apple, Nordstrom, IBM, Lowe's, Publix,

Starbucks, Bank of America, Whole Foods, Costco, and Chipotle (Glassdoor Team, 2020).

Media support the notion of the declining relevancy of degrees by pointing out that a number of high-profile technology titans haven't graduated from college, including Michael Dell (founder, Dell Computers), Daniel Ek (cofounder, Spotify), Bill Gates (founder, Microsoft), Steve Jobs and Steve Wozniak (cofounders, Apple), David Karp (creator, Tumblr), Evan Williams (cofounder, Twitter), and Mark Zuckerberg (founder, Facebook).

Finally, public opinion polls have found that a growing percentage of people believe the value of a college diploma has declined. For example, a 2019 Gallup Poll reported a decreasing proportion of Americans consider a college degree to be very important—51 percent in 2019 versus 70 percent in 2013 (Marken, 2019). An American Media-Hechinger Report poll earlier in year had more positive results, finding only 36 percent of American adults believed college was not worth the cost. But their reasons are worth noting—60 percent said people often graduate without specific job skills and a big amount of debt, and 36 percent agreed that you can get a good job without a college degree (Smith-Barrow, 2019). These are the reasons most often cited for enrolling in certificate programs.

A second cause for a possible reset is that periods of profound change like the present and the Industrial Revolution produce curricular flux. Seemingly every aspect of collegiate education becomes a potential object for innovation and experimentation. During the Industrial Revolution, major changes were made in credentialing. New degrees were established such as the PhD, the associate's degree, and the earned master's degree, previously more honorary than academic. Established degrees became more specialized—scores and scores of new discipline-based baccalaureate degrees came into being, most notably the bachelor of science, which was developed as a means of distinguishing between students who completed a rigorous arts program and those who studied a lesser scientific curriculum. Programs awarding certificates multiplied, too, particularly after the development of continuing education units in the late nineteenth century. And, of course, many, indeed most of the new degrees receded into history such as the sister of arts and the mistress of arts. The bottom line is that this is a period amenable to re-sorting college and university credentials.

The third element is that the demand for just-in-time education will grow much larger. The increasing need for upskilling and reskilling caused by automation, the knowledge explosion, and high pandemic unemployment numbers promises to generate a population seeking just-in-time education, exceeding that currently enrolled in degree programs. Moreover, degree programs are generally discrete, onetime events while just-in-time is likely to occur repeatedly throughout one's lifetime. As with the Coursera example, the credentials awarded by those programs will be better aligned with the job market than most degree programs. Just-in-time education will be increasingly anytime, anyplace, consumer determined, individualized, and unbundled. It will do all of these things and by virtue of its scale normalize such student expectations.

At once higher education is experiencing declining degree stature, rising demand for just-in-time certificate programs, and a period of experimentation in academic practice. At a minimum, in the years ahead, degrees can be expected to lose ground to certificates and microcredentials.

The disruption of the newspaper industry tends to be dismissed as not germane to higher education on the grounds that colleges and universities award degrees and largely have a monopoly on those credentials. Newspapers do not. As microcredentials, which are currently largely unregulated and are awarded by a growing number of nontraditional content providers, increase in status and value, the fate of the newspaper industry grows more and more relevant to higher education.

Impact of the New Realities

These five new realties will transform the industrial era model of higher education and establish the template for its global, digital, knowledge economy successor. The emerging model will have these characteristics.

- Higher education will be based on learning and outcomes. Competency-based education, which is independent of time and process, will become the norm. Students will be required to master specified outcomes or competencies to earn a credential. The Carnegie unit and credit hour, which are time-based, will give way to competencies mastered as the currency and accounting system of higher education.
- Certification can be granted for mastering a single competency such as learning a foreign language or for achieving a set of related outcomes such as the Google IT competences. In short, it is the learner's mastery of competences that will be assessed, certified, credentialed, and recorded on student transcripts.

There are two important caveats here. First, competency-based education (CBE) is now an umbrella term for a panoply of differing practices with strong proponents and opponents. The blurred meaning and controversy surrounding CBE may doom the term, but the focus on learning and outcomes as the foundation of higher education will persist, regardless of what it is called.

Second, the transition to competency-based education will be disorderly and chaotic as was the case with its predecessor, the Carnegie unit in the late nineteenth and early twentieth centuries. These are the early days of defining competencies. Today, there are common terms for competencies such as intercultural communication and data literacy. But there aren't common definitions of what those terms mean, the skills and knowledge they entail, or the tools to assess them. As with the standardization of academic practice, which ultimately produced the Carnegie unit, the process of formulating and gaining consensus for competences will not be quick. Once again, it is likely to be a two-stage process—initially creating and using a multiplicity of differing conceptions for the same competency, followed by movement toward common definitions and practices in order to abate the chaos. As with the Carnegie unit, it is likely to take public and philanthropic support to cross the finish line.

- The universe of higher education providers will expand dramatically to include not only traditional institutions but also a far larger number of nontraditional content producers and distributors, including nonprofits and for-profits, ranging from corporations and museums to television networks and social media platforms. As a result, higher education content will be available digitally, anywhere, at any time. Students will be able to choose from among a plethora of providers, at multiple price points, and access content in the format they prefer in both bundled and unbundled forms and degree and nondegree programs. The competition between traditional and nontraditional providers will be leveled because competency-based education is source agnostic. It assesses only student learning, irrelevant of how it was acquired.
- Demand for just-in-time upskilling and reskilling will

dwarf traditional just-in-case enrollments, shifting the enrollment balance in degree and nondegree programs, raising the status of microcredentials, and spurring the production and distribution of content by nontraditional providers. The pandemic accelerated this because of the tens of millions of unemployed workers it produced.

- Assessment will become largely formative, real time and individualized, seeking to guide students in mastering competencies, which is sometimes called direct and authentic assessment. Earlier, this was likened to the workings of a GPS. Only the final formative assessment will be summative as it demonstrates the student has mastered the competency.

- Certification at least in the short run will be a combination of degrees and microcredentials. The longer-run future of degrees is less certain—a combination of microcredentials in general and specialized studies may achieve the same results as the traditional baccalaureate degree.

- Transcripts will become lifelong records of the competencies people achieve throughout their lives and the certifying authority for each.

- Higher education will shift from the analog to the digital—some institutions using digital technology in support of existing analog programs, others in parallel to current analog programs, and the remainder as replacements for existing analog programs. This will occur in all sorts of permutations within institutions as well.

- The higher education faculty, whose numbers can be expected to decline, is currently composed of subject matter experts engaged in teaching and research. It will be diversified to include learning designers, instructors, assessors, technologists, and researchers, reflecting the demographics of the nation. The competition for this talent both within and outside higher education will be fierce. As in the film industry, talent is likely to over-shadow institutions, and with an abundance of compet-ing providers, an agent may be more valued than tenure.

- Tuition, which is now largely credit-based, will become subscription-based and tied to outcome attainment, which is Coursera's funding model.

As the higher education system of the global, digital, knowl-edge economy coalesces, a number of the historical staples of the industrial model will fade away. They will become the equivalent of buggy whips in the automobile age or slide rules in a time of calculators. No matter how important they were in the past, they will have lost their value in the present and future. Two examples are the time-based practices of colleges and universities and the A–F grading system. For some institu-tions having a costly physical campus could become a liability if students come only to attend classes.

In the industrial model of higher education in which the time and process of education are fixed, it made perfect sense to define and develop academic practice around the clock, but in competency- or outcome-based education the clock becomes irrelevant. As a consequence, historic practices such as credit hours, Carnegie units, credit-based courses, semesters, two- and four-year degrees, measuring faculty workload or student status in credits taught or completed lose their meaning and utility. They become artifacts to be discarded in what Henry Adams called the "ash-heap" of history (2008, 10).

A–F grading is similar. It is a comparative measure of stu-dent performance relative to peers and the subject matter being taught. However, competency-based education, which is rooted in absolute measures, is essentially pass-fail. Students have either mastered a competency or they have not. As a result, A–F grading and the products thereof such as dean's list, class rankings, and graduation honors defined by grade-point average will atrophy as outcome-based education gains in popularity.

Beyond the loss of familiar practices, new methods of quality control can also be expected to emerge. Because content from a multiplicity of providers will be omnipresent and the source of student learning is immaterial in outcome-based education, a new kind of educational institution is likely to emerge—that is, a certifying or validating institution, which does not create or disseminate content, but instead assesses student learning, guides student learning, certifies student learning, credentials student learning, and records student learning. In the short run, one can imagine many such organizations using different definitions of competencies to assess students. As consensus grows regarding those definitions, standards and practices will become increasingly uniform, and the number of such institutions can be expected to decline.

This institution and the shift to outcome-based education will put the current model of accreditation at risk. Accreditation, the peer review, quality improvement, and self-policing agency for the academy, comes in two forms—institutional and program accreditation. Originally created in the late nineteenth and early twentieth century to bring order and common standards to a higher education system lacking in both, accreditation's focus is and has always been on providers, which are still assessed largely on the basis of the best higher education practices of the industrial era. In this time of change and innovation, accreditors and accreditation are increasingly viewed as being slow, outdated, and discouraging of change. This is not surprising because the reason for creating accreditation was to standardize. Unless accreditation is able to shift its focus from the process to the outcomes of education and from institutions and programs to students, it will lose its utility. The time for accreditation to act is short. Accreditation's current power is that Washington relies on institutional accreditation as a condition for students to receive federal financial aid and a number of states mandate accreditation as a means of quality control. Both branches of government are becoming increasingly critical of the enterprise, and other alternatives are being investigated.

Let's turn to the question of how change this deep and this far ranging could possibly occur in higher education.

15

· · · · · · ·

How and When Will Change Occur?

In the introduction, we presented the voices and cases of two opposing camps on the future of higher education. One believed the nation's colleges and universities would be able to adapt successfully to the demographic, economic, and technological challenges they face and the other concluded that higher education would be disrupted by those changes. So who was right? The answer is they both were.

The model of higher education just presented is the product of disruption and mirrors the prognostications of the postsecondary community presented in the introduction. This university is fundamentally different from its industrial era predecessor. The key actor is the student or consumer of higher education, no longer the colleges and universities that provide it. The focus is on learning rather than on teaching. The outcomes of education are fixed instead of time- and process-based. Higher education is primarily digital, no longer principally analog, and content is unbundled rather than consolidated. Competencies replace credits as the currency and accounting system of higher education. Colleges and universities are one of many sources for education rather than the sole provider.

This knowledge economy model of higher education is the end of the story, not the beginning. The first step for organizations faced with unavoidable changes in their environment is adaptation, not disruption. This was the approach the three industries profiled in "Looking Sideways" employed. They adapted to new government regulation, new technologies, and new competitors in piecemeal fashion as each materialized, making the minimal changes necessary to overcome the obstacle.

They did this as long as they possibly could and even beyond when it was no longer effective. They attempted to adapt even when adaptation was no longer sufficient to meet the challenges they faced. Then the three industries broke and were disrupted by digital technology, which imposed a fundamentally different business model than the music, motion picture, and newspaper industries had historically employed.

Higher education can be expected to follow a similar path. Today, the principal mode of responding to the demographic, economic, and first stage of the digital technology revolution has been by adapting. But the end game will vary for different types of institutions. *Higher education* is an umbrella term for a sprawling enterprise composed of more than four thousand, largely independently operating, colleges and universities. To say an industry will be disrupted, does not mean that all of its autonomous subunits will change in a uniform fashion. America's four thousand colleges and universities are headed for very different futures. Those futures may take three different paths.

The first path involves higher education's weakest institutions. For many, adaptation will not be possible. Prior to the pandemic, these colleges were in palpable danger of having to close their doors because of mounting demographic and financial pressures (Zemsky, Shaman, & Baldridge, 2020). However, the pandemic dramatically accelerated the process by decreasing their existing enrollments, reducing foreign student attendance, stripping auxiliary revenues, and diminishing the size of their entering classes. High unemployment rates and business closures also reduced the capacity of students and their families to pay tuition. And evacuating campuses in the middle of a term required colleges to make refunds for room and board, and the longer the campuses stayed closed, the longer their dormitories and cafeterias remained empty. COVID-19 also expanded the number of institutions in this category and their geographic locations, though they were still concentrated in the Northeast, the Midwest, and the mid-Atlantic states. The latest estimates are that 15 percent to 20 percent of colleges could close or merge in the next five years (confidential conversations with state, accrediting, and professional association leaders; Korn, Belkin, & Chung, 2020).

The second category includes institutions or more accurately sectors of higher education that will be able to survive simply by means of adaptation. They will not be disrupted. These colleges and universities, which are wealthier and stronger, bring more to the table. They not only educate students but also offer something else, an additional, greatly valued quality. Two sectors of higher education meet this test.

The first is research universities. They engage in both teaching and research. These universities carry out the basic and applied research that fuels the knowledge economy, and they prepare the people who carry out that work, the next generation of researchers. They are indispensable, but there is a caveat. There are 261 research universities in the United States. In a wired world, that number is likely to prove excessive and based on their productivity, location, and quality can be expected to decline in number.

The second is residential colleges. Contrary to popular perception, less than half (47%) of students are under the age of 25 and attend college on a full-time basis (National Center for Education Statistics, 2020b). Only a fraction of these students reside on campus—across all postsecondary enrollments, only 13 percent of students live on campus (Higher Learning Advocates, 2018). There will continue to be students and families who want the traditional residential college experience. So these colleges will persist but, because of demographics and finances, in significantly reduced numbers. There is also a growing mismatch between the high cost of residential education and the nation's evolving population. The greatest growth will occur among the populations least likely to attend college and to afford the price of a residential college.

However, the research university and residential college will not continue to do business as usual. "Looking Backward" illustrated what can be expected to occur. The higher education transformation during the Industrial Revolution caused colonial colleges with roots in the Middle Ages to become industrial era universities. That change was sweeping and nearly total. Today, St. John's College with its great books curriculum is one of the few institutions in America that resembles its colonial predecessors and while St. John's was founded in the seventeenth century, its great books curriculum dates back to only 1937.

However, more than two hundred colleges founded before the Civil War and the rise of the university still exist today. That would seem a bit of a conundrum. One college looks like its ancestors but hundreds survived. What actually happened is that the other colleges modernized. They dropped their trivium- and quadrivium-based curriculums. They changed their modes of instruction from rote memorization to lectures, labs, and seminars. They offered courses based on Carnegie units and created programs ultimately consisting of general education and majors. They hired faculty with graduate degrees, later with doctorates, and organized them into disciplinary departments. What remained of the colonial college was a four-year residential institution with a liberal arts orientation, often augmented with professional studies. These were the institutions that adapted successfully to the new realities of higher education and industrial America.

Once again, the institutions that survive by adaptation will have to refit themselves for the new world of the global, digital, knowledge economy. They will need to adopt the fundamentals of the new higher education model—become outcome-based with time and process variable curricula; trade Carnegie units for competencies; award both degrees and certificates; and diversify their faculties to include learning designers, instructors, assessors, and technologists that reflect the demographics of the nation. In short, they will take on the characteristics of higher education in the global, digital, knowledge economy but remain research universities and residential colleges.

Two questions arise about the future of higher education. The first, Will liberal arts colleges disappear? The answer is no. Residential liberal arts colleges will persist as they have since the founding of the very first American college but in substantially reduced numbers owing to demographics and finances. This assumes the liberal arts are updated as they have been throughout history to provide the education contemporary students and society need.

A second question is, Will Harvard have to change, or will it and other wealthy, high-status institutions be able to maintain the status quo? The answer is every institution will have to adapt to the new realities as they did in the past. During the Industrial Revolution, Harvard abandoned its classical curriculum, reorganized to become a university, and reconstituted its faculty because the existing model no longer worked. The program, organization, and staffing Harvard adopted in its stead was that of the industrial era university. During that time, Harvard was the leader in diffusing the industrial model to the nation's colleges and universities. The role it will play in the current transformation is uncertain. What we do know is that Harvard will be unable to resist the tide but will have the capacity to adapt to the new realities as Henry Rosovsky claimed at the very beginning of this book. It will have the luxury of moving more slowly than less wealthy and eminent schools, and its standing may permit it to serve as a validator of the changes earlier innovators adopt.

The third category includes institutions that will experience the coming disruption. These colleges and universities are not distinctive, wealthy, or highly selective. They do not have value-added features such as research or residential life. They may be located in demographically challenged areas or offer programs out of step with labor needs and markets. They may have high percentages of students who are older than 25, attend part time, work more than twenty hours a week, and are not engaged in campus life, coming to campus primarily to attend classes. They may offer classes at fixed locations and fixed times, which are not convenient for all students. They may provide higher education principally in just-in-case, degree-based bundles. Classes may be large and oversubscribed; financial aid and admissions services may not be easily accessible. Parking may be difficult to find, and commutes to campus may be long. They may be more expensive than the nontraditional alternatives.

These are the attributes that make institutions ripe for disruption. They don't need to have all of these characteristics. One may be sufficient. The point is that all of these conditions are at odds with the five new realities facing higher education and/ or challenge the efficacy and staying power of the industrial era university. These institutions will face growing competition from lower cost, more convenient, nontraditional providers offering unbundled anytime education and consumers who have changing tastes and more choices. Earlier, this was posed as the dilemma of how the more costly local college with a lengthier program could compete against Google. Or, in the liberal arts, which universities can match the reputation and resources of MOMA in mounting a postwar modern art class?

Relative advantage is the test of which sectors of higher education are most likely to be disrupted. By that standard, the institutions at greatest risk are regional universities and community colleges.

Here are two truisms about higher education that will shape what happens next. The first is that innovation travels from the periphery of higher education to the mainstream. The second is that innovation drives learners from the mainstream to the periphery of higher education. These statements are too long to be epigrams and too esoteric for fortune cookies. Let's consider each in turn.

From the Periphery to the Mainstream

Historically, major change in higher education has begun at its periphery—outside of colleges and universities or in the most marginal units within existing institutions. "Looking Backward" examined how new subject matters and new populations followed this route from the periphery to the center of the enterprise.

In terms of new subject matters, science is exemplary. While many of the classical colleges included natural philosophy in their curriculums and hired scientists to their faculty, they rejected the education of scientists as well articulated in the 1828 Yale Report. The education of scientists began outside higher education, often informally, through scientific academies and societies, continental universities, apprenticeships, applied fields such as agriculture and engineering, and massive technological projects such as the Erie Canal and the railroads.

When science did enter higher education during the Industrial Revolution, it did so through lower-status parallel and partial courses of study and subunits such as the Sheffield School at Yale or Lawrence School at Harvard, which either did not grant degrees or awarded inferior degrees like bachelor of science. Both Sheffield and Lawrence came into being through very large gifts from industrial entrepreneurs. Neither university really wanted a college of science, but the funding was too large to turn down.

New science and technology institutes outside of higher education were also established, many initially subcollegiate. Looked down on by traditional higher education, they included such illustrious future universities as West Point, the Rensselaer School (which would become Rensselaer Polytechnical Institute), Cooper Union (later Institute), and the Massachusetts Institute of Technology. Some pioneering mainstream institutions such as Union College, which was not one of the elite colleges, accorded equal status to its arts and sciences programs but added a healthy dose of the arts curriculum to the sciences.

During the Second Industrial Revolution, the education of scientists became almost inescapable for most of higher education owing to the changing economy, the technology explosion, the rise of the university, and social pressure. The education of scientists moved from the periphery—from a largely informal activity, study abroad, and new nontraditional institutions—to the mainstream and ultimately to the center of higher education, but through lower status curricula and subunits in the universities such as the scientific schools and extension divisions, which embraced research and professional education.

The story of how new groups gained access to higher education is similar and the treatment of women is a good example. In the main, the diversification of higher education has been a process of initial exclusion, then the creation of separate institutions for each new population at the periphery of traditional higher education, and finally gradual, accelerating, and usually incomplete inclusion in the mainstream, beginning with the least selective and most hard-pressed institutions.

Higher education was generally unwilling to accept women until the late nineteenth century. The result is that subcollegiate women's schools—academies and seminaries—sprang up, including Bethlehem Female Academy (1724), Bradford Academy (1802), and Clinton Female Seminary (1821), all of which evolved into women's colleges. Then separate colleges for women were established such as Vassar College (1861), Smith College (1871), and Bryn Mawr College (1885). New coeducational institutions were also founded such as Oberlin (1833) and Cornell (1865).

And finally, the mainstream universities established separate women's subunits, much as they had done with the sciences, including Harvard, Brown, Columbia, and Tulane. Nonetheless, protracted and heated battles over coeducation continued for much of the twentieth century while women's enrollments in mainstream higher education grew to the point that female attendance surpassed male attendance by 1980.

This pattern of innovation entering mainstream higher education from the periphery and traveling from the least selective and most hard-pressed institutions up the status ladder to the most selective and most comfortable universities has been the norm for higher education for most major changes. Today, innovation generally enters the top universities through their least prestigious and most profit-dependent units, often continuing education.

The institutions created to serve excluded populations do

not evaporate as those populations gain access to mainstream higher education. However, their numbers diminish substantially. For instance, there were 281 women's colleges in the 1960s and only 34 today. Black colleges have been an exception. In 1930, there were 121 historically black colleges and universities. Today there are 101. Their persistence is a mark of both their successes and their continuing need in a nation racked by systemic racism.

In the introduction, the postsecondary sector at the periphery of higher education, which comprises a mélange of for-profit and non-profit nontraditional providers, was described as entrepreneurial, historically seeking to capitalize on the perceived shortcomings of colleges and universities. In this sense, the postsecondary sector has become a lab for higher education, experimenting with underserved populations, new curricula and subject matters, new pedagogies and delivery systems, new pricing models, and much more. Higher education observes these innovations, carps, cherry picks, and ultimately adopts what it considers best practices.

This behavior is not unique to higher education. The three case studies in "Looking Sideways" demonstrated the same phenomenon. The music, film, and newspaper industries were forced to adapt their business models to accommodate new competitors, new regulation, and new technologies from outside their industries. They were all disrupted by external organizations—Pandora, Spotify, Netflix, Google, and Facebook.

From the Mainstream to the Periphery

Major innovation drives consumers, according to Clayton Christensen, in the opposite direction, from the center to the periphery of higher education. Christensen told the story of his $2 childhood transistor radio, which was staticky and had terrible reception. He had to stand on a hill and point the radio west if he hoped to hear anything. But it was exactly what Christensen wanted. It was mobile, cheap, and played rock 'n' roll without parental oversight.

His point is that the initial products developed at the periphery are poor in quality and attract previous nonconsumers, individuals who cannot afford the mainstream version or who see real advantage in the alternative. As product quality improves, more and more consumers abandon the traditional product in favor of the new. Mainstream producers do not switch to the new, low-margin, low-quality product because they are so heavily invested in the existing product that the cost would be prohibitive and their consumer base wants the old product. Over time, however, as a growing volume of consumers migrate to the new product, it becomes the principal consumer choice, disrupting the original producer's business model. This is what happened in the music, film, and newspaper industries. In the case of radio, the large vacuum tube–powered pieces of furniture that were radios in Christensen's youth gave way to smaller, cheaper, more portable transistor powered successors (Christensen, 2014).

The same is true of higher education, and online learning is a good example. There is a tendency for each new communications technology to mimic its predecessor. So when radio programming began, it brought the live entertainment people attended—theater, concerts, and sporting events—to the airwaves prior to creating its own unique programming. Television did roughly the same thing, turning popular radio programs into TV shows such as *The Lone Ranger*, *The Goldbergs*, and *The Jack Benny Show*.

The same was true of online courses. In their earliest days, they were existing classes with lectures and readings made digital. The result is that an interactive medium was used for one-way communication, from teacher to student. Not surprisingly, initial reviews were poor. The online courses did not stand up against in-person classes with their opportunities for discussion, teacher-student interaction, and peer-to-peer student contact. It was a lot like Christensen's transistor radio in that the earliest users were students unable to access or afford in-person classes.

For the most part, online education was a product of the periphery of higher education. The first institution to offer a wholly online degree in 1988 was the for-profit University of Phoenix. Nine years later, four new universities or university subunits were created to offer online education—NYU Online, Inc., a for-profit spin off from the university; Western Governors University, an institution founded by nineteen Western governors to break the traditional higher education mold; California Virtual University, a public statewide university offering online classes; and Trident University, also a for-profit internet-based provider. All were peripheral institutions launched in 1997 or 1998; NYU Online and the California Virtual University closed within two years.

Until the pandemic, online enrollments were overwhelmingly concentrated in a small number of colleges and universities, largely at the periphery of higher education. Only 104 institutions offered primarily online degree programs (2.4% of institutions), and 5 percent of those institutions enrolled nearly half of all online degree students. For instance, Western Governors University, which enrolled one hundred twenty thousand students, Southern New Hampshire University with over one hundred fifty thousand students, and the University of Phoenix with ninety-four thousand students, together accounted for 38 percent of online degree enrollment (Blumenstyk, 2020; Lederman, 2019; National Center for Education Statistics, 2018a, 2018b; Seaman, Allen, & Seaman, 2018, 3).

Coronavirus cut two ways on online education. Although

it forced nearly every institution in the country to shift from face-to-face to online instruction, causing its migration from the periphery to the mainstream dramatically faster than any technology innovation discussed in this volume, but in the end, it penalized traditional institutions and rewarded peripheral providers. On average, the former lost enrollment owing to declines in already matriculated students, smaller entering classes, and reduced foreign student enrollment. The latter, which could offer cheaper, more convenient and more established online programs, experienced an enrollment bump. Western Governors University increased by twenty-five to thirty percent, Coursera's enrollment jumped from fifty-three million to seventy-eight million, and a number of other MOOC companies had enrollment increases. For example, FutureLearn, a MOOC platform owned by the British Open University and Australia's Seek Group, reported a 50 percent rise in new students (D'Amico & Hanson, 2020).

The University of the People, a nonprofit that offers its wholly online programs free, charging only an assessment fee for each course, experienced a 75 percent increase in new students. In March and April 2020, Modern States Education Alliance, also a nonprofit, which has a library of online courses that enable students to complete freshman year of college free, gained nine thousand new users, double the number of the prior three months. StraighterLine, a for-profit that offers low-cost online general education courses, had a 40 percent rise from students of nonpartner universities (Blumenstyk, 2020).

Where things stand today is that online degree programs continue to be concentrated at the periphery, less so in the professions. Courses, programs, and even degrees have migrated to the mainstream, but the number of students seeking degrees are still increasing at the periphery.

But the pace of online degree penetration is on the rise in the mainstream. A growing number of traditional institutions are attempting to enter or expand their presence in the online degree marketplace and for-profit online program management firms have sprung up that partner with them to accomplish this. It's a nearly $4 billion growth industry worldwide with leaders such as 2U, Academic Partnerships, Bisk, Noodle, Pearson, and Wiley Education Service and tends to operate on long term contacts and revenue sharing. OPMs generally receive between forty-five and sixty-five percent of the revenue. US Senators Warren and Brown in 2020 wrote the five largest OPMs raising concerns about their business practices. Noodle Partners is unusual in operating on a lower cost fee for services basis.

Deborah Quazzo of GSV says there have been two waves of partnerships between higher education and OPMs. In the first, which she calls the 2U wave after one of the earliest OPM pioneers, it was the OPM's job to support university entry and operations online. The second she labels the Coursera wave in which the OPM assumed a more prominent and visible public role in offering online education, including an increasingly diverse set of products such as short courses and boot camps. Quazzo believes we are beginning an as yet inchoate third wave. The authors wonder whether OPMs will eventually go beyond packaging, marketing, and distributing content to creating their own content utilizing far more sophisticated analytics than typically found on campuses as Netflix did in the film industry, thereby becoming a higher education competitor? Whether they do or do not, the bottom line is that Christensen was right.

The Process of Change

The process of change today can be expected to mirror the seven stages of the industrial era transformation as discussed in chapter five.

1. Demand for change in higher education by government, media, and external stakeholders
2. Denial and resistance of the need to change by higher education
3. Experimentation and reform initiatives inside and outside traditional higher education with a focus on attempting to repair the existing model of higher education
4. Establishment of new models of higher education at the periphery rather than mainstream of the enterprise that seek to replace the existing model rather than repair it
5. Diffusion of the new models with a prestigious institution at the center leading the effort and other mainstream institutions following in adopting the changes in their own fashion
6. Standardizing the hodgepodge of varying practices and policies that diffusion spawned
7. Scaling up and integrating the various pieces of standardized practice and policy to create the industrial era system of higher education

Higher education is in the early stages of the transformation today. The present shows similarities to the pre–Civil War period when American colleges confronted demands for change, the denial of the need to change, and a myriad of institutional experiments. That demand for change is coming, as it did then, from government, business, funders, and students. The issues are the same—cost, failing to keep up with the times, and unwillingness to change. What was referred to as elitism and a need for democratization in the Industrial Revolution has now become equity and access.

Several points from chapter five need to be reaffirmed. There has been no Yale Report, a revered national statement defending the status quo that galvanizes the opponents of change.

Rather as noted in "Looking Backward," resistance to change is now local and campus based and involves clashes between faculty, administration, and trustees over varying issues from the adoption of innovations such as partnerships with for-profit educators and the size and composition of the faculty to institutional governance and budget cuts.

Reform initiatives, largely piecemeal innovations, or at least talk of them aimed at modernizing institutions and often intended to make them more distinctive and competitive are legion. In contrast to David Riesman's notion of the snakelike academic procession, the leadership for change is now based in the tail. Troubled institutions—particularly small, low-endowment, low-selectivity private colleges in the Northeast, Midwest, and mid-Atlantic States, where there are too many colleges and too few students—are in a desperate hunt to find magic bullet innovations to save themselves. As noted, the most successful of these innovations will diffuse up the academic hierarchy, finally being adopted by the least prestigious units of the most prestigious universities. This was the process by which higher education began enrolling nontraditional students—part time, older, working, women—and establishing programs for them in the 1970s.

The other major venue for change will be institutions, principally in the Sunbelt, with the opposite problem, expanding college-aged populations beyond the capacity of their current physical campuses. This will force states to consider a raft of innovations, including virtual campuses, changes in the academic calendar and clock, new approaches to staffing, massive online instruction, and more.

A number of higher education institutions have gained reputations as innovators. Some are engaged in broad-scale changes. Arizona State University is attempting to create what it calls the "Fifth Wave" university combining research excellence, cutting-edge technology, and a culture of diversity and access. Purdue University is focusing on affordability, data and technology, and fusing the worlds of postsecondary and higher education. Southern New Hampshire University and Western Governors University emphasize affordability, access, online instruction, competency-based learning, and a culture of vision and innovation. Some institutions have become known for a specific innovation. Examples, many, many could be cited, include Georgia State University (student success), Hostos Community College (bilingual education), Ivy Tech Community College (access and scale), Minerva (international video seminars), Olin University (redesigning engineering education), Paul Quinn College (turnaround), PennFoster College (career education), University of Maryland, Baltimore County (math/science and underrepresented populations), and University of Texas at El Paso (Latinx and binational education). A small number of universities have created environments that spawn innovation and invention such as Carnegie-Mellon, MIT, Northeastern, and Stanford.

We are not yet at the post–Civil War stages of transformation. Models established by Cornell, Hopkins, and MIT are yet to clearly emerge. But there are candidates just noted that could become potential models, such as Calbright, Coursera, Southern New Hampshire University, University of the People, and Western Governors University. The reason is that each is the embodiment of a solution to a major challenge facing higher education—just-in-time upskilling and reskilling education (Calbright), affordability and mass access (Coursera and University of the People), and competency-based online education at scale (Southern New Hampshire University and Western Governors University). However, the existence of models can only be ascertained by looking backward.

There is also a candidate to lead the transfer and diffusion of the models to mainstream higher education as Harvard did during the Industrial Revolution: MIT. It is a world-class university, which has been guiding higher education into the global, digital, knowledge economy with a series of major innovations in technology, learning sciences, curriculum, instruction, and credentialing. In 2014, it issued an institute-wide task force report on the future of MIT, which, like the Yale Report, also served to chart a course for higher education but in this case a progressive, future-oriented course. In this sense, MIT is reminiscent of Harvard in 1869, one of America's most-respected institutions with a visionary leader and the capacity to diffuse innovation to mainstream higher education. The difference is that MIT is also a leading inventor of 21st century higher education.

Consolidation, standardization, scaling, and integration complete the transformation. As yet, there is nothing to consolidate, standardize, or scale.

When Will Change Occur?

The transformation of higher education has been ongoing for decades, longer than the word *disruption* has had meaning for colleges and universities. It has occurred in big ways and small, as evidenced in:

- The development of innovative practices in the postsecondary sector
- Experiments in competency-based education, technologically based delivery systems, new financing models, new approaches to access, tying higher education more closely with jobs and careers, just-in-time education, anytime-anyplace education, and so much more
- The movement of innovations from the periphery to the

mainstream and the transit of students in the opposite direction

- The creation of new institutions, the transformation of existing institutions, and the closure of troubled institutions
- Government policy and the investment of foundations and philanthropists

It would have continued in this fashion and gained momentum over time as the pace of innovation and the rate of adoption increased, when today's innovations were becoming normalized, and the later adopters were adopting.

But certain social events act as accelerators of change; they speed its pace and scope. The pandemic was one of them. So was the 2008 recession described in chapter seven. As the United States moved from an industrial to a knowledge economy, we knew low-education, low-skill jobs would disappear over time either through automation or by off-shoring jobs. However, the recession telescoped the process and shed millions of jobs in a couple of years that required a high school diploma or less and those lost jobs did not return with the recovery. They were replaced by positions requiring postsecondary education.

The pandemic has played a similar role in higher education. Our analysis found that major changes would occur in higher education. Some institutions would close over the next decade. Colleges and universities would expand their digital presence and their use of online instruction. New, nontraditional providers of higher education content would enter the higher education marketplace. There would be growing demand for worker upskilling and reskilling through short practical programs awarding microcredentials rather than degrees. COVID-19 has accelerated all of these changes.

In this sense, the recession helped us to understand when

change will come to higher education. The recession wasn't felt equally by all Americans. Those with the lowest levels of education experienced the greatest pain and those with the most education the least. The former had the greatest and most permanent job losses during the recession while the latter with graduate degrees actually saw job growth.

Higher education's experience will be similar. The financially weakest and most troubled institutions, largely, the less selective, low endowment private schools in regions of the country with declining college-aged populations, are already experiencing the consequences of the transition to the global, digital, knowledge economy. Closures are on the rise in 2021 and will continue at high rates for the next several years before leveling off.

For the wealthier and more selective research universities and residential colleges, the time frame for change will be longer. In the decade ahead, they will have to adapt by piecemeal reform to a succession of challenges posed by new technologies, changing student demographics and expectations, and growing competition from alternative providers. They will also face shifting employer needs; the transition from time-based to outcome-based education; and growing demands for equity, accountability, and reduced costs as well as changing regulations.

The process will be much like that of the agrarian colleges remaking themselves for industrial America, described earlier in this chapter. When completed, the shell of the house will remain, but the inside will have been largely gutted and refurbished.

There are two caveats. First, the time frame for refurbishing will be considerably shorter than Eliot's four decades at Harvard. However, the wealthiest, most selective, and best geographically situated institutions will have more but still a limited amount of time in comparison with peers to observe before acting. The second caveat is that all colleges and universities that attempt this strategy will not be successful. To put it crassly, they are playing a game of musical chairs. The number of research universities and residential colleges will be reduced in the decades ahead.

The disruption faced by regional universities and community colleges will be a matter of attrition. Their students will move from mainstream institutions to the periphery, to alternative providers for cheaper, more convenient, unbundled, and in some cases higher-quality instruction, better aligned with the street, particularly if degrees diminish in importance, as discussed earlier in this chapter. The length of time for disruption will depend on how quickly students migrate. At the risk of sounding irreverent, the best guidance may come from Ogden Nash's poem about how catsup comes out of a bottle: "First a little, then a lottle." To hold onto their students and escape disruption, these institutions will have to offer some tangible advantage that alternative providers cannot. More on this in the next chapter.

The conclusion is that in the end the industry of higher education will be disrupted. Though every college and university will change, they will get to that end by different routes, over different time frames, and by varying means.

16

· · · · · · ·

What Should Higher Education and Policy Makers Do?

What we have just described is the future of higher education that this analysis reveals. It is not a future the authors are advocating. We are products of traditional higher education and are not comfortable with some of the emerging directions, which we believe have the potential to cause greater educational inequity and social division. The findings are not intended to give a sense of inevitability and powerlessness on the part of institutions and policy makers. This chapter offers recommendations intended to enable institutions to better shape their individual futures and for policy makers to better plan the future of the enterprise. They seek to mitigate the potential dangers, enhance the benefits, and smooth the otherwise rocky and meandering path of the coming transformation of higher education.

What Colleges and Universities Can Do

So far, we have discussed the future of the higher education industry and its various sectors, not the individual futures of the industry's more than four thousand institutions that comprise it. The reality is that most colleges and universities have the capacity to significantly shape their futures. Toward this end, we offer five recommendations.

1. Don't Plan for Business as Usual

While campuses were closed in spring 2020, we spoke with college presidents, the heads of higher education associations, policy makers, and accreditors about COVID-19 and their post-pandemic plans. There were few surprises in what we heard. As might be anticipated, anxiety levels were sky-high. While some of those we spoke to were more optimistic than others, all expected the financial toll and enrollment losses to be extraordinarily high, but how high remained a guessing game. Despite announcements and plans to the contrary, most of the people we spoke with really didn't know when their campuses would truly reopen. A common refrain was that a larger number of campuses will close than projected; seemingly each person we spoke to knew of an institution we would be shocked to hear was discussing closure.

In terms of future plans, most viewed the pandemic as they would a natural disaster—a flood, a tornado, or a hurricane. They wanted to get back to business as soon as possible, clean up the damage, and restore what had been lost.

In this sense, most misunderstood the nature of the pandemic. They viewed it as an interruption in doing business as usual rather than an accelerator of the changes to come. They expected to turn back the clock to 2019, before the pandemic, to recreate their pre-COVID colleges. They wanted to recapture the past, which is no more possible today than it would have been to resurrect lost jobs requiring a high school diploma during the Great Recession.

As the recession revealed a world in the making in which jobs, labor markets, and educational requirements for employment were being recast, the changes in higher education caused by the pandemic will mark the directions colleges and universities can be expected to move in the years ahead. This sadly, given the high price paid for this knowledge, provides an opportunity for institutions as they plan to reopen to ask not simply how they restore what existed prior to COVID-19 but what they want and need to become in the global, digital, knowledge economy.

To look forward rather than backward will require institutions to confront five forces that drive them to focus on the past rather than on the future. One is magical thinking, a belief that the challenges facing their institution will somehow vanish or fail to materialize. A second is complacency and an assumption of institutional exceptionalism, which holds each college to be special, ultimately shielding it from the woes confronting other institutions. Third is short-term rather than long-term vision and planning. Despite the frequency of five-year plans, there is a tendency for most institutions to think about their future a year at time, which discourages creative thinking and investing in the future. Fourth is a tendency to view failed attempts at innovation to be an affirmation of current practices. Finally, there is campus politics and the divides between administrators, faculty, and trustees, which planning for the future and the possibility of making significant changes promises to exacerbate.

However, the future of every institution depends on overcoming these barriers. It's the responsibility of presidents and boards to lead their institutions into the future and to educate their communities about the challenges and opportunities ahead. The pandemic provides the teaching moment to do it.

A former university president, provost, and dean offered us this advice about how to proceed. "Don't fight internal resis-

tance. Work around it." Either create a new subunit, as Southern New Hampshire University did, or a space at the periphery
of the campus outside the academic core for innovation, as MIT
has done. If that isn't feasible, focus on the early or "first adopters." There's no sense trying to make believers of everyone. It
only slows things down. Instead, find, incentivize, reward, and
praise those who adopt new models and let them be the ones to
talk the second wave of faculty into adopting the new.

2. Recognize Higher Education Is in the Education Business, Not the Campus, Degree, or Credit Business

The case study of the newspaper industry is the story of an organization that failed to recognize what business it was in. It
was in the news business but thought of itself as being in the
newspaper business, conflating its business (i.e., producing
news content) with the means for distributing it. The result is
that it was blindsided by the digital platforms that took away its
consumers and advertising revenues.

There are many such stories. The railroads thought they
were in the train business rather than the transportation business and were overtaken by airlines. Carriage makers lost out
to the automobile industry. But the businesses that survived
are instructive. In 1890, there were thirteen thousand wagon
and carriage businesses. Fewer than a handful survived. The
Studebaker Wagon Company is the only one that transitioned
into making cars. The Timken Company, which made roller
bearings for wagons, adapted them for automobile use. And
Westfield Whip Manufacturing shifted its product line from
carriages to equestrian equipment. In short, the survivors
changed their product lines and/or their consumer bases.

The question of "what business are we in" takes on a special urgency in times of profound change when existing institutions are negotiating a shifting terrain in which new competitors, new products, new methods of distribution, and new consumers are emerging. Higher education is in this position today. This is a time in which online and other forms of digital learning are advancing, nondegree programs are expanding, nontraditional providers are entering the higher education marketplace, and credit- and time-based education are receding. Every institution of higher education must ask itself, "What business are we in?" This is not the same as asking, "What business are we in right now?" (for which the newspaper, railroad, and carriage business would have been correct answers).

In examining the business they are in, colleges cannot equate current practices with their business. They have to avoid the error that newspapers made in equating their distribution method—campuses, degrees, and credits—with their business. They have to guard against the mistake made by carriage makers, thinking the product they were producing was the only product they could produce and believing their current consumers were their only possible market. As colleges and universities think about the future, it is essential to recognize that traditional methods of distribution may be liabilities, traditional products may be outdated, and consumer tastes may be changing.

The Yale Report of 1828, while an unabashed defense of existing practice and a curt dismissal of the alternatives, demonstrates how a college might approach the question of what business we are in.

First, the report declared that the wrong questions were being asked by higher education and the public, whether colleges needed to change a lot or a little, immediately or gradually to meet the needs of the times. Rather, the report said there was only one question that needed to be answered: What is the purpose of a college? The academic equivalent of "What business are we in?"

Second, the authors offered a clear and crisp statement of purpose—to provide the discipline and furniture of the mind. It was a single phrase as simple and unadorned as saying the purpose of the New York Yankees is to win baseball games or the purpose of the United Nations is to ensure world peace. It was not the generic page-long mush found in many college catalogs and websites.

Third, Yale operationalized its statement of purpose by determining what program and pedagogy it would be required to enact, which students it would seek to enroll, and what method of distribution it would employ to educate those students: the four-year, residential college.

Fourth, more in theory than in practice, Yale also reviewed the alternatives: different purposes, models, programs, pedagogies, and student bodies other institutions were experimenting with. In truth, Yale actually decided what it would do and then trashed the competition. The ideal time to carry out such a review of alternatives is before creating a business model, when it can actually provide useful guidance.

Fifth, the writing of the Yale Report was an inclusive effort. It was approved unanimously by the entire faculty.

Sixth, the report demonstrated that the question of what business are we in, requires not only an intellectually satisfying but a viable answer. Yale offered a conservative defense of the classical college. As one of the nation's most eminent colleges, it thrived as a consequence, but many institutions that rallied around the Yale Report, particularly in the Midwest and South, did not fare well. The Yale Report was in reality an outdated defense of past practices rather than present needs. It dragged down the less eminent institutions that followed its recommendations. The lesson is that the Yale Report was viable for one institution, not all.

These six steps define how colleges and universities can determine what business they are in. One additional element is necessary—data, which we turn to next.

3. Know Tomorrow Will Not Be a Repeat of Yesterday

Higher education is in the midst of a transformation. Of course, tomorrow will not be a repeat of yesterday. So in the words of Wayne Gretzky—higher education has to "skate to where the puck is going, not to where it has been." The question is, Where is the puck going to be? While this is a book about where the puck is going to be for the higher education industry, the puck will be at different places for every institution, varying by institutional type, mission, location, selectivity, demographics, and resources.

Every institution or institutions in partnership need to establish a skunkworks to continuously determine where the puck is going to be, both in the short and long run—that is, a unit charged with monitoring the institution's environment and developing solutions to respond to changes. This unit should track demographics and changes in consumer needs, tastes, and demands. It should study the economy and the changing requirements of the job market and employers. It should monitor technology and its potential impact and application to education. It should closely observe existing and emerging competitors to the institution. It should follow public policy at the national, state, and local levels.

The job of the skunkworks is to communicate its findings to the institution, to use its research to identify the challenges and the opportunities facing the institution, to formulate the actions the institution should consider, and to serve as an incubator for new ideas flowing from that research.

Southern New Hampshire University established a model skunkworks named the Sandbox colLABorative. It is the research, development, and incubation arm of the university, engaging in environmental scanning and discovering, examining and testing promising innovations with the aim of improving existing programs and modes of instruction, and discovering opportunities for developing cutting-edge approaches to education and untapped markets for the university to pursue. Former Sandbox director Michelle Weise put it this way: "We're trying to be an incubator.... If we do land on something that could be a new viable business model for education, the lab will incubate the idea until it's ready to be pushed out on its own" (Hart, 2016, para. 7).

As a result, when American higher education was frantically attempting to move from face-to-face classes to online instruction, Southern New Hampshire University was seeking to create the next generation of online instruction. When colleges and universities were trying to manage their way through the pandemic, Southern New Hampshire University was studying the impact of prior disasters on higher education and the strategies that proved most effective in dealing with them.

4. Restore the Connection with the Street

Earlier, it was said that higher education is most successful when it has one foot in the library (human heritage) and the other foot in the street (the real world). In times of deep and rapid change, higher education loses traction with the street; it changes more slowly than the society around it, so that higher education is perceived as out of step with the times.

Today, that disconnect is most apparent in career education, which is exacerbated by an oft held belief in the academy that practical and vocational education are a debasement of higher education's commitment to pursue knowledge for knowledge's sake. This is a misreading of history, which documents unambiguously that, since the earliest universities, students have come to college to prepare for jobs. Any lingering distaste for career, professional, and practical education is fake history and a liability, too. The dichotomy between education for personal enrichment and education for participation in society, including the labor market, has always been a false one.

Restoring the connection between education and work requires colleges and universities to build on the research of the skunkworks. It means continually updating and modernizing existing programs, including nonvocational areas such as general education, which needs to incorporate twenty-first-century skills; dropping outdated curricula; and filling emerging career curricular gaps. It necessitates strong apprenticeship, internship, and cooperative programs; practical minors for liberal arts students; and a career center on steroids that begins working with students and faculty from the day they arrive on campus and continues for students postgraduation. It demands the cutting-edge facilities and technology employers use and a faculty current in their fields and knowledgeable about emerging developments.

Only the wealthiest colleges and universities will be able to do this alone. Consortia among institutions and partnerships with alternative and specialized providers of the types discussed in this chapter will be essential for most institutions. At bottom, all institutions have to establish mutually beneficial affiliations with employers, beginning with those in areas in which students live, study, and work and those that the skunkworks identifies as future high-growth fields.

5. Make Institutions Distinctive, Give Them a Value Added or Plus That Distinguishes Them from Peers

This analysis found that the rise of the global, digital, knowledge economy will disrupt higher education and only two sectors of the industry have the capacity to adapt to the changes without disruption: research universities and residential colleges. The reason is that both have a distinctive and value-added feature, discussed earlier, that distinguishes them from other institutions.

Not long ago, Arthur had lunch with a board member of a somewhat selective liberal arts college. Enrollment was declining and efforts to stanch the tide had not worked. They had tried online programs, added more career education, and sought to attract adult, minority, and foreign students.

Prior to the meeting, Arthur perused the institution's website and public data on its students. The reason for the decline was that, in a region of the country with an oversupply of higher education, there was nothing special about the college and no way to distinguish it from peers. The focus of much of the institution's public relations was on its long history, which while interesting probably had little impact on the students and families it hoped to recruit and might actually have been a negative in the post–George Floyd era. The college was more expensive than the public alternatives and high discount rates didn't seem to be making it more competitive. Attrition and graduation rates were not as strong as some of its liberal arts competitors, which offered roughly the same program and had comparable faculties with similar student/faculty ratios. It was an attractive campus, but not eye popping in terms of appearance or facilities.

There was really nothing distinctive about the college. The actions this college had taken, throwing a bunch of new programs at the wall, hoping each would add a few students, don't work. Many colleges are doing exactly the same thing with exactly the same programs and achieving exactly the same results. With worsening institutional finances, this college is a candidate for closure.

What residential and research universities demonstrate is that the difference must be meaningful, unique, and highly valued. There are needs in higher education that are not being met that could be the basis for institutional distinctiveness—low cost/high quality, upskilling and reskilling, career education, use of digital technology to support face-to-face instruction, underserved populations, and a subject focus such as climate change. It is not enough to patch together a few courses in an area. These are the gaps nontraditional providers are seeking to fill.

The distinction need not be a dramatic departure from current practice. For instance, one can imagine a college's distinction as a focus on excellence in teaching and learning, which would be infused into the fabric of the institution.

On the teaching side, ads for new faculty might state that preference will be given to faculty who have won teaching awards. Search committees need to reiterate this and act on it. All institutional promotional materials from admissions and development brochures to the campus letterhead and seal would proclaim the commitment. The reward system of the institution, salaries and promotion, would be tied not to conventional metrics such as research output but to teaching quality. Authentic assessment of teaching and learning would be built into the core of the institution. There could be a department of learning sciences and an array of more traditional departments that make teaching and learning a centerpiece of their work such as a psychology department that studies adolescent development and learning.

There might be a center or, more accurately, a lab located at the heart of the campus, which works with every faculty and staff member on teaching excellence from the day they arrive on campus to the day they retire. It might prepare faculty to serve as mentors for colleagues in their departments. It might serve as an incubator for innovative practices and provide grants to faculty for research and development in teaching and learning. The center itself might engage in and support research on teaching and learning, recruit departmental faculty to participate in their work, and keep the campus and the world informed of advances in learning sciences, learning technology, and teaching through presentations, social media, blogs, and webinars. The institution might provide professional development programs and online resources for faculty and staff from other institutions. The end result should be a new kind of instructor: one who has cultivated proficiencies not only in their subject matter but also in pedagogy, learning sciences, and educational technology.

On the learning side, as at Georgia State University, student learning would be personalized and the services that Course Hero provides, making learning resources, tutoring, problem solving, and lesson support available online to students and faculty around the clock, would become staples. Course Hero shows these services can be individualized and offered at low cost. It is difficult to imagine that legislators, students and families, and donors would not find such a campus distinctive and attractive.

For community colleges, the uniqueness could be being local and inextricably intertwined with its community. This means serving employers with up-to-date, jointly constructed programs tied to the needs of their industries. It means being the go-to place for upskilling and reskilling. For the community, it means providing services, facilities, expertise, and resources that serve its traditional and emerging needs. It may mean serving as a lab for innovation and a center for community research with the ability to fulfill an early warning function, making the community aware of what is coming and its best responses. For students, it means offering programs and services rooted in their needs and abilities, being learner centered, and providing the just-in-time education they will require. This college is indispensable to its community, not merely physically located there.

There is historical precedent for such a college. In 1904, Charles Van Hise, president of the University of Wisconsin, unveiled a radical vision of higher education, the "Wisconsin Idea." The campus of his institution would become the state of Wisconsin, applying the university's research, teaching, and service to the problems of the state. Several years later, testifying before the Wisconsin legislature, Van Hise was asked what contribution the university made to the state. He said—we invented the cow. He wasn't far off. The university's research had transformed cow breeding, productivity, economics, and public health, among other things. Its experiment and extension services brought the research to farmers. Its classrooms educated farmers, researchers, and agriculture policy makers and administrators.

And agriculture was not a one-off. The University of Wisconsin brought its entire body of knowledge and capacity to experiment, teach, and apply it to the state, including bringing government officials to campus to teach and faculty to government offices to staff and advise. The University of Wisconsin made itself indispensable to the state.

What Policy Makers and Funders Can Do

The focus shifts here from individual colleges and universities to issues facing the higher and postsecondary education industries and the sectors that constitute it. Four issues stand out.

1. Ensuring Educational Equity

The term *educational equity* needs to be redefined. The current definition is a product of the industrial era and focuses on providing all students with access to the same educational process for the same length of time. The goal is to ensure that each student receives equal resources and experiences.

In the global, digital, knowledge economy, the emphasis shifts to outcomes. In this world, equity takes on a new meaning—ensuring equal access to the same learning outcomes, providing students with the differential resources they require to achieve the same result. This is an approach the courts are commonly taking to adjudicate school fiscal equity lawsuits in the states.

This definition of equity makes universal access to postsecondary education essential. As discussed in chapter seven, in the aftermath of the 2008 recession, education beyond high school became a necessity for getting a good job in the United States and made postsecondary accessibility essential for every American who could benefit from it. We have a long way to go to make this a reality, particularly for our fastest-growing and most economically disadvantaged populations. Just how far is discussed in chapter six.

College promise programs, which generally offer high school graduates free tuition for the first two years of college, provide a means to close the gap. The initial program was established in 2005 in Kalamazoo, Michigan, enabling local secondary school graduates to attend in-state colleges with tuition reductions ranging from two-thirds to 100 percent. Today, there are more than 320 such state, regional, and city programs, which operate with differing funding sources and widely varying designs.

The industrial era brought free education through grade twelve. The global, digital, knowledge economy requires that free education be extended to grade fourteen. The states have taken the lead in making this a reality, beginning with Tennessee, which made its community colleges free in 2014. The federal government could spur similar initiatives by providing incentives to the states to adopt promise programs.

With the massive COVID-19 unemployment numbers, this could be equivalent to the 1944 G.I. Bill, which provided unprecedented educational opportunity to veterans but was created to head off the massive unemployment that followed World War I. It's important for states to embrace promise programs for a very pragmatic reason. Their economic futures are tied to having an educated labor force and educating that labor force is a better investment than paying wages to unemployed workers.

But increasing access begins not with the colleges but with schools. Say Yes to Education, which launched promise programs in Buffalo, Cleveland, Guilford County, and Syracuse, has emphasized school wraparound services such as tutoring, mentoring, after-school programs, assessment of student progress, and pro bono legal and mental health support. The goal has been to drive up student achievement and high school graduation rates as perquisites for maximizing access.

President Truman's 1947 Commission on Higher Education identified five barriers to college access—family income, race, gender, religion, and geography. The pandemic spotlighted a sixth—technology. Well before COVID-19, there were frequent studies documenting disparities in access to digital technology and the internet by family income, zip code, and race. When the pandemic closed schools and colleges in 2020, forcing instruction online, those studies were translated by the media into real people with names, faces, and stories told by the students themselves, their teachers, and their families. They were stories about children unable to attend school, to carry out assignments, and to turn in homework for lack of digital technology and internet access. News footage showed whole families crowded into cars for hours in parking lots outside stores where the Wi-Fi could be tapped.

If college access is to be a reality for the most disadvantaged Americans, the most underrepresented populations in higher education, the digital divide must be closed. The federal government has to take the lead in partnership with the states. In the industrial era, government built highways. In the twenty-first century, government needs to make a comparable investment in digital highways, as President Biden has proposed.

We need to provide all students not only with access to higher education but also with choice among higher education providers. The Truman Commission recommended this almost eight decades ago, saying not only did college access need to be dramatically expanded but it was essential that students be able to attend the college best meeting their needs and talents. The commission saw access and choice as coequal needs. But as a matter of federal and state policy, only the access provision was enacted, beginning with the 1965 Higher Education Act.

Today, choice takes on a special urgency because there is a danger that the emerging postsecondary education system, consisting of both traditional and nontraditional providers, will exacerbate inequality in higher education by establishing two separate and unequal models of higher education. One for the affluent would have campuses, face-to-face instruction, residences, and all the trappings of traditional collegiate education. The other, far cheaper in price, for lower-income students would be virtual, digital, and online. The former would emphasize four year, full-time degree programs, and the latter would favor shorter-term, part-time certificates.

To make choice a reality, traditional institutions must reconfigure their activities to meet the needs of students who are not full time and residential, providing the convenience, service, instructional quality, and affordability of their nontraditional competitors. Federal, state, and promise financial aid programs need to expand beyond access to incorporate choice if they have not done so already.

2. Speed the Transition

Chapter fifteen discussed the seven stages by which higher education's transformation can be expected to occur. It concluded the transformation is in the third and fourth stages of the change: experimentation with new practices and creating models based on the successful innovations. The next stage would be diffusion of those models, or what many funders call scaling up. The point is that we cannot scale up until we know which of the myriad of experiments being undertaken actually work. Accordingly, the critical work of funders, individually but better collectively, now is to support experimentation and the assessment of the success of the various experiments and wide distribution of the results. Where funders are convinced the data actually demonstrate the efficacy of an innovation, the next task is for them to support the development of one or more models that can be used to promote scaling up.

By way of example, during the Industrial Revolution, there were many experiments at adding graduate education to the classical American college. Out of their successes and failures and the existence of exemplary university programs abroad came a model graduate school in the United States, Johns Hopkins University. Its creation required a combination of philanthropic dollars, a study of best practices, and hiring experienced talent to lead it. The model provided the grist for diffusing, establishing quality standards, and scaling up graduate education in the United States.

Several areas are now ripe for funders to support. With the waning of time-based education and the rise of outcome-based education, the highest priority is developing the fundamentals required for the transition—common definitions of competencies or outcomes, methods to assess them, credentials to certify their mastery, and a mechanism to record the competencies mastered throughout life. Recall the industrial era alternative, which was chaotic decades of individual institutions, associations, and governments enacting competing and conflicting policies regarding matters as rudimentary as the definition of a course and a measure of academic progress. This can be avoided.

3. Reexamine Current Industrial Era Higher Education Regulations

Current government regulations were designed for the colleges and universities of the national, analog, industrial economy. Regulations necessarily lag behind societal change as was the case during the Industrial Revolution. The existing laws and regulations of agrarian America didn't fit the industrial age with its giant corporations, new technologies, and changed working conditions. A new regulatory framework was required. It evolved slowly and painfully, in a reactive rather than an active manner.

We can do better during the current transformation. We know what is coming. The current set of higher education laws, regulations, and public funding models were created for accredited two- and four-year colleges attended by full-time, degree-seeking students, who progress academically by accumulating credits. Over the years, the regulations have been adjusted modestly to accommodate new populations such as part-time students and to permit experimentation in areas such as outcome-based education.

However, the years ahead will bring massive changes to higher education that will require comparable changes in government regulation. The current accounting system for higher education and financial aid is credit-based. Government will need an outcome- and learning-based accounting system to replace it, which was discussed earlier.

The current system for determining which institutions qualify for government financial aid is rooted in government recognition and institutional accreditation. The immediate question is how to respond to the multiplying numbers of non-traditional providers, the panoply of different formats of education they offer, and the capacity of students to study at several simultaneously. How should financial aid be distributed when businesses such as Google, Alibaba, and Danone are providing the content and assessment of learning? Does accreditation, which was established to standardize higher education, still make sense as the assurance of quality in a time that demands major innovation? In the longer run, given that outcome-based education is agnostic regarding the source of student learning, should financial aid continue to be tied to a set of approved institutions? Is there a role for accreditation in this new world?

Government commonly roots financial aid in degree programs and student academic progress in those programs according to the number of courses or credit hours they complete. In a time when enrollments in just-in-time certificate programs promise to eclipse those in traditional degree programs, government needs to reconfigure financial aid to support studies of variable length that grant microcredentials. At the moment, unlike degrees, microcredentials are unregulated. Do they need to be standardized? Unlike degrees, in today's knowledge economy where the half-life of knowledge is getting shorter and shorter, just-in-time education for the purposes of upskilling and reskilling will be recurrent throughout a lifetime. There is the question of who should pay for it—government; workers, employed and unemployed; and/or employers? What is the right combination? Should every American be given an education account to be used throughout life to pay for the education they choose?

Government financial aid is intended to make college accessible, which requires that it be affordable. This takes on a special urgency today because postsecondary education has become mandatory for obtaining a good job in America. However, the cost of college is soaring, far out of the reach of higher education's most underrepresented populations who are low income and nonwhite. And students are graduating from college with dramatically greater loan debt than ever before. This is unjust, politically unacceptable, and deleterious to the knowledge economy. It's also a fundamental failing in the goals for financial aid.

To reverse this, two actions are essential. The parties involved in financial aid are the federal government, the states, institutions, and students. At the moment, each party acts independently. Federal financial aid has failed to keep up with inflation, the states have reduced higher education support, and colleges have raised their prices far higher than inflation. It is a system in which increases in government support for financial aid provide an incentive for colleges to raise their tuition. The parties need to come together and coordinate their funding. The growing number of promise programs provides an opportunity to do this.

Additionally, government needs to place caps on higher education prices if institutions do not. This should be made a condition for participating in government financial aid programs. It requires a commitment from Washington and the states to provide the student support to make that possible.

The balance between student grants and loans has shifted dramatically beginning in the 1980s on the grounds that the primary beneficiary of college is the student. Before, a college education was thought to be a social good benefiting the nation. In the knowledge economy, higher education is both a social good and the equivalent in importance to free public schools. It's time to rebalance, which will dramatically reduce postgraduate loan debt, expand access to underrepresented populations, and move in the direction of equity.

• •

There is an even greater challenge ahead. Today's financial aid programs are rooted in the industrial era definition of equity. The redefinition discussed earlier will require a transformation of financial aid, which is now time based.

The bottom line is that the shift of higher education to a global, digital, knowledge economy requires a fundamental rethinking of current industrial era policies. It's time to launch that process and to institute three-year audits of current policy, emerging policy needs, and progress in meeting those needs.

4. Promote Shared Social Bonds

The common bonds that Americans once shared have grown frayed. The population is growing increasingly atomized in terms of its beliefs, values, confidence in public institutions, media consumption, and accepted truths.

The directions in which higher education is moving threaten to exacerbate these divisions. The common collegiate experience and the core curriculum are long gone. The modestly common baccalaureate course of studies, consisting of general education (rooted in the shared human heritage) and a major (specialized studies elected by students) is fading. At most colleges and universities, general education has become a distribution requirement with wide variation in content and little in the way of commonality. In the years ahead, as higher education becomes more individualized and just-in-time education expands, which is largely technical and professional, general education will decline even further.

In ever-diminishing degree, the historic role of higher education in promoting common learning and developing shared bonds among its graduates has diminished. Boyer and Levine (1981) found that movements to strengthen general education occur at times when social division is high and individualism overshadows community. In times when conditions are reversed, colleges and universities dilute their general education programs by reducing requirements and permitting greater student election. In this manner, general education has served as a counter to social splintering and uniformity. In short, this is a time for higher education to revive general education, to build bridges and reduce divisions by offering a common general education curriculum in its degree programs, firmly planted in the library and in the street, providing students with the skills and knowledge needed to thrive in the future individually and socially as members of a commonweal.

However, as postsecondary education becomes more individualized and providers multiply, fewer students will be exposed to general education in college. This means the last common educational experience Americans will have is K–12 education. Our schools must be a bastion for building the bonds that unite us. Rather than teaching students the familiar disciplines and subject matters, general education should focus on the shared human experience—linking our past with our present and future, our heritage with the realities that will confront us today and tomorrow.

This is the last opportunity for students to learn about the common bonds that join us. What might those studies include? Were it up to us, we would suggest five subjects:

1. Communication using words, numbers, images, and digital tools;

2. Our shared heritage, institutions, activities, and planet—aesthetically, scientifically, and socially;
3. How to thrive in a diverse, interconnected, multicultural world;
4. How to live in a time of profound change and the essential skills it demands: creativity, critical thinking, and continuous learning; and
5. Ethics and values: the difference between right and wrong, the distinction between truths and falsehoods, the contrast between fact and opinion, the ability to identify logical fallacies, and the capacity to make wise judgments.

Henry Adams, scion of a family that produced two presidents, attended Harvard in the mid-nineteenth century. He lamented the fact that he received an eighteenth-century education that failed to prepare him for a world plunging into the twentieth century. Henry Adams went to college at a time when the classical college was dying and the university was not yet born. The models that would guide the future had not yet been created.

It was a time much like the present, an age of continuity and experimentation. We know a transformation is to come. The present cannot be sustained. The transformation will require innovators to launch and pragmatic dreamers to bring it to fruition.

Higher education professionals, policy makers, and funders are being presented with a daunting and extraordinary opportunity to create the colleges of the global, digital, knowledge age. We cannot turn our backs on change. It will come anyway. This generation can shape the future of higher education or it will be shaped in spite of us. Only one other generation in US history has had such a moment.

BIBLIOGRAPHY

Introduction. Where You Look Determines What You See

Baer, J., & Martel, M. (2020, November). Fall 2020: International student enrollment snapshot. Institute of International Education. Retrieved from https://www.iie.org/-/media/Files/Corporate/Open-Doors /Special-Reports/Fall-2020-Snapshot-Report—-Full-Report.ashx ?la=en&hash=D337E4E9C8C9FACC9E3D53609A7A19B96783C5DB.

Brint, S. (2019, January 9). Is this higher education's golden age? *Chronicle of Higher Education*. Retrieved from https://www.chronicle.com/article /is-this-higher-educations-golden-age/.

Craig, R. (2015). *College disrupted: The great unbundling of higher education*. St. Martin's Press.

Craig, R. (2018). *A new U: Faster + cheaper alternatives to college*. BenBella Books.

Desjardins, J. (2017, August 2). Here's why small businesses fail. *Business Insider*. Retrieved from https://www.businessinsider.com/why-small -businesses-fail-infographic-2017-8.

Korn, M., Belkin, D., & Chung, J. (2020, April 30). Coronavirus pushes colleges to the breaking point, forcing "hard choices" about education. *Wall Street Journal*. Retrieved from https://www.wsj.com/articles /coronavirus-pushes-colleges-to-the-breaking-point-forcing-hard -choices-about-education-11588256157.

Lederman, D. (2017, July 19). The culling of higher education begins. *Inside Higher Ed*. Retrieved from https://www.insidehighered.com /news/2017/07/19/number-colleges-and-universities-drops-sharply -amid-economic-turmoil.

National Center for Education Statistics. (2019a). Enrollment in elementary, secondary and degree-granting postsecondary institutions by level and control of institutions: Selected years 1869–70 through fall 2029. Table 105.30. *Digest of education statistics*. Retrieved from https:// nces.ed.gov/programs/digest/d19/tables/dt19_105.30.asp?current=yes.

National Center for Education Statistics. (2019b). Degrees conferred
by postsecondary institutions by level of degree and sex of student:
Selected years, 1869–70 through 2029–30. Table 318.10. *Digest of education statistics*. Retrieved from https://nces.ed.gov/programs/digest
/d19/tables/dt19_318.10.asp?current=yes.

O'Neil, K. (2019, June 28). *Virtual reality training helps medical students
develop real empathy*. Georgetown University Medical Center. Retrieved
from https://gumc.georgetown.edu/gumc-stories/virtual-reality
-training-helps-medical-students-develop-real-empathy/.

Schubarth, C. (2013, February 7). Why Apple, Tesla, VCs, and academia
may die. *Silicon Valley Business Journal*. Retrieved from https://
www.bizjournals.com/sanjose/news/2013/02/07/disruption-guru
-christensen-why.html.

Seltzer, R. (2017, November 13). Days of reckoning. *Inside Higher Ed*.
Retrieved from https://www.insidehighered.com/news/2017/11
/13/spate-recent-college-closures-has-some-seeing-long-predicted
-consolidation-taking.

Study International Staff. (2018, May 2). Which country is home to the
largest international student population. *SI News*. Retrieved from
https://www.studyinternational.com/news/country-home-largest
-international-student-population/.

US Department of Education. (2006). A test of leadership: Charting the
future of US higher education. *A report of the commission appointed by
Secretary of Education Margaret Spellings*. US Department of Education.

Chapter One. The Industrial Revolution and
the Transformation of America

Ayers, R. U. (1989). *Technological transformations and long waves* (RR
89-1). International Institute for Applied Systems Analysis.

Gordon, S. H. (1997). *Passage to union: How the railroads transformed
American life, 1829–1929*. Ivan R. Dee.

Haines, M. R. (2000). The population of the United States, 1790–1820. In
S. L. Engerman & R. E. Gallman (Eds.), *The Cambridge economic history
of the United States* (Vol. 2). Cambridge University Press.

Hindle, B., & Lubar, S. D. (1986). *Engines of change: The American Industrial Revolution 1790–1860*. Smithsonian Institution Press.

Irving, W. (2011). *Rip Van Winkle and other stories*. Penguin UK.

Kennedy, P. (1987). *The rise and fall of the great powers*. Random House.

Lebergott, S. (1966). Labor force and employment, 1800–1960. In D. S.
Brady (Ed.), *Output, employment, and productivity in the United States
after 1800* (pp. 117–204). National Bureau of Economic Research.

Margo, R. A. (1992). *The labor force in the nineteenth century* (No. h0040). National Bureau of Economic Research.

Mooney, C. (2011). *The industrial revolution.* Nomad Press.

Morris, C. R. (2012). *The dawn of innovation: The first American Industrial Revolution.* PublicAffairs.

Olson, J. S., & Kenny, S. L. (2014). *The Industrial Revolution: Key themes and documents.* ABC-CLIO.

National Park Service. (2015). *Civil War facts: 1861–1865.* National Park Service. Retrieved from https://www.nps.gov/civilwar/facts .htm.

Taylor, G. R. (2015). *The transportation revolution, 1815–60.* Routledge.

US Census Bureau. (1975). *Historical statistics of the United States, colonial times to 1970* (No. 93). US Department of Commerce.

US Census Bureau. (2012). *Population and housing unit counts: 2010 census of population and housing.* United States summary: 2010. US Department of Commerce. Retrieved from https://www2.census.gov /library/publications/decennial/2010/cph-2/cph-2-1.pdf.

Chapter Two. Criticism, Denial, and Innovation

Bronson, W. C. (1914). *The history of Brown University 1764–1914.* Brown University.

Day, J., & Kingsley, J. L. (1829). Original papers in relation to a course of liberal education. *American Journal of Science, 15,* 297–351.

Faculty of Amherst College. (1827). *The substance of two reports of the faculty of Amherst College to the board of trustees with the doings of the board of trustees.* Carter and Adams.

Fox, D. R. (1945). *Union College: An unfinished history.* Graduate Council, Union College.

Geiger, R. L. (2015). *The history of American higher education: Learning and culture from the founding to World War II.* Princeton University Press.

Hislop, C. (1971). *Eliphalet Nott.* Wesleyan University Press.

Levine, A. (2012). Clark Kerr and the Carnegie Commission and Council. In S. Rothblatt (Ed.), *Clark Kerr's world of higher education reaches the 21st century* (pp. 43–60). Springer.

Levine, A., with the assistance of Zolner, J. (1994). *Locke College.* Harvard Education Publishing Group.

Murray, J. O. (1891). *Francis Wayland.* Houghton Mifflin.

Rudolph, F. (1990). *The American college and university: A history.* University of Georgia Press.

Urofsky, M. I. (1965). Reforms and response: The Yale report of 1828. *History of Education Quarterly, 5*(1), 53–67.

Wayland, F. (1842). *Thoughts on the present collegiate system in the United States*. Gould, Kendall & Lincoln.

Chapter Three. New Models and Diffusion

Bishop, M. (2014). *A history of Cornell*. Cornell University Press.

Brubacher, J. S., & Rudy, W. (1997). *Higher education in transition: A history of American colleges and universities*. Transaction Publishers.

Edison, T. A. (1929). Edison Papers (Folder 30, Box 3). Henry Ford Library.

Eliot, C. (1869a, February). The new education. *Atlantic Monthly*.

Eliot, C. (1869b, March). The new education. *Atlantic Monthly*.

Eliot, C. W. (1869c). *Addresses at the inauguration of Charles William Eliot as president of Harvard College, 1869*. Sever and Francis.

Flexner, A., Pritchett, H., & Henry, S. (1910). *Medical education in the United States and Canada* (Bulletin Number Four) (The Flexner Report). Carnegie Foundation for the Advancement of Teaching.

Geiger, R. L. (2015). *The history of American higher education: Learning and culture from the founding to World War II*. Princeton University Press.

Gilman, D. C. (1872). *Report on the national schools of science*. US Government Printing Office.

Massachusetts Institute of Technology. (1894). *Annual report of the president and treasurer*. Massachusetts Institute of Technology.

Morrill Act, Public Law 37-108. 15 STAT 503 (1862).

National Center for Education Statistics. (1993). *120 years of American education: A statistical portrait*. US Department of Education.

Veblen, T. (1918). *The higher learning in America: A memorandum on the conduct of universities by business men*. The Perfect Library.

Chapter Four. Standardization, Consolidation, and Scaling

Boyer, J. W. (2015). *The University of Chicago: A history*. University of Chicago Press.

Flexner, A., Pritchett, H., & Henry, S. (1910). *Medical education in the United States and Canada* (Bulletin Number Four) (The Flexner Report). Carnegie Foundation for the Advancement of Teaching.

Levine, A. (1978). *Handbook on undergraduate curriculum*. Jossey Bass.

Levine, A. (1987). Clark Kerr: The masterbuilder at 75. *Change: The Magazine of Higher Learning, 19*(2), 12–35.

National Center for Education Statistics. (1993). *120 years of American education: A statistical portrait*. US Department of Education.

Slosson, E. E. (1910). *Great American universities*. Macmillan.

Veblen, T. (1918). *The higher learning in America: A memorandum on the conduct of universities by business men*. The Perfect Library.

Chapter Five. Transformation

National Center for Education Statistics (2019c). Degree-granting postsecondary institutions by control and level of institution, selected years 1949–50 through 2018–19. Table 317.10. *Digest of education statistics, 2019.*. Retrieved from https://nces.ed.gov/programs/digest/d19/tables /dt19_317.10.asp?current=yes.

Chapter Six. A Demographic Sea Change

American Community Survey. (2019). 2019: ACS 1-year estimates selected population profiles. Table S0201. US Census Bureau. Retrieved from https://data.census.gov.

Barshay, J. (2018, September 10). College students expected to fall by more than 15% after the year 2025. *The Hechinger Report.* Retrieved from https://hechingerreport.org/college-students-predicted-to-fall-by -more-than-15-after-the-year-2025.

Fain, P. (2017, October 17). Default crisis for black student borrowers. *Inside Higher Ed.* Retrieved from https://www.insidehighered.com /news/2017/10/17/half-black-student-loan-borrowers-default-new -federal-data-show.

Frey, W. H. (2018, March 14). *The US will become "minority white" in 2045: Census projects.* Brookings Institution. Retrieved from https://www .brookings.edu/blog/the-avenue/2018/03/14/the-us-will-become -minority-white-in-2045-census-projects/.

Grawe, N. D. (2018). *Demographics and the demand for higher education.* Johns Hopkins University Press.

Hussar, W. J., & Bailey, T. M. (2018). *Projections of education statistics to 2026* (NCES 2018-019). National Center for Education Statistics.

Hussar, W. J., & Bailey, T. M. (2019). *Projections of education statistics to 2027.* National Center for Education Statistics: Institute of Education Sciences. Retrieved from https://nces.ed.gov/pubs2019/2019001.pdf.

Kelchen, R. (2017, October 6). New data on long-term student loan default rates. *Kelchen on Education.* Retrieved from https://robertkelchen.com /2017/10/06/new-data-on-long-term-student-loan-default-rates/

Korn, M., Belkin, D., & Chung, J. (2020, April 30). Coronavirus pushes colleges to the breaking point, forcing "hard choices" about education. *Wall Street Journal.* Retrieved from https://www.wsj.com/articles /coronavirus-pushes-colleges-to-the-breaking-point-forcing-hard -choices-about-education-11588256157.

Lederman, D. (2017, July 19). The culling of higher education begins. *Inside Higher Ed.* Retrieved from https://www.insidehighered.com /news/2017/07/19/number-colleges-and-universities-drops-sharply -amid-economic-turmoil.

Levine, A., & Dean, D. R. (2012). *Generation on a tightrope: A portrait of today's college student*. John Wiley & Sons.

Mitchell, M., Leachman, M., & Masterson, K. (2017). *A lost decade in higher education funding*. Center on Budget and Policy Priorities. Retrieved from https://www.cbpp.org/research/state-budget-and-tax/a-lost -decade-in-higher-education-funding.

Mitchell, T. (2020, August 11). The biggest danger to U.S. higher education? Losing 20 years' worth of gains in access for first-generation and minority students. The Hechinger Report. Retrieved from https://hechingerreport.org/opinion-the-biggest-danger-to-u-s -higher-education-losing-20-years-worth-of-gains-in-access-for-first -generation-and-minority-students/.

Mortenson, T. G. (2012). State funding: A race to the bottom. *The Presidency, 15*(1), 26–29.

National Center for Education Statistics. (2019b). Degrees conferred by postsecondary institutions by level of degree and sex of student: Selected years, 1869–70 through 2029–30. Table 318.10. *Digest of education statistics, 2019*. Retrieved from https://nces.ed.gov/programs /digest/d19/tables/dt19_318.10.asp?current=yes.

National Center for Education Statistics. (2019e). Average undergraduate tuition and fees and room and board rates charged for full-time students in degree-granting postsecondary institutions, by level and control of institution: Selected years, 1963–64 through 2018–19. Table 330.10. *Digest of education statistics, 2019*. Retrieved from https://nces .ed.gov/programs/digest/d19/tables/dt19_330.10.asp?current=yes.

National Center for Education Statistics. (2019g). Degree-granting postsecondary institutions, by control and classification of institution and state or jurisdiction: 2018–2019. Table 317.20. *Digest of education statistics, 2019*. Retrieved from https://nces.ed.gov/programs/digest /d19/tables/dt19_317.20.asp?current=yes.

National Center for Education Statistics. (2020a). *The condition of education 2020*. US Department of Education. Retrieved from https://nces.ed .gov/pubsearch/pubsinfo.asp?pubid=2020144.

Pew Research Center. (2014, January 30). Dependency ratios in the U.S. and globally. In *Attitudes about aging: A global perspective*. Retrieved from https://www.pewresearch.org/global/2014/01/30/chapter-4 -population-change-in-the-u-s-and-the-world-from-1950-to-2050/ #dependency-ratios-in-the-us-and-globally.

President's Commission on Higher Education. (1947). *Higher education for American democracy: A report of the president's commission on higher education*. US Government Printing Office.

Seltzer, R. (2017, November 13). Days of reckoning. *Inside Higher Ed*.

Retrieved from https://www.insidehighered.com/news/2017/11
/13/spate-recent-college-closures-has-some-seeing-long-predicted
-consolidation-taking.

Snyder, T. D., de Brey, C., & Dillow, S. A. (2019). *Digest of education statistics 2018* (NCES 2020-009). National Center for Education Statistics, Institute of Education Sciences, U.S. Department of Education.

Toynbee, A. (1884). *Lectures on the industrial revolution in England.* Rivingtons.

US Census Bureau. (1961). *Statistical abstract of the United States: 1961.* US Census Bureau. Retrieved from https://www.census.gov/library /publications/1961/compendia/statab/82ed.html.

US Census Bureau. (2018b). *Older people projected to outnumber children for first time in U.S. history.* US Census Bureau. Retrieved from https:// www.census.gov/newsroom/press-releases/2018/cb18-41-population -projections.html.

US Census Bureau. (2019). *U.S. population growth by region.* US Census Bureau. Retrieved from https://www.census.gov/popclock/data_tables .php?component=growth.

US Census Bureau. (2020). *Annual estimates of the resident population by sex, age, race, and Hispanic origin for the United States: April 1, 2010 to July 1, 2019* (NC-EST2019-ASR6H). US Census Bureau, Population Division. Retrieved from https://www2.census.gov/programs-surveys /popest/tables/2010–2019/national/asrh/nc-est2019-asr6h.xlsx.

US Centers for Disease Control and Prevention. (n.d.). *Population by age groups, race, and sex for 1960–97.* Retrieved from https://www.cdc.gov /nchs/data/statab/pop6097.pdf.

US Department of Education. (2017). 2003–04 beginning postsecondary students longitudinal study, second follow-up. U.S. Department of Education. Retrieved from https://nces.ed.gov/datalab/powerstats /output.aspx.

Vespa, J., Armstrong, D. M., & Medina, L. (2018). *Demographic turning points for the United States: Population projections for 2020 to 2060.* US Department of Commerce, Economics and Statistics Administration, US Census Bureau. Retrieved from https://www.census.gov/library /publications/2020/demo/p25-1144.html.

World Population Review. (2020a). *Asian population by state 2020.* Retrieved from http://worldpopulationreview.com/states/asian -population/.

World Population Review. (2020b). *Black population by state 2020.* Retrieved from http://worldpopulationreview.com/states/black -population-by-state/.

World Population Review. (2020c). *Hispanic population by state 2020.*

Retrieved from http://worldpopulationreview.com/states/hispanic
-population-by-state/.

World Population Review. (2020d). *Native American population 2020.*
Retrieved from http://worldpopulationreview.com/states/native
-american-population/.

World Population Review. (2020e). *Median age by state 2020.* Retrieved
from https://worldpopulationreview.com/states/median-age-by-state/.

Wozniak, A. (2018, March 22). Going away to college? School distance
as a barrier to higher education. Econofact. Retrieved from https://
econofact.org/going-away-to-college-school-distance-as-a-barrier-to
-higher-education.

Zumeta, W., & Kinne, A. (2011). The recession is not over for higher education. *The NEA 2011 Almanac of Higher Education,* 29–41.

Chapter Seven. An Emerging Knowledge Economy

Carnevale, A. P., Jayasundera, T., & Gulish, A. (2016a). America's divided
recovery: College haves and have-nots. *Georgetown University Center
on Education and the Workforce.* Retrieved from https://files.eric.ed.gov
/fulltext/ED574377.pdf.

Carnevale, A. P., Jayasundera, T., & Gulish, A. (2016b). America's divided
recovery: College haves and have-nots: Jobs are back, but they're not
the same ones that were lost [Infographic]. Retrieved from https://
1gyhoq479ufd3yna29x7ubjn-wpengine.netdna-ssl.com/wp-content
/uploads/DR-infographics-2.pdf#zoom=250.

US Bureau of Labor Statistics. (2020). Employees on nonfarm payrolls by
industry sector and selected industry detail, not seasonally adjusted.
Table B-1b, d. *Current employment statistics: Employment and earnings
table.* US Bureau of Labor Statistics. Retrieved from https://www.bls
.gov/web/empsit/ceseeb1b.htm#ce_ee_table1b.f.3.

Chapter Eight. A Technological Revolution

Anderson, M., & Jiang, J. (2018, May 31). Teens, social media, & technology
2018. Pew Research Center. Retrieved from https://www.pewinternet
.org/2018/05/31/teens-social-media-technology-2018.

Bauer-Wolf, J. (2020, January 2020). Coursera launches first US online
bachelor's degree. Education Dive. Retrieved from https://www
.educationdive.com/news/coursera-launches-first-us-online-bachelors
-degree/571069/.

Best Colleges. (2018). 2018 online education trends report. Best Colleges.
Retrieved from https://www.bestcolleges.com/perspectives/annual
-trends-in-online-education/.

Best Colleges. (2019). 2019 online education trends report. Best Colleges.

Retrieved from https://res.cloudinary.com/highereducation/image
/upload/v1556050834/BestColleges.com/edutrends/2019-Online
-Trends-in-Education-Report-BestColleges.pdf.

Chappell, B. (2019, December 10). University of Phoenix reaches $191
million settlement with FTC, including debt relief. NPR. Retrieved from
https://www.npr.org/2019/12/10/786738760/university-of-phoenix
-reaches-191-million-settlement-with-ftc-including-debt-rel.

Desilver, D. (2017, July 25). Most Americans unaware that as US manufacturing jobs have disappeared, output has grown. Pew Research Center.
Retrieved from https://www.pewresearch.org/fact-tank/2017/07/25
/most-americans-unaware-that-as-u-s-manufacturing-jobs-have
-disappeared-output-has-grown/.

Domo. (2019). Data never sleeps 7.0: How much data is being generated
every minute [Infographic]. Domo. Retrieved from https://www.domo
.com/learn/data-never-sleeps-7.

Facebook IQ. (2017, January 9). How virtual reality facilitates social
connection. Facebook IQ. Retrieved from https://www.facebook
.com/business/news/insights/how-virtual-reality-facilitates-social
-connection.

Frey, C. B., & Osborne, M. A. (2013). The future of employment: How
susceptible are jobs to computerisation? *Technological Forecasting and
Social Change, 114*, 254–280.

Hicks, M. J., & Devaraj, S. (2015). *The myth and reality of manufacturing in
America*. Ball State University, Center for Business and Economic Research. Retrieved from http://projects.cberdata.org/reports/MfgReality
.pdf.

ICEF Monitor. (2020, January 14). Slower growth in new MOOC degrees
but online learning is alive and well. ICEF Monitor. Retrieved from
https://monitor.icef.com/2020/01/slower-growth-in-new-mooc
-degrees-but-online-learning-is-alive-and-well/.

Levine, A., & Dean, D. R. (2012). *Generation on a tightrope: A portrait of
today's college student*. John Wiley & Sons.

Manyika, J., Chui, M., Miremadi, M., Bughin, J., George, K., Willmott, P.,
& Dewhurst, M. (2017). *A future that works: Automation, employment,
and productivity*. McKinsey Global Institute. Retrieved from https://
www.mckinsey.com/~/media/McKinsey/Featured%20Insights/Digital
%20Disruption/Harnessing%20automation%20for%20a%20future
%20that%20works/MGI-A-future-that-works_Full-report.ashx.

National Center for Education Statics. (2019f). Number and percentage
of students enrolled in degree-granting postsecondary institutions, by
distance education participation, location of student, level of enrollment, and control and level of institution: Fall 2017 and fall 2018.

Table 311.15. *Digest of education statistics, 2019.* Retrieved from https://nces.ed.gov/programs/digest/d19/tables/dt19_311.15.asp?current=yes.

National Commission on Technology, Automation, and Economic Progress. (1966). *Technology and the economy.* US Government Printing Office. Retrieved from https://files.eric.ed.gov/fulltext/ED023803.pdf.

O'Dea, S. (2020, February 27). Smartphone ownership in the U.S. 2015–2018, by age group. Statista. Retrieved from https://www.statista.com/statistics/489255/percentage-of-us-smartphone-owners-by-age-group/.

Perrin, A., & Anderson, M. (2019, April 10). Share of U.S. adults using social media, including Facebook, is mostly unchanged since 2018. Pew Research Center. Retrieved from https://www.pewresearch.org/fact-tank/2019/04/10/share-of-u-s-adults-using-social-media-including-facebook-is-mostly-unchanged-since-2018/.

Petrov, C. (2020, July 19). 25+ impressive big data statistics for 2020. Tech Jury. Retrieved from https://techjury.net/blog/big-data-statistics/#gref.

Raconteur. (2019). A day in data [Infographic]. Raconteur. Retrieved from https://www.raconteur.net/infographics/a-day-in-data.

Ritholtz, B. (2017, July 6). The world is about to change even faster. Bloomberg. Retrieved from https://www.bloomberg.com/opinion/articles/2017-07-06/the-world-is-about-to-change-even-faster.

Robles, P. (2018, October 1). China plans to be a world leader in artificial intelligence by 2030. *South China Morning Post.* Retrieved from https://multimedia.scmp.com/news/china/article/2166148/china-2025-artificial-intelligence/index.html.

Seaman, J. E., Allen, I. E., & Seaman, J. (2018). Grade increase: Tracking distance education in the United States. Babson Survey Research Group. Retrieved from https://onlinelearningsurvey.com/reports/gradeincrease.pdf.

Seamans, R., & Zhu, F. (2013). Responses to entry in multi-sided markets: The impact of Craigslist on local newspapers. *Management Science, 60*(2), 476–493.

Shah, D. (2019a, December 1). Coursera's 2019: Year in review. Class Central. Retrieved from https://www.classcentral.com/report/coursera-2019-year-review/.

Shah, D. (2019b, December 1). EdX's 2019: Year in review. Class Central. Retrieved from https://www.classcentral.com/report/edx-2019-year-review.

Southern New Hampshire University. (2020). About us: Expanding the boundaries of higher education. Southern New Hampshire University. Retrieved from https://www.snhu.edu/about-us.

University of Maryland Global Campus. (2020). Facts at a glance. University of Maryland Global Campus. Retrieved from https://www.umgc.edu/administration/policies-and-reporting/institutional-data/facts-at-a-glance.cfm.

US Bureau of Labor Statistics. (2020). Employees on nonfarm payrolls by industry sector and selected industry detail, not seasonally adjusted: Employment and earnings. Table B-1b. *Current employment statistics.* US Bureau of Labor Statistics. Retrieved from https://www.bls.gov/web/empsit/ceseeb1b.htm#ce_ee_table1b.f.3.

Western Governors University. (2019). *WGU 2019 annual report.* Western Governors University. Retrieved from https://www.wgu.edu/content/dam/western-governors/documents/annual-report/annual-report-2019.pdf.

Zimmerman, E. (2018, July 13). More students rely on mobile devices to complete online classes. *EdTech.* Retrieved from https://edtechmagazine.com/higher/article/2018/07/more-students-rely-mobile-devices-complete-online-classes.

Chapter Ten. *The Music Industry*

Gibson, M. (2015, January 13). Here's why music lovers are turning to vinyl and dropping digital. *Time Magazine.* Retrieved from http://time.com/3663568/vinyl-sales-increase/.

Gillett, C. (1971). *The sound of the city.* Sphere Books.

Graham, G., Burnes, B., Lewis, G. J., & Langer, J. (2004). The transformation of the music industry supply chain. *International Journal of Operations & Production Management.*

Ingraham, N. (2013, April 26). iTunes store at 10: How Apple built a digital media juggernaut. The Verge. Retrieved from https://www.theverge.com/2013/4/26/4265172/itunes-store-at-10-how-apple-built-a-digital-media-juggernaut.

Johnson, N. (2016, August 15). What about the end? The evolution from mixtape to playlist. Medium. Retrieved from https://medium.com/applaudience/what-about-the-end-the-evolution-of-the-playlist-5261fb8b7555.

Lule, J. (2016). *Understanding media and culture: An introduction to mass communication.* University of Minnesota Libraries Publishing.

Madden, M. (2009). The state of music online: Ten years after Napster. Pew Internet. Retrieved from http://www.pewinternet.org/files/old-media/Files/Reports/2009/The-State-of-Music-Online_-Ten-Years-After-Napster.pdf.

Mann, C. C. (2000, September). The heavenly jukebox. *The Atlantic.*

Retrieved from https://www.theatlantic.com/magazine/archive/2000
/09/the-heavenly-jukebox/305141/.

Medium. (2014, June 7). History of the recording industry, 1877–1920s.
Medium. Retrieved from https://medium.com/@Vinylmint/history-of
-the-record-industry-1877-1920s-48deacb4c4c3.

Newman, K. (2014, February 28). The end of an era: The death of the
album and its unintended effects. *Gnovis*, Georgetown University.
Retrieved from http://www.gnovisjournal.org/2014/02/28/the-end-of
-an-era-the-death-of-the-album-and-its-unintended-effects/.

Nicolaou, A. (2017, January 16). How streaming saved the music industry.
Financial Times. Retrieved from https://www.ft.com/content/cd99b95e
-d8ba-11e6-944b-e7eb37a6aa8e.

Nielsen. (2020). Year-end music report: U.S. 2019. The Nielsen Company.
Retrieved from https://static.billboard.com/files/pdfs/NIELSEN_2019
_YEARENDreportUS.pdf.

Rose, J. (2011, March 16). For better or worse, MP3s are the format of
choice. NPR. Retrieved from https://www.npr.org/sections/therecord
/2011/03/18/134598010/for-better-or-worse-mp3s-are-the-format-of
-choice.

Sanchez, D. (2018, January 16). What streaming music services pay
[Updated for 2018]. *Digital Music News*. Retrieved from https://www
.digitalmusicnews.com/2018/01/16/streaming-music-services-pay
-2018/.

Siwek, S. E. (2007). The true cost of sound recording piracy to the US
economy. Institute for Policy Innovation. Retrieved from http://www
.ipi.org/ipi_issues/detail/the-true-cost-of-sound-recording-piracy-to
-the-us-economy.

Tschmuck, P. (2012). *Creativity and innovation in the music industry* (2nd
ed.). Springer Netherlands.

Warr, R., & Goode, M. M. (2011). Is the music industry stuck between rock
and a hard place? The role of the internet and three possible scenarios.
Journal of Retailing and Consumer Services, 18(2), 126–131.

Wikström, P. (2014). Change: The music industry in an age of digital distribution. BBVA OpenMind. Retrieved from https://www
.bbvaopenmind.com/wp-content/uploads/2014/03/BBVA-OpenMind
-Technology-Innovation-Internet-Informatics-Music-Patrik-Wikstr
%C3%B6m-The-Music-Industry-in-an-Age-of-Digital-Distribution
.pdf.

Xroads. (n.d.). *Radio in the 1920s: Emergence of radio in the 1920s and
its cultural significance*. University of Virginia. Retrieved from http://
xroads.virginia.edu/~ug00/3on1/radioshow/1920radio.htm.

Chapter Eleven. The Film Industry

Baldwin, R. (2012, November 29). Netflix gambles on big data to become the HBO of streaming. *Wired*. Retrieved from https://www.wired.com /2012/11/netflix-data-gamble/.

Boddy, W. (1985). The studios move into prime time: Hollywood and the television industry in the 1950s. *Cinema Journal*, 23–37.

Chong, C. (2015, July 17). Blockbuster's CEO once passed up a chance to buy Netflix for only $50 million. *Business Insider*. Retrieved from http://www.businessinsider.com/blockbuster-ceo-passed-up-chance -to-buy-netflix-for-50-million-2015-7.

Demain, B. (2018, June 7). How Mister Rogers saved the VCR. Mental Floss. Retrieved from http://mentalfloss.com/article/29686/how-mister -rogers-saved-vcr.

Downes, L., & Nunes, P. (2013, November 7). Blockbuster becomes a casualty of big bang disruption. *Harvard Business Review*. Retrieved from https://hbr.org/2013/11/blockbuster-becomes-a-casualty-of-big -bang-disruption.

Eyemen, S. (1997). *The speed of sound: Hollywood and the talkie revolution: 1926–1930*. Simon and Schuster.

Kaplan, S. (2011, October 11). How not to get "Netflixed." *Fortune*. Retrieved from http://fortune.com/2011/10/11/how-not-to-get-net flixed/.

Liedke, M., & Anderson, M. (2010, September 23). Blockbuster tries to rewrite script in bankruptcy. Associated Press. Retrieved from http:// archive.boston.com/business/articles/2010/09/23/blockbuster_tries _to_rewrite_script_in_bankruptcy/.

Madrigal, A. C. (2012, January 10). The court case that almost made it illegal to tape TV shows. *The Atlantic*. Retrieved from https://www .theatlantic.com/technology/archive/2012/01/the-court-case-that -almost-made-it-illegal-to-tape-tv-shows/251107/.

National Association of Theatre Owners. (2020). Annual U.S./Canada admissions. Retrieved from https://www.natoonline.org/data /admissions/.

Pautz, M. C. (2002). The decline in average weekly cinema attendance, 1930–2000. *Issues in Political Economy*, 11.

Petraetis, G. (2017, July 13). How Netflix built a house of cards with big data. CIO. Retrieved from https://www.cio.com/article/3207670/big -data/how-netflix-built-a-house-of-cards-with-big-data.html.

Rodriguez, A. (2020, January 21). Netflix crushed growth targets internationally during Q4 but missed in the US, where rivals like Disney Plus emerged. *Business Insider*. Retrieved from https://www.businessinsider

.com/netflix-q4-2019-earnings-results-subscriber-growth-revenue
-analysis-2020-1.

Schatz, T. (2008). The studio system and conglomerate Hollywood. In
P. MacDonald and J. Wasko (Eds.), *The contemporary Hollywood film
industry* (pp. 13–42). Blackwell Publishing.

Chapter Twelve. The Newspaper Industry

Butler, J. K., & Kent, K. E. (1983). Potential impact of videotext on newspapers. *Newspaper Research Journal, 5*(1), 3–12.

Carey, L. (2018, October 28). One-fifth of U.S. newspapers close in last 14
years. *Daily Yonder*. Retrieved from https://dailyyonder.com/one-fifth
-u-s-newspapers-close-last-14-years/2018/10/22/.

Clark, L. S., & Marchi, R. (2017). *Young people and the future of news: Social
media and the rise of connective journalism*. Cambridge University Press.

Edgecliffe-Johnson, A. (2005, November 24). Murdoch predicts demise
of classified ads. *Financial Times*. Retrieved from https://www.ft.com
/content/6b49e6ba-5d11-11da-a749-0000779e2340.

Herndon, K. (2012). *The decline of the daily newspaper: How an American
institution lost the online revolution*. Peter Lang.

Jenkins, S. (1997, January 4). No plug, no wires, no rivals. *The Times*.

Kennedy, D. (2018). *The return of the moguls: How Jeff Bezos and John
Henry are remaking newspapers for the twenty-first century*. University
Press of New England.

Meisler, S. (1986, September 12). News, games, dating: Videotext—in
France, it's the rage. *Los Angeles Times*. Retrieved from https://www
.latimes.com/archives/la-xpm-1986-09-12-mn-11878-story.html.

National Humanities Center. (2006). Publick occurrences both forreign
and domestick. Retrieved from http://nationalhumanitiescenter.org
/pds/amerbegin/power/text5/PublickOccurrences.pdf.

O'Barr, W. M. (2010). A brief history of advertising in America. *Advertising
& Society Review, 11*(1).

Perrin, N. (2019, November 4). Facebook-Google Duopoly won't crack this
year. eMarketer. Retrieved from https://www.emarketer.com/content
/facebook-google-duopoly-won-t-crack-this-year.

Pew Research Center. (2019). Newspaper fact sheet. Pew Research Center.
Retrieved from https://www.journalism.org/fact-sheet/newspapers/.

Schudson, M. (1981). *Discovering the news: A social history of American
newspapers*. Basic Books.

Seamans, R., & Zhu, F. (2013). Responses to entry in multi-sided markets:
The impact of Craigslist on local newspapers. *Management Science,
60*(2), 476–493.

Shearer, E. (2018, December 10). Social media outpaces print newspapers in the U.S. as a news source. Fact Tank, Pew Research Center. Retrieved from https://www.pewresearch.org/fact-tank/2018/12/10/social-media-outpaces-print-newspapers-in-the-u-s-as-a-news-source/.

Stamm, M. (2011). *Sound business: Newspapers, radio, and the politics of new media.* University of Pennsylvania Press.

Chapter Fourteen. What Will Change?

Adams, H. (2008). *The education of Henry Adams.* Oxford University Press.

Bustamante, J. (2019, June 8). College graduation statistics. Education Data. Retrieved from https://educationdata.org/number-of-college-graduates/.

Geiger, R. L. (2015). *The history of American higher education: Learning and culture from the founding to World War II.* Princeton University Press.

Glassdoor Team. (2020, January 10). 15 more companies that no longer require a degree—Apply now. Glassdoor. Retrieved from https://www.glassdoor.com/blog/no-degree-required/.

Gordon, S. H. (1997). *Passage to union: How the railroads transformed American life, 1829–1929.* Ivan R. Dee.

Levine, A. (1978). *Handbook on undergraduate curriculum.* Jossey Bass.

Levine, A., & Dean, D. R. (2012). *Generation on a tightrope: A portrait of today's college student.* John Wiley & Sons.

Marken, S. (2019, December 30). Half in U.S. now consider college education very important. Gallup. Retrieved from https://www.gallup.com/education/272228/half-consider-college-education-important.aspx.

Perrin, A., & Turner, E. (2019, August 20). Smartphones help blacks, Hispanics bridge some—but not all—digital gaps with whites. Pew Research Center. Retrieved from https://www.pewresearch.org/fact-tank/2019/08/20/smartphones-help-blacks-hispanics-bridge-some-but-not-all-digital-gaps-with-whites/.

Smith-Barrow, D. (2019, March 11). Despite high costs, new poll shows most young adults think a four-year degree is worth it. *Hechinger Report.* Retrieved from https://hechingerreport.org/despite-high-costs-new-poll-shows-most-young-adults-think-a-four-year-degree-is-worth-it/.

Sylla, R., & Wright, R. E. (2012). Early corporate America: The largest industries and companies before 1860. *Finance Professionals' Post.*

Chapter Fifteen. How and When Will Change Occur?

Blumenstyk, G. (2020, April 29). "Alt-ed" ventures could gain traction in an uncertain fall. *Chronicle of Higher Education.* Retrieved from https://www.chronicle.com/article/Alt-Ed-Ventures-Could/248653.

Chappell, B. (2019, December 10). University of Phoenix reaches $191 million settlement with FTC, including debt relief. NPR. Retrieved from https://www.npr.org/2019/12/10/786738760/university-of-phoenix -reaches-191-million-settlement-with-ftc-including-debt-rel.

Christensen, C. (2014). *The future of higher education in a digital age* [Recorded lecture]. Retrieved from https://www.youtube.com/watch?v =mnMvEP2OTIM.

D'Amico, C., & Hanson, A. (2020, June 24). *Public viewpoint webinar: Reskilling and changing careers in the midst of COVID-19* [Webinar]. Strada Education Network. https://www.stradaeducation.org/video /june-24-public-viewpoint-webinar-reskilling-and-changing-careers -in-the-midst-of-COVID-19/.

Higher Learning Advocates. (2018, October). Today's students: Pop culture vs. reality. Higher Learning Advocates. Retrieved from https:// higherlearningadvocates.org/wp-content/uploads/2018/10/10-18-HLA -TodaysStudents-Survey-Deck-FINAL.pdf.

Holon IQ. (2019, February 14). The anatomy of an OPM and a $7.7B market in 2025. Holon IQ. Retrieved from https://www.holoniq.com /news/anatomy-of-an-opm/.

Institute-wide Task Force on the Future of MIT Education: Final report. (2014). MIT. Retrieved from http://web.mit.edu/future-report/Task ForceFinal_July28.pdf?

Korn, M., Belkin, D., & Chung, J. (2020, April 30). Coronavirus pushes colleges to the breaking point, forcing "hard choices" about education. *Wall Street Journal*. Retrieved from https://www.wsj.com/articles /coronavirus-pushes-colleges-to-the-breaking-point-forcing-hard -choices-about-education-11588256157.

Lederman, D. (2019, December 17). The biggest movers online. *Inside Higher Ed*. Retrieved from https://www.insidehighered.com/digital -learning/article/2019/12/17/colleges-and-universities-most-online -students-2018.

Metaari. (2020, July 13). First half 2020 learning technology investment surged to $11.6 billion. PRWeb. Retrieved from https://www.prweb .com/releases/first_half_2020_learning_technology_investment _surged_to_11_6_billion/prweb17252510.htm.

Nash, O. (n.d.). The catsup bottle. Retrieved from https://allpoetry.com /The-Catsup-Bottle.

National Center for Education Statistics. (2018a). *Selected characteristics for degree-granting institutions that primarily offer online programs, by control of institution and selected characteristics: Fall 2017 and 2016–17*. Table 311.33. Retrieved from https://nces.ed.gov/programs /digest/d18/tables/dt18_311.33.asp.

National Center for Education Statistics. (2018b). *Number and percentage of students enrolled in degree-granting postsecondary institutions, by distance education participation, location of student, level of enrollment, and control and level of institution: Fall 2016 and fall 2017*. Table 311.15. Retrieved from https://nces.ed.gov/programs/digest/d18/tables /dt18_311.15.asp.

National Center for Education Statistics. (2020b). *Total fall enrollment in degree-granting postsecondary institutions, by attendance status, sex, and age of student: Selected years, 1970 through 2029*. Table 303.40. Retrieved from https://nces.ed.gov/programs/digest/d19/tables/dt19 _303.40.asp?current=yes.

Seaman, J. E., Allen, I. E., & Seaman, J. (2018). Grade increase: Tracking distance education in the United States. Babson Survey Research Group. Retrieved from https://onlinelearningsurvey.com/reports /gradeincrease.pdf.

Southern New Hampshire University. (2020). About us: Expanding the boundaries of higher education. Southern New Hampshire University. Retrieved from https://www.snhu.edu/about-us.

US Department of Education. (2020). National Center for Education Statistics, Integrated Postsecondary Education Data System (IPEDS) [Fall 2018]. Students enrolled exclusively in distance education courses. Retrieved from https://nces.ed.gov/ipeds/datacenter/MasterVariableList .aspx?changeStep=YES&stepId=2.

Western Governors University. (2019). *WGU 2019 annual report*. Western Governors University. Retrieved from https://www.wgu.edu/content /dam/western-governors/documents/annual-report/annual-report -2019.pdf.

Zemsky, R., Shaman, S., & Baldridge, S. C. (2020). *The college stress test: Tracking institutional futures across a crowded market*. Johns Hopkins University Press.

Chapter Sixteen. What Should Higher Education and Policy Makers Do?

Boyer, E. L., & Levine, A. (1981). *A quest for common learning: The aims of general education*. Carnegie Foundation for the Advancement of Teaching.

Hart, M. (2016, April 27). Incubating innovation at Southern New Hampshire University. Campus Technology. Retrieved from https:// campustechnology.com/articles/2016/04/27/incubating-innovation-at -southern-new-hampshire-u.aspx.

President's Commission on Higher Education. (1947). *Higher education for American democracy: A report of the president's commission on higher education*. US Government Printing Office.

INDEX

The letter *t* following a page number signifies a table.

About the Authors

Arthur Levine

Arthur Levine is Distinguished Scholar of Higher Education at New York University. He is also senior fellow and President Emeritus of the Woodrow Wilson National Fellowship Foundation (now Institute for Citizens and Scholars) and President Emeritus of Teachers College, Columbia University. Levine has been a faculty member and chair of the Institute for Educational Management at the Harvard Graduate School of Education, president of Bradford College, and senior fellow at the Carnegie Foundation. He was also the founder and first president of the High Meadows Graduate School of Teaching and Learning. Levine has authored twelve books and published scores of articles in venues such as the *Wall Street Journal, New York Times, Washington Post, Los Angeles Times,* Politico, the *Chronicle of Higher Education, Education Week,* and *Inside Higher Education.* He has appeared on shows such as *60 Minutes,* the *Today Show, All Things Considered, Morning Edition, Open Mind,* and *Fox News.* Levine has received a number of awards, including twenty-six honorary degrees and Carnegie, Fulbright, Guggenheim, and Rockefeller Foundation Fellowships. He is a member of the American Academy of Arts and Sciences.

Scott Van Pelt

Scott Van Pelt is a higher education professional and instructor who has held a variety of administrative and teaching positions during the past ten years, including roles in the areas of academic advising, admissions, student life, instructional technology, and curriculum design. A graduate of the MA and EdM programs in Higher and Postsecondary Education from Teachers College, Columbia University, Scott's academic interests lie at the intersection of technology and pedagogy.

Currently, Scott is a lecturer and associate director with the Wharton Communication Program at the Wharton School of the University of Pennsylvania. In this role, Scott designs and implements the curricula for communication courses within the MBA core curriculum. He also teaches several courses in the program.